Dedicated to John Lewis,
Congressman, U.S. House of Representatives,
for his exemplary efforts to advance
equality, justice, and human rights in the United States.

Sociology for a
New Century Series

SOCIOLOGY FOR A NEW CENTURY

SOCIOLOGY AND HUMAN RIGHTS

A Bill of Rights for the Twenty-First Century

Judith Blau

The University of North Carolina at Chapel Hill

Mark Frezzo

University of Mississippi

Editors

Los Angeles | London | New Delhi
Singapore | Washington DC

Los Angeles | London | New Delhi
Singapore | Washington DC

FOR INFORMATION:

Pine Forge Press

An Imprint of SAGE Publications, Inc.

2455 Teller Road

Thousand Oaks, California 91320

E-mail: order@sagepub.com

SAGE Publications Ltd.

1 Oliver's Yard

55 City Road

London EC1Y 1SP

United Kingdom

SAGE Publications India Pvt. Ltd.

B 1/I 1 Mohan Cooperative Industrial Area

Mathura Road, New Delhi 110 044

India

SAGE Publications Asia-Pacific Pte. Ltd.

33 Pekin Street #02-01

Far East Square

Singapore 048763

Acquisitions Editor: David Repetto

Editorial Assistant: Maggie Stanley

Production Editor: Libby Larson

Copy Editor: Melinda Masson

Typesetter: C&M Digitals (P) Ltd.

Proofreader: Wendy Jo Dymond

Indexer: Terri Corry

Cover Designer: Candice Harman

Marketing Manager: Erica DeLuca

Permissions Editor: Karen Ehrmann

Copyright © 2012 by Pine Forge Press, an Imprint of SAGE Publications, Inc.

Printed in the United States of America

Library of Congress Cataloging-in-Publication Data

Sociology and human rights: a Bill of Rights for the twenty-first century /

editors Judith Blau, Mark Frezzo.

p. cm.—(Sociology for a new century)
Includes bibliographical references and index.

ISBN 978-1-4129-9138-4 (pbk.)

1. Sociology. 2. Human rights. 3. Globalization—Social aspects. I. Blau,

Judith R., 1942- II. Frezzo, Mark.

HM585.S632 2012
323—dc22
2011000024

This book is printed on acid-free paper.

11 12 13 14 15 10 9 8 7 6 5 4 3 2 1

Contents

Foreword

There Is No Other Option!

Shulamith Koenig

We live in a world without moral borders. Many of us who are engaged in interdisciplinary analysis combined with social activism have abandoned (or never fully held) the holistic approach in assessing symptoms and causes, urgencies, and/or long-term solutions theoretically or practically to this challenging development. It is not often that the interconnectedness and interrelatedness of human rights concerns become part of a genuine systemic analysis that stands to avail us with the necessary compass for real economic and social transformation. Yet the increasing complexity of the world demands this holistic response to its many challenges.

Many around the globe whose rights are not actively protected become vulnerable to the three Ps: Patriarchy, Power, and Politics. What is most disheartening is the lack of an ongoing dialogue throughout all sectors of society about human rights. This volume tries to redress this gap. We who are facilitating learning processes at the community level speak of developing Human Rights Cities through learning human rights as a way of life. In 20 years of working around the world, I have witnessed firsthand how the vision and mission of human rights answers the dreams, hopes, and expectation of humanity, moving charity to dignity.

The reader for whose attention this volume most likely vies is a scientist engaged in *the study of human society, social relations, and change—of the beliefs and values, of societal groups, and of the processes governing social phenomena—and is willing to view the social world from the perspective of others, addressing social structure with interrelated parts.*

These words describe succinctly the purpose, the processes, and the phenomena of social structures as understood by the framers of the Universal Declaration of Human Rights. They give credibility to people's own hopes, their values, and their dignity and make the promise for human rights to serve humanity. Indeed, the holistic human rights framework guides communities into a journey of hope that informs societal development and positive change toward economic and social justice and the closing of the widening gap of dignity around the world.

More than 2 billion people live in cities today. Cities are a microcosm of a state with all its promises and concerns. Four billion people will live in cities within 15 to 20 years. With the multitudes of people and issues interacting and interrelating, there is no inherent knowledge, support system, or guidance regarding how to live with one another in dignity and how practically to abide by moral values in today's fast-changing and harsh world. The multiple and pluralist realities of people in the information age and the growing number of people (of which 50 percent are under 25 years old) need urgently to be attended to, morally and politically. Scientists and researchers devoting their lives to learn about, analyze, and *understand* societies must learn about human rights and bring the message to a world that is yearning for change.

To move from the vision to a practical mission that enables people to belong to a community in dignity, with trust and respect for others, a new phenomenon has begun to take form, in some cities in Latin America, Africa, and recently the United States. Community activists working alongside local authorities are developing programs that will have their citizens learn about, know, and own human rights and take actions to change their lives guided by the human rights framework. Certain cities have chosen to call themselves "Human Rights Cities" when they aspire to become centers for knowledge. These cities encourage their citizens to work together to build communities based on economic and social justice, equality, and non-discrimination, realizing that we have no other option but human rights as a way of life.

In Human Rights Cities, we remind ourselves what a true human rights educator is: *a person, a woman or a man, who is capable of evoking systemic analysis and critical thinking, at the community level, guided by the fully comprehensive human rights framework that leads to action.* This is a tall order both for the educator and for the learner. Yet the call of Nelson Mandela to develop a new political culture based on human rights is being investigated and implemented by, for, and with the people as they become mentors and monitors in a Human Rights City.

The assumptions being made in developing human rights cities are as follows:

- Every woman, man, youth, and child knows when injustice and/or justice is present.
- Every human being expects to live in dignity and free from humiliation.
- The holistic human rights framework provides a viable guideline for economic, societal, and human development.
- Millions of people will be born and die and will never know that they are owners of human rights that they can claim as their own to break through the vicious cycle of humiliation.
- Human rights represent not only a litany of their violations but strategies for social and economic development.
- People belong in dignity in community with others, women and men alike.
- If we are to achieve economic and social justice, no one human right can violate another, and all conflicts must be solved within the human rights framework.
- Democracy, to be true to its mission, must be a delivery system of human rights to all, in full equality and without discrimination.
- People can move power to human rights—moving from patriarchal verticality to human rights horizontality.

In a Human Rights City, people consciously internalize and socialize to overcome fear and impoverishment. The city provides human security—access to food, housing, education, health care, and work at liveable wages—sharing these resources with all citizens, not as a gift but as the realization of human rights. A Human Rights City is a practical, viable model that demonstrates that developing and living in such a society is possible. Often joined by the local authorities and law enforcement agencies, residents work together with a wide array of stakeholders and organizations to devise and design a dialogue and learning programs in the neighborhoods. The purpose of these is to instill a sense of ownership of human rights as a way of life as relevant to people's concerns. The city, its institutions, and its residents, as a complex social economic and political entity, become a model for citizens' participation in their social, economic, and cultural development. This process leads to the mapping and analysis of causes and symptoms of violations such as poverty and patriarchy and work by citizens to design ways and means to achieve the well-being of every person in their city.

As human rights are realized, people no longer live in fear and desperation, so conflict is often avoided altogether. Appropriate conflict resolution is an inevitable consequence of the learning process as women and men work to secure the sustainability of their community as a viable, creative, and caring society.

Steering committees in Human Rights Cities represent public sector employees; religious groups, nongovernmental organizations (NGOs), and community groups; community activists working on the issues of women, children, workers, indigenous peoples, poverty, education, food, housing, health care, environment, and conflict resolution; and all other nonaffiliated inhabitants. These committees work together to design the process of learning and reflecting about the ownership of human rights as significant to the decision-making process. Together they design actions that ensure that democracy abides by human rights principles, norms, and standards and that these are integrated in the policies that guide the life of the city. They work to strengthen activities that ensure community development and accountability. Individuals and groups take part in the action—every citizen is considered a creative partner of sustainable change. And, as they identify needs, they adopt this inclusive framework, giving momentum to attain a better life for future generations.

After learning about the various human rights treaties that their government has ratified, an analysis with a human rights perspective would examine the following:

- The laws of the city. Do these abide by human rights?
- The policies that guide the life of the city. Are they guided by the obligations undertaken and commitments made?
- The relationships in the city, in the community, and with the authorities. Are they developing a community guided by the human rights principles?

To achieve these goals the democratic committees create a vertical and horizontal progressive learning process. Step by step, neighborhoods; schools; political, economic, and social institutions; and NGOs examine the human rights framework, relating it to their traditional beliefs, collective memory, and aspirations with regard to environmental, economic, and social justice issues and concerns. As agents of change, they learn to identify, mentor, monitor, and document their needs and engage in one of the most important actions in the city: developing alternative participatory budgets progressively to realize the human rights needs of the community, thus moving power to human rights.

It is important to note that human rights learning and socialization highlights the normative and empirical power of human rights as a tool in individual and collective efforts to address inequalities, injustices, and abuses at home, in the workplace, in the streets, in prisons, in courts, and more. Even in recognized democracies, citizens and policymakers must learn to understand human rights and the obligations and responsibilities they represent in a holistic and comprehensive way. In Human Rights Cities people learn to enforce human rights effectively. As an integral part of social responsibility, citizens can demand that their cities ratify various human rights covenants and conventions to accordingly scrutinize domestic laws, policies, resources, and relationships.

Finally, it must be noted that the Human Rights Cities are not an urban or a utopian agenda. Cities are microcosms of states. And as with the state, the city and its institutions are complex social, economic, and political entities. All the usual day-to-day economic problems, societal dilemmas, and stressful issues of inequality, discrimination, violence, and poverty that are present in a state are present in cities with greater intensity.

In summary, it is evident that all political, civil, economic, social, and cultural human rights concerns for which human rights norms and standards have been elaborated are present in the life of the city. Social responsibility is a major result of these activities where people own and claim their human rights and those of others, within their social and economic realities. And most important, people will experience the power that grows from the knowledge that each individual can make a difference.

This is not about Utopia. This is about hope—a new understanding of human rights to change the world.

Preface

For intellectual and practical reasons, there is no better partnership than sociology and human rights. Sociologists are concerned with human welfare and decent societies. By this we mean that sociologists want to understand how societies can promote nondiscrimination, social equality (the right to food, housing, and education), labor rights, cultural rights, civil and political rights, the right to information, migrants' rights, and economic justice. Many sociologists are now becoming interested in how humans and their habitats can adjust to climate change and alter its effects. This volume is an expression and celebration of that partnership. Needless to say, the authors recognize that the field of human rights is interdisciplinary, with anthropology, political science, law, philosophy, and other disciplines making significant contributions. Nevertheless, sociologists place a distinct emphasis on human welfare and societies (including the communities of which they are composed), instead of, say, the legal frameworks of human rights or their philosophical underpinnings.

Human rights scholars are intellectually rigorous, and many use sophisticated quantitative techniques that are prevalent in the sciences, including the social sciences. Still, scientific work that presupposes human rights assumptions differs from mainstream scientific work in that it explicitly affirms human values and does not pretend to be neutral. Far from being idiosyncratic, these values are universal and formalized in international human rights laws. For this reason, the partnership of human rights and science ought to have broad legitimacy. For example, people may not agree about how to craft school policies and funding mechanisms, but they do agree that education should be provided to all youngsters. Thus, research dedicated to the aim of bringing the right to education to fruition should be universally welcome.

The subtitle for our book—*A Bill of Rights for the Twenty-First Century*—reflects our view that the U.S. Constitution needs to robustly reflect current international laws about human rights. Most governments have ratified human rights treaties and have incorporated them into their constitutions. The constitutions of most rich countries, such as Spain and Sweden, and those of most poor countries, such as Bolivia and Croatia, enumerate the social and economic rights to which all their citizens ought to enjoy. Of course, not all people in Bolivia and Croatia have attained the security and well-being that accompany these rights, and neither have all the people in Spain and Sweden. Nevertheless, articulating such rights in a constitution provides people with shared principles and makes governments accountable. In this volume, authors discuss the human rights treaties that have shaped countries' constitutional provisions, suggesting the implications for the U.S. Constitution, or an expanded Bill of Rights.

The partnership between sociology and human rights is a new one, especially in the United States, which is the motivation for this book. We provide readers with a wide-ranging collection of topics, each covered by experts in their fields. An organization that has accelerated and strengthened sociologists' interest in the field has been the scholarly NGO Sociologists without Borders/Sociólogos sin Fronteras, or SSF. In addition to its webpage and an interactive space,[1] it has a peer-reviewed, open-access journal.[2] Because SSF is global, it is a space where people from all over the world can discuss and debate issues related to human rights with interesting detours into the topics of public goods, the environment, and culture. Both editors have been involved with SSF, as well as with the Human Rights Section of the American Sociological Association and the Thematic Group on Human Rights and Global Justice in the International Sociological Association. Blau has also been active in the Science and Human Rights Coalition of the American Association for the Advancement of Science.

We both acknowledge our students for their inquisitiveness, their eagerness to learn, and their openness to human rights assumptions. We are especially appreciative and thankful for the support and professionalism of the editorial and production staff of Pine Forge Press: Libby Larson, Melinda Masson, Dave Repetto, and Maggie Stanley. As all contemporary authors and editors probably know, it takes an e-village to "raise" a book. Blau would like to thank Rafael Gallegos, who has been the teaching assistant for her course on human rights for two years and is associate director for the Human Rights Center. There are many others to thank for their devoted work at the center, especially Nancy Hilburn and Alfonso Hernandez. She also thanks the nearly 150 University of North Carolina students who have contributed to its programs over the last two years. Frezzo would like to thank his "virtual colleagues" in the fields of human rights and peace studies for encouraging—whether directly or indirectly—his scholarly and pedagogical pursuits.

Judith Blau
Mark Frezzo

1. http://sociologistswithoutborders.org/; http://www.ssfthinktank.org/

2. http://societieswithoutborders.org/

/

PART I

What Are Universal Human Rights?

1

Introduction

Mark Frezzo

The Definition of Human Rights

We begin with the most fundamental question in the field: What are human rights? By definition, human rights are a set of protections and entitlements held by all members of the human species—irrespective of race, class, gender, sexual orientation, cultural background, or national origin. If membership in the human community is the only precondition for human rights, then the same protections and entitlements should be available across the global system. In appealing to universalism—the regulative idea that all humans have the same fundamental needs, deserts, and aspirations—rights discourse stresses the importance of eliminating inequalities not only within nation-states, but also between them. In light of its intrinsic and irreducible universalism, rights discourse has a direct bearing on the policies and practices of intergovernmental organizations, nation-states, transnational corporations, nongovernmental organizations (NGOs), community groups, and individuals. In short, human rights norms constrain and facilitate the undertakings of both state and nonstate actors; offer inspiration to scholars, policymakers, and activists; and provide a grammar and vocabulary for the articulation of demands and the settlement of disputes.

What kinds of protections do human beings have? In principle, human beings are supposed to be protected from abuse or exploitation imposed by

by who?

national governments, corporations, organizations, groups, and individuals. Known as "negative rights"—that is, rights that may not be denied by state or nonstate actors—these protections include the rights to life, bodily integrity, dignity, due process of law, association, assembly, free speech, religious affiliation (or nonaffiliation), and representation in government. Taken together, these civil and political rights guarantee not only the individual's safety, security, personality, and conscience but also his or her participation in public life and freedom from undue interference on the part of the state.

What kinds of entitlements do human beings have? In principle, human beings are entitled to economic structures and social programs that provide them with access to the means of subsistence, allow them to develop their bodies and minds, facilitate access to trades and professions, provide them with leisure time, and protect them from a range of catastrophes (including fluctuations of the market, human-made crises, and natural disasters). Known as "positive rights"—that is, rights that must be provided by public authorities—these entitlements include the rights to food, clothing, housing, health care, an education, employment, unemployment and disability insurance, social security, and a minimum standard of living. Taken together, these economic and social rights promote longevity and self-actualization among individuals. Alternatively, the objectives of longevity and self-actualization can be conceptualized as "rights bundles"—packages of rights that imply or necessitate one another. While the objective of longevity—the ability to lead a long, healthy life—presupposes access to food, water, shelter, proper hygiene, a clean environment, and health care, the objective of self-actualization—the ability to develop one's talents, personality, interests, and tastes—presupposes access to education, training, information, and a range of choices in defining one's identity. Far from being exclusively economic and social in character, both rights bundles—longevity and self-actualization—are filtered through culture.

What does culture—defined as a collection of shared values, symbols, and practices within a group or society—have to do with human rights? The category of positive rights includes cultural rights, as well as economic and social rights. In principle, all human beings—whether in the Global North or the Global South and irrespective of social standing within nation-states—are entitled to have a culture; to inhabit ancestral lands (where applicable); to affirm the rituals, practices, and customs of their ethnic group, tribe, or clan (where applicable); and to learn and speak a minority language in school (where applicable). By design, these entitlements promote the preservation of the world's cultural diversity—a crucial objective in a globalized age marked by the deepening of consumerism, the homogenization of cultures, and grave threats to the life-ways of indigenous peoples and peasants, as well as to racial, ethnic, linguistic, and religious minorities. While globalization—defined as increased interdependency among the world's peoples—has produced new opportunities for transnational cooperation in the name of human rights, social justice, and peace, it has also endangered the world's cultural diversity. For this reason, sociologists of human rights—following the example of their counterparts in anthropology—have devoted considerable attention to cultural rights.

The Foundation of Human Rights

What makes someone so human?

Having defined the basic forms of human rights, we can proceed to the next fundamental question in the field: Where do human rights—whether negative or positive, civil and political, economic and social, or cultural—come from? In answering this question, Turner (2006) advances the following argument:

> The study of human rights places the human body at the center of social and political theory, and it employs the notion of embodiment as a foundation for defending universal human rights. My argument is based on four fundamental philosophical assumptions: the vulnerability of human beings as embodied agents, the dependency of humans (especially in their early childhood development), the general reciprocity and interconnectedness of social life, and, finally, the precariousness of social institutions. (P. 25)

In a nutshell, the foundation of human rights can be found in the human body and its fundamental needs. Though nurtured differently according to culture and geography, the human body—in its intrinsic vulnerability—constitutes the basis for universalism.

In answering the question of the foundation of human rights from a different angle, Ishay (2008) advances the following argument:

> Human rights are rights held by individuals because they are members of the human species. They are rights shared equally by everyone regardless of sex, race, nationality, and economic background. They are universal in content. Across the centuries, conflicting political traditions have elaborated different components of human rights or differed over which elements have priority. In our day, the manifold meanings of human rights reflect the process of historical continuity and change that helped shape their present substance and

helped form the Universal Declaration of Human Rights adopted by the General Assembly of the United Nations in 1948. (P. 3)

Though consistent with Turner's (2006) ontological approach, Ishay's (2008) historical approach emphasizes the role of past struggles—on the part of workers in the socialist movement, women in the feminist movement, popular forces opposing colonialism, and a host of other activists—in expanding the scope of human rights. In effect, the human rights available to the inhabitants of the early twenty-first century—the civil and political, economic and social, cultural, and other forms of rights examined in this book—can be seen as the accumulation of social knowledge from previous generations. What is the origin of this social knowledge? Over time, social movements—in laying claim to Enlightenment doctrine while exposing the limitations of existing forms of government—have greatly expanded what are thinkable and realizable as human rights. Accordingly, in documenting the range of human rights available to the inhabitants of the United States, this book points to the need to reflect on the possibility of revising the Constitution in keeping with contemporary thinking in the field.

Sociology, Human Rights, and the U.S. Context

This volume is intended not only for undergraduate and graduate students in the social sciences but also for scholars, policymakers, and activists in the broader domain of human rights. As a contribution to the sociology of human rights—a growing academic field that analyzes the social conditions under which human rights norms emerge, evolve, and inspire the creation of laws, social programs, and institutions—this volume proposes a comprehensive revision of the U.S. Constitution (1787) to reflect recent innovations in civil and political rights, economic and social rights, nondiscrimination, the rights of vulnerable people, cultural rights, immigrants' rights, environmental rights, and a range of other rights. While these innovations in rights thinking have been incubated largely outside of the United States (especially in Latin America, with the recent proliferation of social movements and the growth of the World Social Forum), they harbor profound ramifications for U.S. society, politics, and law. More to the point, the adoption of new conceptions of human rights represents the key to the deepening of democracy in the United States.

In tracing the practical applications of cutting-edge rights thinking for the U.S. context, this volume explains the conventional categories of rights (i.e., first-generation civil and political rights, second-generation economic and social rights, and third-generation cultural rights), while exploring the recently postulated right to a clean environment and other "fourth-generation" rights. At the same time, this volume affirms the indivisibility of rights: civil and political rights—including the freedoms of association, assembly, and speech, along with the right to vote—acquire considerably more substance when articulated with such economic and social rights as subsidized food and housing, medical care, education, disability and unemployment insurance, and social security; meanwhile, an expanded social safety net—though crucial to the promotion of longevity and self-actualization across the population (without regard to race, class, gender, sexual orientation, or national origin)—must be supplemented by the right to have a culture, the protection of indigenous practices, the right to inhabit an ancestral land, and the right to learn and speak a minority language in school. In sum, these rights form the basis of a pluralistic and participatory democracy—pluralistic insofar as the government protects the diversity of the U.S. cultural landscape and participatory insofar as the government brings more voices into the decision-making process (e.g., through federal, state, and local referenda on public policies). In short, though we may place rights in distinct categories for analytic and pedagogical purposes, we must also recognize the inextricability of rights in the "real world."

Notwithstanding the powerful legacy of rights-oriented movements (organized by workers, women, African Americans, the LGBTQ community, environmentalists, and many other constituencies), along with previous proposals for an "Economic Bill of Rights" to advance the interests of poor and working-class citizens and an "Equal Rights Amendment" to advance the interests of women, U.S. scholars and activists alike have proved reluctant to embrace the idea of amending the Constitution to accommodate demands that would have been unimaginable in the time of the founders. Instead, scholars and activists have tended to support legislative change—the addition or subtraction of federal, state, and local laws in accordance with changing tides. Well documented by sociologists of law and social movement researchers, the legislative strategy—that is, the utilization not only of the voting booth but also of cyber-activism, public protests, building occupations and sit-ins, labor slowdowns and strikes, boycotts of prominent corporations, and other tactics to pressure elected officials in Congress, state legislatures, and city councils to (a) ratify laws that mitigate inequalities of race, class, gender, sexual orientation, national origin, and physical disability and (b) repeal laws that calcify or exacerbate such inequalities—would be more effective if it included a demand for constitutional amendments. Arguably, the aforementioned tactics would exert more influence if they were linked to an explicit demand for the revision of the Constitution.

Bringing Human Rights Back Home

One of the major arguments of this book is that lawmakers should craft constitutional amendments that render such United Nations (UN) treaties as the 1966 International Covenant on Civil and Political Rights (ICCPR) and the 1966 International Covenant on Economic, Social, and Cultural Rights (ICESCR) legally binding on U.S. soil. As the authors in this volume demonstrate, the constitutional strategy would serve three significant functions. First, it would cement the achievements of past movements in the United States. Second, it would create a platform—or, more precisely, a political opportunity structure—for future movements in the United States. Third, in keeping with a cosmopolitan vision that has been alternately nurtured and suppressed since the Enlightenment, a decision on the part of U.S. policymakers to adopt and enforce the ICCPR and the ICESCR would expand and intensify the connections between the inhabitants of the United States and their counterparts in the rest of the world.

Since the ratification of the ten amendments that compose the Bill of Rights in 1791, four amendments have testified to the existence of political opportunity structures or conjunctions between movements in civil society and progressive forces in the federal government: the Thirteenth Amendment abolishing slavery in 1865, the Fourteenth Amendment guaranteeing equal protection under the law in 1868, the Fifteenth Amendment granting African Americans and other racial minorities the right to vote in 1870, and the Nineteenth Amendment giving women the right to vote in 1920. Subsequently, the New Deal, the civil rights movement, the Great Society, the "new social movements" of the late 1960s and early 1970s, and the spate of subsequent legislation to mitigate inequalities of race, class, gender, and sexual orientation—though successful in many ways—have fallen short of producing constitutional change.

Why is it problematic that the aforementioned currents failed to change the Constitution? It is widely acknowledged that the most significant legacy of the New Deal—namely, the Social Security system established in 1935— could be abolished by an act of Congress. In fact, recent years have witnessed considerable debate on the future of Social Security and other social programs. But it is often forgotten that the two most significant legal contributions of the civil rights movement—the Civil Rights Act of 1964, which abrogated the "Jim Crow laws" and banned segregation in schools, workplaces, and other public accommodations, along with the Voting

Rights Act of 1965, which reinforced the Fifteenth Amendment and banned the discriminatory practices that had prevented African Americans from voting—could be overturned by an act of Congress. This is the rationale for current proposals to (a) cement the achievements of the New Deal in an "Economic Bill of Rights" (akin to the amendments President Franklin Delano Roosevelt had proposed in 1944 amid preparations for the postwar reconstruction of the global economy and the interstate system around the principle of "One World"); (b) extend the accomplishments of the civil rights movement in amendments banning racial discrimination in education, employment, and the enjoyment of public life; and (c) solidify the gains of the women's movement in an "Equal Rights Amendment" (akin to the declaration drafted by suffragette Alice Paul in 1923, entertained by public officials in the 1960s, approved by Congress in 1972, and ratified by 35 of the necessary 38 states before its expiration date in 1982).

In light of the precariousness of the aforementioned legislative gains, this book argues for the need to formalize the past accomplishments and facilitate the future undertakings of popular movements by amending the Constitution. If U.S.-based scholars and activists have fallen out of the habit of proposing amendments to the Constitution, where might they turn for ideas on how to proceed? In a plea to U.S.-based scholars and activists to join forces in reinterpreting the Constitution, the authors draw on the advanced thinking and social learning that have accumulated not only in Latin America (where the World Social Forum has built on the previous efforts of the Landless Rural Workers' Movement in Brazil and popular mobilizations in neighboring countries), but also in Africa and Asia. If recent university conferences on human rights and the 2007 and 2010 installments of the US Social Forum are any indication, U.S.-based scholars and activists have begun to strengthen their ties not only to one another but also to their colleagues abroad. In the process, they have been the beneficiaries of novel ideas from human rights advocates across the globe.

At the very least, it is clear that the process of transnational coalition building can be facilitated through the adoption of the malleable language of human rights. It is instructive that an array of grassroots movements, NGOs, and UN agencies—though vastly different in worldview, mandate, and power—have articulated their demands and policy proposals in the language of human rights. In implying a complex universalism that allows for geographic variation and cultural specificity, the adoption of human rights as a "master frame" has cultivated transnational alliances among a diversity of actors (including indigenous peoples; peasants; workers; racial, ethnic, and religious minorities; women; and LGBTQ communities). In sum, grassroots groups and their NGO partners have grappled with the enduring contradictions of Enlightenment thought—including the articulation of an emancipatory project alongside the preservation of colonialism, slavery, and other forms of domination, exploitation, and exclusion—in renovating the cosmopolitan vision for the twenty-first century. As if to respond to the trenchant critiques of Enlightenment thought offered by poststructuralism and postmodernism, postcolonial theory and subaltern studies, Third World and global feminism, and other schools of contemporary social theory, popular forces and intellectuals in the Global South have advanced a new form of universalism. In principle, there is no reason why this new universalism should not take root in the United States—after all, the U.S. university system has, for some time, been the world leader of research and innovative ideas.

While U.S.-based scholars and activists have grown accustomed not only to supporting imperiled academics, intellectuals, journalists, political leaders, and movement organizers but also to providing material and logistical assistance to community groups, social movement organizations, and NGOs elsewhere in the world—examples include Amnesty International campaigns on behalf of prisoners of conscience, the Zapatista solidarity network, campaigns launched by United Students Against Sweatshops and other challenges to the labor and environmental practices of transnational corporations, and coalitions against human trafficking and sexual slavery—they have not regained the habit of importing new conceptions of human rights to the United States. Phrased differently, the outflow of solidarity (as manifested in the provision of material, logistical, and moral support) to the Global South has only recently been accompanied by a backflow of ideas to the United States. In essence, this book is designed to facilitate the transmission of human rights-oriented ideas across the United States.

Although an explanation of the aforementioned phenomenon falls beyond the purview of this book, it is worthwhile to mention two contributing factors. First, the residues of positivism (i.e., the belief that the social sciences should be value-free) and relativism (i.e., the belief in the impossibility or undesirability of making value judgments across cultural contexts) have, until recently, prevented social scientists from building an explicit concern for human rights into their research (Turner 2006). Second, in the world of activists, the daily grind for resources and publicity—exacerbated by a history of competition between groups, infighting within groups, and a marked susceptibility to identity politics—has impeded the formation of enduring alliances among factions. In this light, the emergence of the public sociology initiative in the American Sociological Association (ASA) in 2004 and the US Social Forum three years later marked a significant breakthrough for academics and activists, respectively. It comes as no surprise, therefore, that a large number of scholars have participated in the activities of the US Social Forum.

To date, the sea change among scholars and activists has exerted little or no influence on the Democratic and Republican parties in the United States. Notwithstanding its tendency—especially since the administration of President Jimmy Carter (1976–1980)—to invoke the language of human rights in justifying a foreign policy that often conflicts with the rights of peoples elsewhere in the world, the U.S. government has carefully avoided using human rights terminology in its articulating of domestic policy. Recognizing the paradoxical role of the United States as a founder and chief sponsor of the UN and yet a reluctant party to international treaties that would provoke the reconsideration or transformation of domestic policy, this book aims to bring human rights "back home." This process entails sustained reflection on the history, structure, and mandate of the UN—not least because UN declarations serve as reference points for human rights advocates across the world.

Designed not only to manage the interstate system but also to promote national self-determination, nation building, and development in the Global South, the UN has, throughout its 65-year history, served as a cauldron for research and debate on human rights. Reflected in the 1948 Universal Declaration of Human Rights (UDHR), the 1966 ICCPR, the 1966 ICESCR, and an array of other declarations, the knowledge-producing function of the UN should not be ignored. On one hand, the UDHR, the ICCPR, and the ICESCR can be characterized as the intellectual expressions of popular mobilizations for human rights, peace, and justice. On the other hand, these documents can be characterized as springboards for new forms of advocacy and movement activity. In short, even though the UN has outstripped the United States in rights thinking—in part by sponsoring conferences for academics, policymakers, NGO staff, and activists across the world—there exists no formal obstacle to applying the insights of the UN and its intellectual orbit in the U.S. context. Hence the question arises: What would happen if the United States took seriously the ICCPR and the ICESCR? Phrased differently, how would the implementation of these treaties affect U.S. society, politics, and law? How might the United States contribute to the debate on the contents of such treaties? It is incumbent upon us to explore such questions without fear of seeming utopian or out of touch with domestic norms, customs, and practices.

Building on a series of projects associated with the scholarly NGO Sociologists without Borders[1]—including the journal *Societies without Borders: Human Rights and the Social Sciences*[2]; a number of panels at the annual meetings of the ASA, the International Sociological Association (ISA), and other disciplinary organizations; and the collected volume *The*

Leading Rogue State: The U.S. and Human Rights (Blau et al. 2008)—the present book emphasizes three interrelated questions. First, how might we apply sociological expertise in illuminating recent advances in the theory and practice of human rights? Second, how might we draw on innovations in rights thinking in updating the Constitution to meet the demands of a changing global economy, interstate system, and global civil society? Third, what are the implications of the rights project for sociology as a discipline? In answering these questions, the present book argues that the tools of sociology are well suited to elucidate the invariably complex and often contradictory interactions among academics, policymakers, and activists operating in the field of human rights. Consequently, the present book can be seen as a corollary of the ongoing efforts of the Human Rights Section of the ASA[3] and the Thematic Group on Human Rights and Global Justice in the ISA[4] to systematize the sociology of human rights.

In conceptualizing the human rights community as a knowledge movement—a transnational consortium of university researchers, UN officials, NGO staff, and movement organizers citing the ICCPR and the ICESCR as touchstones—this book excavates the idea systems, institutions, and policies associated with a vision of human rights that has evolved markedly since the founding of the UN system in 1945. In addition, this book argues for the need to import rights thinking from abroad in an effort to breathe new life into the U.S. Constitution. In principle, there is no reason why the United States cannot follow the example of countries that have revised their constitutions.[5] Finally, this book argues for the abandonment of a social problems approach that presumes value neutrality in favor of a human rights approach that affirms such values as equality, solidarity, diversity, and sustainability as objectives of scholarly research, teaching, and service.

In building a concern for human rights into the conduct of social science, we find support not only in the ASA's (2009) "Statement Affirming and Expanding the Commitment to Human Rights,"[6] but also in the American Anthropological Association's (1999) "Declaration on Anthropology and Human Rights"[7] and the Science and Human Rights Program launched by the American Association for the Advancement of Science (2009).[8] Taken together, the efforts of these organizations to incorporate values into social and natural scientific research can be seen as a movement beyond the false opposition between positivism and relativism. It is possible to reconcile scientific rigor with the advocacy of human rights; social and natural scientists can—and should—have it both ways. More broadly, it is clear that a number of events—including financial crises from East Asia to Russia, to Latin America, and more recently to the United States and the European Union; social unrest across the Global South; the U.S. wars in Iraq and Afghanistan;

increasing environmental degradation; the rapid spread of treatable diseases across sub-Saharan Africa; civil wars and genocides in poor countries; and the disastrous effects of Hurricane Katrina on the inhabitants of New Orleans and the coastal communities of Louisiana and Mississippi—have prompted many social and natural scientists in the United States to become advocates of human rights. This represents an extremely important development. As the case of Katrina and its aftermath suggests, the next step is for social and natural scientists to apply their growing awareness of human rights problems to the U.S. context. Alas, human rights issues exist not just "over there," in the Global South, but also "right here," in the United States. In this light, low life expectancy, high infant mortality, and limited access to educational and professional opportunities among poor and working-class people; the persistence of discrimination on the basis of race, gender, and sexual orientation; and the rapid advance of environmental degradation can be defined as human rights issues. This is the essence of the human rights approach to sociology.

Conclusion

As this chapter has argued, the constitutional strategy—that is, codifying the achievements of social movements at the level of the Constitution—would present three significant advantages over the legislative strategy. First, it is appreciably more difficult to repeal constitutional amendments than it is to overturn legislation. For example, a civil rights amendment would concretize the rights of African Americans, Latinos, and other racial and ethnic minority groups appreciably more than existing legislation outlawing discrimination in education, work, and the public sphere. Similarly, an equal rights amendment would secure women's rights to a much greater degree than existing legislation banning sexual discrimination and harassment in schools, workplaces, and other public institutions. Second, constitutional amendments pertaining to human rights would have the effect of legitimizing and enabling social movements pursuing projects of emancipation or pushing for the expansion of democracy. For example, a constitutional amendment banning discrimination and harassment according to sexual orientation and legalizing same-sex marriage would, in all likelihood, provide momentum for the LGBTQ movement in its pursuit of other objectives. Third, constitutional amendments would offer the possibility of linking domestic law to international law in a more robust way. Phrased differently, constitutional amendments on civil rights for African Americans, Latinos, and other minority groups; equal rights for women; and an array of rights for the LGBTQ community would serve to bring the United States into a more productive dialogue not only with nation-states that have revised their constitutions but also with a spectrum of NGOs and UN agencies operating in the field of human rights. This would allow the United States—a hegemonic power with an extensive university system (including numerous law schools), a high number of NGOs and other civil society organizations, a dense concentration of foreign embassies and consulates in Washington, D.C., and a massive conglomeration of foreign missions to the UN in New York—to participate more fruitfully in debating, enacting, and enforcing international law. It is high time for the United States to mobilize its vast reservoir of talent and its substantial infrastructure for the cause of human rights.

Notes

1. http://www.sociologistswithoutborders.org/
2. http://societieswithoutborders.org/
3. http://www.asanet.org/sections/humanrights.cfm
4. http://www.isa-sociology.org/tg03.htm
5. See the University of Richmond Constitution Finder: http://confinder.richmond.edu/
6. http://asanet.org/about/Council_Statements.cfm
7. http://www.aaanet.org/stmts/humanrts.htm
8. http://shr.aaas.org/

References

American Anthropological Association. 1999. "Declaration on Anthropology and Human Rights." Retrieved January 6, 2011 (http://www.aaanet.org/stmts/humanrts.htm).

American Association for the Advancement of Science. 2009. "Science and Human Rights Program." Retrieved January 6, 2011 (http://shr.aaas.org).

American Sociological Association. 2009. "Statement Affirming and Expanding the Commitment to Human Rights." Retrieved January 6, 2011 (http://asanet.org/about/Council_Statements.cfm).

Blau, Judith, David L. Brunsma, Alberto Moncada, and Catherine Zimmer, eds. 2008. *The Leading Rogue State: The U.S. and Human Rights*. Boulder, CO: Paradigm.

Ishay, Micheline. 2008. *The History of Human Rights: From Ancient Times to the Globalization Era*. Berkeley: University of California Press.

Turner, Bryan. 2006. *Vulnerability and Human Rights*. University Park: Pennsylvania State University Press.

University of Richmond. 2010. "Constitution Finder." Retrieved January 6, 2011 (http://confinder.richmond.edu/).

2

Deepening Civil and Political Rights

Mark Frezzo

The Sociological Approach

Drawing on the sociology of human rights—a field that analyzes the world historical conditions under which human rights declarations are drafted, debated, implemented, and enforced—this chapter examines the origins and impact of the most important documents produced by the United Nations (UN): the 1948 Universal Declaration of Human Rights (UDHR), which established a framework for the implementation of human rights across the world and became an important reference point, not only for the UN and its member nations, but also for national liberation movements in the Global South, and subsequently for such nongovernmental organizations (NGOs) as Amnesty International and Human Rights Watch; the 1966 International Covenant on Civil and Political Rights (ICCPR)[1], which delineated first-generation rights to liberty and security of the person (to be achieved through safeguards on individuals); and the 1966 International Covenant on Economic, Social, and Cultural Rights (ICESCR), which delineated second-generation rights to equality (to be achieved through a range of social programs) and third-generation rights to solidarity (to be achieved through the official recognition of group identities). Though often separated by scholars for analytic purposes—and by policymakers and activists for political purposes—the three generations of human rights are indivisible.

One of the major objectives of the sociological approach is to illuminate the connections among civil and political rights, economic and social rights, cultural rights, and environmental rights. As Blau and Moncada (2006) have argued, "The human rights perspective does not abstract people according to their functional role in the polity or the economy, but rather grants persons their freedoms and self-determination and recognizes their integral social, economic, and cultural needs and their social, economic, and cultural responsibilities" (p. 234).

It follows that such civil and political rights as the right to life and security of the person, the right to due process of law, the right to vote in free and fair elections, freedom of religion, freedom of speech, freedom of association, and freedom of assembly—the most prominent features of the ICCPR—are conducive to the realization of other rights. Though significant in themselves, civil and political rights have the effect of augmenting participation democracy; in turn, the expansion and intensification of popular participation in democratic institutions and practices stand as the precondition for the achievement of such social entitlements as government-funded health care and child care, paid maternity and paternity leave, and a living wage.

After all, every social movement needs the freedom of association to recruit members, the freedom of assembly to mount protests in public spaces, and the freedom of speech to articulate its demands for economic, social, and cultural rights. In the course of U.S. history, these civil liberties have facilitated the undertakings of activists for working-class rights, civil rights for racial minorities, women's rights, peace, LGBTQ rights, and environmental justice. If these movements have achieved more expansive rights—including a social safety net and legislation barring discrimination according race, sex, and sexual orientation—it is because they have maximized whatever civil liberties were available to them in their times. In forging connections with like-minded forces overseas, these movements have often made reference to transnational norms—including the ones embedded in such vaunted documents as the UDHR, the ICCPR, and the ICESCR.

Far from trivializing the UDHR, the ICCPR, and the ICESCR as reflections of utopian sentiment or echoes of high-minded "rights talk," the sociological approach recognizes that such documents play an important role in regulating the undertakings of nation-states, nonstate actors, and individuals. This raises the following question: In what sense do UN documents have power? Clearly, national governments, NGOs, popular movements, and ordinary people appeal to such documents—declarations, treaties, and research reports—in the quest for legitimacy; by the same token, they wish to avoid condemnation in reference to such documents. While it would be naïve to assume that UN documents in themselves could govern the inter-state system or the global economy, it would be equally problematic to deny the role of norms in influencing the conduct of governments, civil society actors, and individuals (Khagram, Riker, and Sikkink 2002). Thus, the sociological approach treats UN documents as if they were material mani-festations of transnational norms. In effect, such documents can be inter-preted not only as the buildup of "social learning" from past debates, but also as a platform for future debates. What are thinkable as human rights in the twenty-first century represent the accumulation of past struggles—including the efforts of the heavily cited Enlightenment philosophers and revolu-tionaries of the late eighteenth century, along with the underacknowledged or even anonymous working-class militants, anticolonialists, civil rights advocates, indigenous rights activists, partisans of women's rights, LGBTQ campaigners, peacemakers, and environmentalists of subsequent centuries (Ishay 2008).

What connects these movements—across historical time, geographic space, and a diversity of evolving cultures—is their use of the language of human rights to articulate their grievances, demand concessions from nation-states, appeal to NGOs and the UN to pressure nation-states on their behalf (in the quest for what is known as the "boomerang effect"), and draft blueprints of a more inclusive, democratic, and just world. In fact, it is difficult—if not impossible—for such movements to avoid invok-ing human rights as a "master frame." Moreover, by invoking the discourse of rights—and thereby animating the specter of past struggles—such movements routinely create new "bundles" of rights that cut across the conventional categories employed by scholars and policymakers. One example comes in the form of the right to longevity, which presupposes the rights to food, water, health care, and a clean environment. Another example comes in the form of the right to self-actualization or to the free development of the personality, which presupposes the rights to an educa-tion, job training, information, equality of opportunity, and an identity (based on gender, sexual orientation, ethnicity, etc.). Arguably, the rights to longevity and self-actualization fall equally into the categories of first-, second-, and third-generation rights. In the process of creating such bun-dles, movements have effectively transformed the syntax and semantics of rights beyond what any Enlightenment philosopher or any militant in the nineteenth-century working-class movement could have imagined. It is through this lens that we must examine the role of the UDHR, the ICCPR, and the ICESCR in crystallizing what have "counted" as human rights from 1945 to the present day.

The International Bill of Rights

Although the UDHR effectively prefigured the three generations of human rights—raising the celebrated slogan of the French Revolution, "Liberty, Equality, Fraternity," to the level of international law—the ICCPR and the ICESCR offered important, and yet highly contested, elaborations of human rights. Conceptualized as the three planks of an "International Bill of Rights," the UDHR, the ICCPR, and the ICESCR were designed not only to constrain but also to facilitate the undertakings of nation-states (embedded in an interstate system), nonstate actors (including NGOs and other civil society entities), and individuals. Though cut from the same cloth—namely, the debates that accompanied the drafting, promulgation, and ratification of the UDHR—the ICCPR and the ICESCR followed separate trajectories. Phrased differently, the theoretical and practical indivisibility of human rights—though consistent with the original intentions of U.S. planners and recognized by the founders of the UN—was obscured by the geopolitics and national politics of the United States. It is important, therefore, for sociologists to excavate the world historical conditions under which civil and political rights were separated from economic and social rights. Notwithstanding its role in planning the International Bill of Rights—a project that involved former First Lady and pioneer of civil rights and women's rights Eleanor Roosevelt—the United States developed an attitude of ambivalence toward the ICCPR, along with an attitude of hostility toward the ICESCR.

As the Cold War grew more intense and the demands of social movements (including those pushing for *decolonization, civil rights,* working-class rights, and women's rights) grew louder, the United States recoiled from the implications of the ICCPR and the ICESCR alike. In contrast, such allies of the United States as France, Germany, Italy, Spain, the United Kingdom, and every other Western European state (except for the Holy See) ratified both the ICCPR and the ICESCR. Doubtless, this reflected differences in how the historic compromise between capital and labor was implemented in the United States versus Western Europe. Notwithstanding the status of the New Deal as a pioneering experiment in social planning, the United States was quickly outstripped by Western Europe in terms of social entitlements. In the United States, efforts to expand human rights were impeded by divisions in the Democratic Party—especially concerning the status of African Americans in the southern states; in Western Europe, such efforts were accelerated by the presence of labor, social democratic, socialist, and communist parties in parliament. Over time, most nations—from Africa to Asia, Latin America, and beyond—ratified the two covenants. While it would be naïve to imagine that merely ratifying the covenants would suffice to bring the three generations of rights to fruition on a national scale, it is significant that the United States—a forerunner in the cultivation of human rights norms and practices—would opt to remain an outlier. The peculiar status of the United States as both a forerunner and an outlier in the field of human rights—a phenomenon that this chapter calls the "U.S. paradox"—requires further analysis.

The United States and the ICCPR

Notwithstanding its pivotal role in founding the UN and promoting the UDHR, the United States displayed considerable ambivalence about the ICCPR and opted, ultimately, to reject the ICESCR altogether. More precisely, the United States signed the ICCPR in 1976, but waited until 1992 to ratify the treaty. Moreover, in ratifying the covenant, the United States added five reservations, five understandings, and four declarations—including the stipulation that the ICCPR would not be self-executing, and hence would have no bearing on the creation, interpretation, or enforcement of U.S. laws. Meanwhile, although President Jimmy Carter signed the ICESCR in 1979, he opted not to present the treaty to the Senate for "advice and consent," thereby preventing it from being considered for ratification. By all accounts, Carter recognized that there was little support in the Senate for the human rights-oriented foreign policy he envisaged; it would have complicated matters if Carter had taken the next step in legitimizing economic and social rights at home. In all likelihood, the ICESCR would have suffered the same fate as the ICCPR, since the United States had routinely maintained that international treaties should not be self-executing. In practice, this meant that the United States—in its capacity as a hegemonic power—granted itself an exemption from such treaties.

Since the United States has always considered itself a bastion of civil and political rights, its ambivalent position vis-à-vis the ICCPR deserves further scrutiny. In its first reservation, the Senate rejected Article 20—the prohibition of war propaganda, along with "any advocacy of national, racial or religious hatred that constitutes incitement to discrimination, hostility or violence"—on the grounds that such a provision would constitute an abridgement of the freedom of speech.[2] In its second, third, fourth, and fifth reservations, the Senate rejected the ICCPR's prohibition of the death penalty, along with its proposals for penal reforms.[3] In its five understandings, the Senate proposed highly restrictive interpretations of the ICCPR's language.[4] Doubtless, the Senate's reservations and understandings could be defended within the conception of civil and political rights that has prevailed in the United States since the Revolution. As a consequence, legal scholars have debated this issue in considerable detail. Nevertheless, the Senate's first declaration—"that the provisions of Articles 1 through 27 of the Covenant are not self-executing"—has received widespread criticism for preventing the ICCPR from having an impact on the Constitution or laws of the United States.[5] Similarly, the Senate's proviso—"nothing in this Covenant requires or authorizes legislation, or other action, by the United States of America prohibited by the Constitution of the United States as interpreted by the United States"—formally precludes the ICCPR from altering the U.S. legal system.[6]

It has been a long-standing policy of the U.S. government to promote human rights treaties abroad while refusing to apply them at home. This policy stems not only from a deeply ingrained belief in "American exceptionalism"—the idea that the United States should play a prominent role in defining the rules of the interstate system and orchestrating the affairs of other nations, while considering itself above international law—but also from a tendency to treat the U.S. Constitution as if it were a sacred document requiring no revisions. However, as its 27 amendments—including the 17 added since the ratification of the Bill of Rights in 1791—testify, the Constitution is a living, breathing, and evolving document. In fact, the framers of the Constitution—including its principal author James Madison, who coauthored the touchstone of U.S. political theory, *The Federalist Papers*, in 1787 and 1788 and served as President from 1809 to 1817—claimed neither infallibility for themselves nor perfection for their document.

Notwithstanding the contentions of "strict constructionists"—legal scholars, jurists, policymakers, and lobbyists who advocate a "faithful" interpretation of the Constitution in accordance with the "original intent" of the "Founding Fathers," while opposing the "judicial activism" of those who propose to alter the Constitution—there exists a broad consensus on the malleability of the Constitution. Indeed, this consensus flows through all channels of U.S. society. In the contemporary period, how many Americans would oppose the Thirteenth Amendment abolishing slavery, the Fourteenth Amendment guaranteeing equal protection under the law, the Fifteenth Amendment ensuring African Americans and other racial minorities the right to vote, or the Nineteenth Amendment granting women the right to vote? Who would deny that these amendments—in advancing the civil and political rights of African Americans, other racial and ethnic minorities, and women—made the United States a more inclusive, democratic, and just nation? Furthermore, if we accept that the Thirteenth, Fourteenth, Fifteenth, and Nineteenth amendments improved U.S. society, what prevents us from speculating about how future amendments might serve the same purpose? What prevents us from updating our Constitution in accordance with the prevailing norms on human rights? As Blau and Moncada (2006) have contended, the U.S. Constitution seems antiquated when compared to newer constitutions.[7]

Taken literally, the term *constitution* denotes an ongoing process by which people expand their rights; in theory, this process is permanent insofar as the realization of rights inevitably creates a demand for more rights. In this light, the ICCPR can be seen as an important reference point for those who aspire to update the U.S. Constitution. In focusing on the social context of the ICCPR—understood as a cutting-edge document that crystallizes the aspirations of human rights advocates across the world—this chapter explores the following questions: Why did the United States decide to sign the ICCPR with reservations, understandings, and declarations? What were the ramifications of the U.S. decision? How might the ICCPR—if taken seriously by policymakers, courts, and ordinary people in the United States— contribute to the revision or reinterpretation of the U.S. Constitution? Why might it be beneficial to the inhabitants of the United States to bring the Constitution and domestic laws into compliance with the ICCPR?

In answering these questions, this chapter examines the role of the UN in bolstering U.S. power, while creating a forum for the expression of dissent on the part of the Soviet Bloc and the nations of the non-Western world. Whether by design or by accident, the UN played the role of a pressure-release valve in the postwar system—alleviating tensions stemming from the Cold War and the North-South divide. In the process, the UN served not only as an arbiter of international disputes, a peacekeeper, and a conduit to development in the Global South, but also as a laboratory for new ideas on human rights. Manifested in conferences, scholarly research, and advocacy, the intellectual function of the UN deserves further exploration—not least because it caused the UN to drift away from the United States. In achieving a modicum of autonomy and giving voice to anticolonial forces in the Global South, the UN emphasized the deep connection between human rights and development—encapsulated in the principle of the "right to development." Over time, the UN's influence spread to civil society groups in the Global North—including the United States. In recent years, the UN has been joined by NGOs, social movement organizations (SMOs), and community groups across the world in rethinking, debating, and transforming the doctrine of human rights. With the growth of the US Social Forum—established in

2007 to promote dialogue among NGOs, SMOs, community groups, and scholar-activists on the prospects for deepening human rights and augmenting popular participation in democracy—the process has come full circle.[8] In narrating the story of U.S.-UN relations and the trajectory of human rights thinking, this chapter lays the groundwork for an open-ended debate—among people from all walks of life—on the future of civil and political rights in the United States.

U.S. Hegemony and the UN

Using the sociological approach to human rights, this chapter examines the evolution of civil and political rights since the founding of the UN in 1945—a process that was spearheaded by the U.S. government and its wartime allies in an effort not only to restore order to the interstate system, but also to establish a framework for human rights (including civil, political, economic, social, and cultural rights), national self-determination, nation building, development, conflict resolution, and peacekeeping. Finding its precursors in Enlightenment philosopher Immanuel Kant's "cosmopolitan ethic," U.S. President Woodrow Wilson's liberal internationalism (with its institutional offshoot, the League of Nations), U.S. President Franklin Delano Roosevelt's vision of "One World"—inclusive of the former Axis Powers, the rival Union of Soviet Socialist Republics (USSR), and peoples living under colonial rule—prepared the ground for the institutionalization of the UN. In Roosevelt's view, the UN would serve not only to legitimize U.S. leadership in the interstate system and the global economy but also to accord representation to other nations—wealthy and poor alike—in a forum for debate, conflict resolution, and decision making. Implicit in Roosevelt's vision was the need not only for national self-determination for colonized peoples but also for civil and political rights—including the right to life and security of the person, the right to due process of law, voting rights, freedom of religion, freedom of speech, freedom of association, and freedom of assembly for the entire human community. Delivered prior to the official entrance of the United States into the Second World War in 1941—when the resolution of the conflict remained in doubt—Roosevelt's famous "Four Freedoms" speech echoed Wilsonian internationalism and its ill-fated institutional offshoot, the League of Nations, while prefiguring a new form of internationalism that would manifest itself in the UN:

> We look forward to a world founded upon four essential human freedoms. The first is freedom of speech and expression—everywhere in the world. The

second is freedom of every person to worship God in his own way—everywhere in the world. The third is freedom from want—which, translated into world terms, means economic understandings which will secure to every nation a healthy peacetime life for its inhabitants—everywhere in the world. The fourth is freedom from fear—which, translated into world terms, means a world-wide reduction of armaments to such a point and in such a thorough fashion that no nation will be in a position to commit an act of physical aggression against any neighbor—anywhere in the world. That is no vision of a distant millennium. It is a definite basis for a kind of world attainable in our own time and generation.[9]

In addition to marking a turning point in U.S. and world history, Roosevelt's speech is notable in its emphasis on the need for an institutional framework for the realization of the freedom of speech, the freedom of religion, the freedom from want, and the freedom from fear. In light of its influence on subsequent thinking in the fields of human rights, development, and global governance, Roosevelt's speech merits further attention. Whereas the freedom of speech and the freedom of religion fall into the category of first-generation civil and political rights, the freedom from want—that is, the right to a job or unemployment insurance in lieu of a job, along with a social safety net to mitigate the fluctuations of the economy— falls into the category of second-generation economic and social rights. But where does the freedom from fear fit? Arguably, the freedom from fear— that is, the right to inhabit a peaceful world that engenders the self-actualization of individuals and societies—can be categorized as a third-generation right. But what does the right to peace entail? In essence, the right to peace presupposes an organizational architecture that ensures the right to national self-determination, assistance in nation building, respect for national sovereignty, a forum for open diplomacy and conflict resolution, and a mechanism for peacekeeping. In sum, Roosevelt's speech anticipated the UN and its major documents, the UDHR, the ICCPR, and the ICESCR, in important ways. In addition, the speech influenced subsequent scholarship on human rights.

Following the "Four Freedoms" speech and other wartime declarations, Roosevelt's State of the Union Address in 1944 called for a "Second Bill of Rights"—a formal revision of the Constitution that would codify the achievements of the New Deal and set the stage for the addition of new social programs in the postwar period.[10] Drawing on the "pursuit of happiness"—a principle that had figured prominently in the Declaration of Independence—Roosevelt argued that "political rights proved inadequate to assure us equality in the pursuit of happiness."[11] Accordingly, in an effort to make political rights more meaningful, Roosevelt proposed the rights to employment (with a living wage), unemployment and disability insurance, housing, medical care, and education. Far from being mere social programs—subject to adjustment or abolition according to the whims of succeeding administrations and congresses—these addenda would be treated as inalienable rights. In the conclusion of his speech, Roosevelt argued that "these rights spell security . . . and without security here at home there cannot be lasting peace in the world."[12] In short, Roosevelt connected his proposal to extrapolate the New Deal with his vision of the postwar reconstruction around the UN and a globally binding human rights code. Although Roosevelt's proposal for a Second Bill of Rights was never brought to fruition by the U.S. government, it has served as an important reference point for human rights advocates in the United States.

In reflecting cutting-edge thinking on human rights in the 1940s, Roosevelt's vision represented a challenge to the community of nation-states, popular forces pushing for decolonization in the non-Western world, and the citizens of the United States to bring to fruition the promises of the Enlightenment. Nevertheless, in criticizing the Roosevelt administration for the deficiencies of the New Deal in addressing the civil and political status of African Americans in the South, human rights advocates of the time recognized the contradiction between U.S. support for civil and political rights abroad and the continued segregation and disenfranchisement of African Americans at home. In exploring the contradiction that defined U.S. efforts to promote human rights in the aftermath of the Second World War, Piven (2008) states,

> In fact, the grounds for American moral hubris were always shaky. How could the United States be a champion of human rights in the world when for two centuries the fundamental human rights embedded in the US Constitution, in US political culture, and in US laws had never been widely honored? Think of the right to vote, perhaps the foundational right in a democracy, and certainly the animating aspiration of the common people—the "people out of doors"—who fought the American Revolution. (P. 2)

This contradiction reached a fever pitch in the late 1940s, as nascent movements for national independence—especially the Indian mobilization, with its renowned leader Mahatma Gandhi—made contact with the embryonic civil rights movement in the United States. In explaining the connection between decolonization and civil rights, Winant (2005) has argued that a "worldwide racial break" accompanied the post-1945 reconstruction:

> There is a parallel between the post-Second World War dismantling of the old imperialism and reform of state racial policies in the United States during the

same period. Elsewhere I have written extensively on the worldwide racial "break" or rupture set in motion during and after the war (Winant 2001). In the postwar period, antiracist and anticolonial movement interacted extensively (Dudziak 2002). Consider Dr. King's denunciation of the Vietnam War in this regard, a position that was seen as controversial at the time. Similarly, postcolonial reform regimes and post-civil rights era racial policies exhibit numerous similarities: both achieved the incorporation of a range of movement demands (generally the more mainstream or moderate ones) in state policy and both also experienced the inclusion (or co-optation) of former insurgents and movement leaders in postcolonial and post-civil rights state apparatuses (in government executives or leaderships, as legislators and officials, etc.). (Pp. 124–25)

How can we account for this rupture in race relations—both on a global scale and within the United States? In recruiting for the war effort, France and the United Kingdom drew not only on their domestic populations, but also on their colonial subjects. For its part, the United States drew not only on its majority white population, but also on African Americans and other racial minorities in building its armed forces. Thus, France, the United Kingdom, and the United States mobilized diverse—yet segregated—militaries in the name of such vaunted ideals as freedom and democracy. Moreover, in joining the multinational and multiethnic USSR in the struggle against fascism, the United States reaffirmed its opposition to colonialism. Owing to their invocation of the language of human rights to legitimize the war effort, France and the United Kingdom unwittingly encouraged popular unrest in their colonies. In a similar fashion, the United States unintentionally lent doctrinal support for the embryonic civil rights movement at home. As a consequence, support for decolonization and civil rights—whether rhetorical or substantive—would figure prominently in securing *U.S. hegemony* after the cessation of hostilities in 1945.

In the academic domains of sociology, political science, law, and peace studies, the term *hegemony* is often used to denote the combination of force and consent, hard and soft power, necessary for a nation-state to occupy a leadership position in the global system. As Wallerstein (2006) has noted, the term "refers to those situations in which one state combines economic, political, and financial superiority over other strong states, and therefore has both military and cultural leadership as well. Hegemonic powers define the rules of the game" (p. 94). Accordingly, this chapter explores the relationship between U.S. hegemony and the transnational norms that became prominent after 1945. Hence the question arises: To what extent was U.S. hegemony based on support for national self-determination, human rights, and global governance? Far from being predicated exclusively on military might and economic power, the Pentagon and Wall Street, U.S. hegemony entailed the use of soft power—diplomatic persuasion, ideological legitimization, and appeals to moral and legal authority—in the creation of such intergovernmental organizations (IGOs) as the UN, the International Monetary Fund (IMF), the World Bank (WB), and the General Agreement on Tariffs and Trade (GATT). In the vision of U.S. planners, these IGOs would manage the interstate system and the global economy, thereby codifying the lessons of the preceding 30 years (Arrighi 1999; McMichael 2008). In sum, the postwar system accommodated the strategic and economic interests of the United States; incorporated the defeated powers (Germany and Japan); regulated the rivalry between the United States and the USSR; established the parameters for the dissolution of the colonial empires of France, the United Kingdom, and Portugal; created a mechanism for the resolution of interstate disputes; and facilitated the implementation of a new set of financial and trade policies across national boundaries. Whether by design or by accident, the postwar system also set the stage for the rise of transnational corporations (based primarily in the United States, Western Europe, and Japan), the spread of U.S. popular culture, and the creation of a global public sphere.

In the name of enlightened self-interest, the United States would serve as the most significant donor to the UN—an institution that would be housed in New York. In addition, the United States would serve on the UN Security Council, along with its wartime allies, France, the United Kingdom, the USSR, and China. Similarly, the United States would maintain the largest number of shares and hence de facto veto power in the IMF and the WB—institutions that would be housed in Washington, DC. In theory, the UN would have authority over the IMF and the WB. In practice, however, the IMF and the WB quickly achieved autonomy from the UN and worked closely with the U.S. government (especially the Department of the Treasury) in designing, implementing, and monitoring development programs in the Global South. Though significant in itself, the practical separation of the UN from the IMF and the WB was intensified not only by the Cold War and the concomitant arms race, but also by U.S. and Soviet interventions in decolonization conflicts and civil wars across the Global South—seemingly in violation of the vaunted principle of national sovereignty. To make matters more complicated, the USSR became a major player in the UN Security Council and General Assembly, while remaining outside the IMF and the WB. This created an incongruity between the management of an interstate system that incorporated the USSR as a major power and the management of a global economy that marginalized the USSR and its Eastern European client states. In retrospect, three factors—the relative autonomy of the UN from the U.S. government; the tensions within the UN system among the delegations from the United States, the USSR, and the emerging nations of the Global South; and the conflict between the UN and the IMF/WB—caused the postwar order to evolve in a manner that U.S. planners could not have predicted. Phrased differently, the jagged structure of the postwar system—with the UN and the IMF/WB maintaining conflicting visions of development in the Global South—produced an array of unintended consequences.

What was the impact of the unanticipated conflict between the UN and the IMF/WB? From the late 1940s through the early 1970s, the widening divide between the UN and the IMF/WB had a profound effect on the implementation of the right to development in the Global South. It was in a world historical context defined by U.S. support for IGOs, structural tensions among IGOs, the Cold War, and movements for decolonization throughout the Global South that development—a right that presupposed national self-determination (i.e., the overturning of colonial rule), nation building (i.e., the construction of a national identity, state machinery, and a legal system), and the formal recognition of civil, political, economic, social, and cultural rights—became the order of the day. In a sense, development—understood as industrialization, protectionism, the recognition of certain civil and political rights (especially the rule of law, property rights, and hence enforceable contracts), the establishment of social programs (especially in the areas of health and education), the creation of a consumer market, and, most important, the reconfiguration of the national economy in the pursuit of growth in gross domestic product (GDP)—served as a point of convergence between the interests of the United States and those of anticolonial movements in the non-Western world. To the end of cementing its hegemonic status—while containing the influence of the USSR—the United States acknowledged the legitimacy of decolonization movements across the non-Western world.

As the next section of this chapter demonstrates, the United States found itself caught in a paradox. On the one hand, the United States spearheaded the construction of a postwar system based on the UN and such norms as national self-determination and human rights. On the other hand, the United States reserved the right to intervene—either unilaterally or in concert with its allies and client states—in the affairs of other nations and proved reluctant to implement the ICCPR, the ICESCR, and other international treaties on the domestic front. In sum, the U.S. paradox—the tension between the hegemonic power's calculated support for international law and its refusal to allow the resulting treaties to influence U.S. law—had a profound impact on the world order. More precisely, while U.S. rhetorical advocacy of human rights would impose a normative logic on the postwar system and activate the movements for decolonization and civil rights, the hegemonic power's refusal to bring its Constitution and laws into conformity with the ICCPR, the ICESCR, and other international treaties would place severe limitations on the evolution of politics and civil society at home. Arguably, the reluctance of the United States to apply the ICCPR and the ICESCR domestically contributed to the erosion of the hegemonic power's legitimacy in the eyes of the world. Indeed, many analysts and observers have wondered, "What happens if the hegemonic power fails to apply the values it purports to affirm?" From 1945 to the present day, this question has preoccupied human rights advocates and peace activists across the world.

The U.S. Paradox

In exploring the role of the United States as a leader in global affairs, a sponsor of the UN, and a propagator of transnational norms, Donnelly (2008) has captured the essence of the *U.S. paradox:*

> The United States government applies international human rights standards freely, and at times even forcefully, to other countries. For example, for thirty years, the State Department, by congressional mandate, has produced annual human rights reports on the practices of all states that receive foreign assistance. And since the end of the Cold War, human rights diplomacy has become not merely a concern of "liberal" administrations but a nonpartisan element of American foreign policy. Yet international human rights norms are treated as if somehow not relevant to the domestic practices of the United States. (P. 239)

As Donnelly (2008) suggests, it is noteworthy that the United States routinely reviews the human rights records of recipients of development aid. Thus, in principle, the United States considers respect for human rights—especially such first-generation civil and political rights as association, assembly, expression, and voting—obligatory for beneficiaries of development assistance. Nevertheless, the United States tends not only to apply these standards selectively to nations in the Global South—with strategic considerations figuring prominently in the decision-making process—but also to exempt itself from the ICCPR, the ICESCR, and other international treaties.

What were the causes and effects of the U.S. paradox? In essence, the story begins with the end of the Interregnum (1914–1945)—one of the most violent, destructive, and tumultuous periods in human history. What lessons had U.S. planners learned from the First World War, the Great Depression, and the Holocaust and the Second World War? First, they recognized the need to reconstruct the interstate system in accordance with the emerging transnational norms of national self-determination and human rights. In practice, this meant that all nation-states should support the right of colonized peoples to govern themselves, respect the sovereignty of other nation-states, and institutionalize, promote, and enforce human rights within their borders. Second, U.S. planners acknowledged the importance of rebuilding the global economy—along with national economies—according to Keynesian and developmentalist principles. In practice, this meant not only that the IMF, the WB, the GATT, and other institutions should regulate the global economy to promote industrialization, trade, investment, and hence growth in GDP, while mitigating uncertainty and preventing the global economy from slipping into another depression, but also that all national governments, irrespective of their economic standing, should provide a social safety net—in the form of basic provisions for health, education, and welfare—for their citizens.

Notwithstanding attempts by scholars and policymakers to tailor the new principles for different geographic, geopolitical, and cultural contexts, the postwar consensus on national self-determination, human rights, and Keynesianism-developmentalism produced uneven results across the world. This unevenness derived from substantial differences in the nature and extent of colonial exploitation, position in the global economy, access to natural resources, previous experiences with industrialization, politics, gender relations, and culture. Irrespective of the intentions of U.S. planners and other advocates of development, the implementation of the paradigm was impeded by positivism (i.e., the belief in the scientific character of development thought), economism (i.e., the belief in GDP growth as the be-all and end-all of economic life), gender neutrality (i.e., the belief that gender relations on the ground were of little or no consequence), and Eurocentrism (i.e., the belief that all nations could or should follow the same path from "barbarism" to "civilization" as Europe and the United States).

Notwithstanding interwar debates on how to "modernize" the economies of the former European colonies in Africa, Asia, and the Caribbean, the postwar development project as such received its first sophisticated articulation in President Harry S. Truman's 1949 Inaugural Address (McMichael 2008; Rist 2002). Injecting a heavy dose of realism into Roosevelt's idealistic blueprint of the postwar order (Arrighi 1999), Truman's speech was divided into four points: first, a declaration of support for the UN as a mechanism for undertaking open diplomacy and settling conflicts without recourse to war; second, a declaration of support for the Marshall Plan as a means of financing the reconstruction of Europe—including defeated and occupied Germany—and thereby internationalizing the New Deal (with the newly invented IMF and WB serving as conduits for U.S. assistance); third, a declaration of support for the North Atlantic Treaty Organization (NATO) as a security arrangement for the United States and its closest allies amid the growing antagonism with the USSR and the Soviet Bloc; and, fourth, support for the economic reconstruction and transformation of the poorer regions of the globe. In offering a definitive response to the USSR and its version of development, Truman's words reverberated across the world:

> We must embark on a bold new program for making the benefits of our scientific advances and industrial progress available for the improvement and growth of underdeveloped areas . . . Our aim should be to help the free peoples of the world, through their own efforts, to produce more food, more clothing, more materials for housing, and more mechanical power to lighten their burdens.[13]

Known thereafter as Truman's Point Four Program—a sustained effort to assist the Global South in "catching up" to the standard of living enjoyed in the United States and Western Europe—the U.S.-sponsored development project would spark research and deliberation among policymakers; IMF, WB, and UN staff; elites in the Global South; and scholars in the emerging interdisciplinary field of development studies. Indeed, the spirit of development would animate the postwar reconstruction, fostering intense debate on the relationship between different forms of human rights. It was widely assumed that development—defined as programmed industrialization—entailed the right to national self-determination, along with basic civil and political rights (including the rights to security of the person, due process of law, and private property). Similarly, it was widely believed that the development of productive forces (including such infrastructure innovations as roads, bridges, tunnels, electrification, and factories)—in retooling economies to produce commodities first for domestic consumption and later for export—would prepare the ground for the realization of such economic and social rights as health care and education. In sum, the development project—though predicated on industrialization as a means of achieving sustained economic growth—implied civil and political rights, along with economic and social rights.

Taken together, the UN-managed interstate system and the IMF/WB/GATT-managed global economy can be seen as the institutional pillars of U.S. hegemony. As Cold War tensions between the superpowers deepened, the United States emphasized the NATO and other military alliances, arms shipments abroad, and weapons stockpiling at home in the quest for stability in what Truman and others called the "free world." Whereas the UN included the USSR and its Eastern European satellites, NATO, the IMF, the WB, and the GATT excluded the Soviet Bloc. This had a pronounced effect on the trajectory of the UN. Entrusted with the difficult task of bridging two divides—that between the capitalist West and the socialist East and that between the Global North and the Global South—the UN served not only as a forum for negotiation, debate, and research on such issues as interstate relations, decolonization, nation building, and development but also as a source of funding for projects launched by emerging nation-states and NGOs. Meanwhile, the IMF, the WB, and the GATT provided policy advice, technical assistance, and financial aid—first to war-torn countries and later to the nations of the "Third World."

In effect, the emergence of the Third World—a diverse array of poor, nonaligned, and postcolonial nations in Africa, Asia, and Latin America pursuing such development policies as rapid industrialization and protectionism—rivaled the Cold War as the most significant story of the postwar period (Rist 2002). Notwithstanding differences in ideology and interest, U.S. planners; officials from the UN, the IMF, the WB, and the GATT; public policymakers; NGO staff; and scholars in the interdisciplinary field of development studies pointed to the historical, geographic, geopolitical, and cultural factors that distinguished the poor nations of the Third World from the wealthy nations of the "First World" (primarily the United States, Western Europe, and Japan) and the socialist states of the "Second World" (primarily the USSR and its satellites in Eastern Europe). While there was consensus on the importance of development—defined as planned economic, political, and social change to assist the Third World in "catching up" to the standard of living enjoyed in the United States and Western Europe—there were significant differences between the UN camp and the IMF/WB/GATT camp. Over time, as the development project ran its course, tensions between the two camps grew considerably. Though significant in its own right, the decision on the part of the United States to reject the UN's Declaration on the Establishment of a New International Economic Order (NIEO) and related proposals in 1974 falls beyond the purview of this chapter. For the present study, it suffices to mention that the failure of the NIEO marked a watershed not only in U.S.-UN relations, but also in the history of human rights thinking. Thenceforth, UN agencies, NGOs, and SMOs would shift their emphasis from development (in the conventional sense of the term) to human rights (conceived in terms of such "bundles" as the rights to longevity and self-actualization). Most important for the present study, this transition—from development as the prescription for the Global South to human rights as the medicine for the entire world—has begun to influence grassroots organizations and scholar-activists in the United States.

Bringing the ICCPR Back Home

What are prospects for bringing the ICCPR to bear on the U.S. legal system? In recent years, transnational coalitions of SMOs, NGOs, and UN agencies—in transforming the language of human rights—have begun to influence grassroots politics and scholar activism in the United States. As the example of the US Social Forum attests, community groups, independent activists, and intellectuals in the United States have imported conceptions of human rights from the Global South. Having been planted in U.S. soil, these seeds promise to produce new species of flowers. The emergence of the *US Social Forum*—an offshoot of the World Social Forum, whose 2001 Charter of Principles[14] echoes UN documents—has renewed interest among Americans in the UDHR, the ICCPR, the ICESCR, and other international treaties. In accordance with a holistic vision of human rights and a practical emphasis on rights bundling, this chapter has proposed longevity and self-actualization as suitable objectives on both a national scale and a global scale.

In the United States, the removal of the non-self-executing clause from the ICCPR—a document that remains powerful and instructive despite its age—would constitute an important step en route to these objectives. If the United States were to enforce the ICCPR at home, it would stimulate productive debate on (a) the relationship between the United States and the UN, (b) the contradictions between the U.S. Constitution and the ICCPR, and (c) the implications of expanding civil and political rights for the realization of economic, social, cultural, and environmental rights. If, as this chapter has argued, U.S. hegemony was bolstered by its initial support for the UN, it seems likely that the United States could improve its standing in the world by moving closer to the UN—perhaps to the point of participating more actively and constructively in the push to reform the UN (e.g., by abolishing the Security Council or by turning the General Assembly into a World Parliament). Similarly, if the United States were to bring its Constitution and legal system into conformity with the ICCPR, it would provide a set of tools for the empowerment of its citizens.

Far from being confined to the freedom of conscience, security of the person, voting rights, the right to property, and other forms of individual liberty, first-generation civil and political rights have a decisive bearing on the capacity of individuals—in this case, U.S. citizens—to participate in democracy. With greater participation in democracy—beyond voting every two, four, or six years for representatives from the two major political parties—U.S. citizens would find themselves in a better position to demand such social entitlements as government-funded health care (a precondition for longevity) and education/training/information (a precondition for self-actualization or the full development of the personality). In sum, the ratification and enforcement of the ICCPR—though insufficient in itself—would serve as a prelude to the revitalization of democracy in the United States.

Discussion Questions

1. What was the connection between decolonization movements in the Global South and the civil rights movement in the United States? To what extent did UN declarations and treaties—including the UDHR, the ICCPR, and the ICESCR—reflect and affect these movements?

2. How did the new intergovernmental organizations—including the UN, the IMF, and the WB—bolster *U.S. hegemony?* How did the United States use "soft power"—understood as ideology, diplomatic persuasion, and moral authority—to secure and maintain hegemony in the global system?

3. Explain the origins and implications of the *U.S. paradox.* How might we resolve the paradox?

4. In the light of the recent accomplishments of the *US Social Forum,* what are the prospects for deepening civil and political rights in the United States?

Notes

1. http://www2.ohchr.org/english/law/ccpr.htm
2. http://www1.umn.edu/humanrts/usdocs/civilres.html
3. Ibid.
4. Ibid.
5. Ibid.
6. Ibid.
7. The texts of every constitution in the world can be found at the following website: http://confinder.richmond.edu/
8. http://www.ussf2010.org
9. http://docs.fdrlibrary.marist.edu:8000/od4frees.html
10. http://teachingamericanhistory.org/library/index.asp?document=463
11. Ibid.
12. Ibid.
13. http://www.let.rug.nl/usa/P/ht33/speeches/truman.htm
14. http://www.forumsocialmundial.org.br/main.php?id_menu=4&cd_language=2

References

Arrighi, Giovanni. 1999. *The Long Twentieth Century.* London: Verso.
Blau, Judith and Alberto Moncada. 2006. *Justice in the United States.* Oxford, UK: Rowman & Littlefield.

Donnelly, Jack. 2008. "Postscript." Pp. 239–40 in *The Leading Rogue State: The U.S. and Human Rights,* edited by Judith Blau, David L. Brunsma, Alberto Moncada, and Catherine Zimmer. Boulder, CO: Paradigm.

Ishay, Micheline. 2008. *The History of Human Rights: From Ancient Times to the Globalization Era.* Berkeley: University of California Press.

Khagram, Sanjeev, James V. Riker, and Kathtryn Sikkink, eds. 2002. *Restructuring World Politics: Transnational Social Movements, Networks, and Norms.* Minneapolis: University of Minnesota Press.

McMichael, Philip. 2008. *Development and Social Change: A Global Perspective.* Los Angeles: Pine Forge Press.

Piven, Frances Fox. 2008. "Introduction." Pp. 1–3 in *The Leading Rogue State: The U.S. and Human Rights,* edited by Judith Blau, David L. Brunsma, Alberto Moncada, and Catherine Zimmer. Boulder, CO: Paradigm.

Rist, Gilbert. 2002. *The History of Development: From Western Origins to Global Faith.* London: Zed Books.

Roosevelt, Franklin Delano. 1941. "Annual Address to Congress." Retrieved January 6, 2011 (http://docs.fdrlibrary.marist.edu:8000/od4frees.html).

Roosevelt, Franklin Delano. 1944. "State of the Union Address." Retrieved January 6, 2011 (http://teachingamericanhistory.org/library/index.asp?document=463).

Truman, Harry S. 1949. "Inaugural Address." Retrieved January 6, 2011 (http://www.let.rug.nl/usa/P/ht33/speeches/truman.htm).

United Nations. 1966. "International Covenant on Civil and Political Rights." Retrieved January 6, 2011 (http://www2.ohchr.org/english/law/ccpr.htm).

U.S. Senate. 1992. "Advice and Consent on the International Covenant on Civil and Political Rights." Retrieved January 6, 2011 (http://www1.umn.edu/humanrts/usdocs/civilres.html).

US Social Forum. 2010. "Home Page." Retrieved January 6, 2011 (http://www.ussf2010.org).

Wallerstein, Immanuel. 2006. *World-Systems Analysis: An Introduction.* Durham, NC: Duke University Press.

Winant, Howard. 2005. "Globalization and Racism: At Home and Abroad." Pp. 121–130 in *Critical Globalization Studies,* edited by Richard P. Appelbaum and William I. Robinson. New York: Routledge.

World Social Forum. 2001. "Charter of Principles." Retrieved January 6, 2011 (http://www.forumsocialmundial.org.br/main.php?id_menu=4&cd_language=2).

3

Ensuring Economic and Social Rights

Louis Edgar Esparza

A t the 2004 meetings of the World Social Forum, Arundhati Roy told us that

> to imagine that a leader's personal charisma and a c.v. of struggle will dent the corporate cartel is to have no understanding of how capitalism works, or for that matter, how power works. Radical change will not be negotiated by governments; it can only be enforced by people. (Democracy Now! 2004)

As long as people do not take steps to ensure economic and social rights, persons of economic and social privilege will have greater influence over how the world is shaped than the rest. Economic rights, such as the rights to be free from economic oppression, to work, to have fair labor standards, and to earn a decent living, are necessary in order for all persons to have an equal chance of personal fulfillment and agency. The rights to food, housing, health, and education serve to reduce inequality and flatten authority structures that are incompatible with the goals that these rights assert.

International law already protects many of these rights. For instance, the International Covenant on Economic, Social, and Cultural Rights (ICESCR) (see Box 3.1), the Universal Declaration of Human Rights, and agreements from the International Labour Organization (ILO) all speak to the universality and inalienability of these rights. ILO Social Policy Convention 117 states that "the improvement of standards of living shall be regarded as the principal objective in the planning of economic development." Economic and social rights are human rights that each individual is born with. Grassroots activists around the world, many without much formal education, know exactly when it is that their economic and social rights are being violated and when economic development is undertaken that does not improve the standard of living of most people. Even without training in the details of international human rights law, many activists defend their rights when states, corporations, or armed groups violate them. To them, human rights are bound up in fighting against injustice and inequality. They realize that economic and social rights do not exist without mobilizing to *ensure* that they are in place.

taking action

BOX 3.1: ICESCR

PART III

Article 6

1. The States Parties to the present Covenant recognize the right to work, which includes the right of everyone to the opportunity to gain his living by work which he freely chooses or accepts, and will take appropriate steps to safeguard this right.

[...]

The States Parties to the present Covenant recognize the right of everyone to the enjoyment of just and favourable conditions of work which ensure, in particular:

(a) Remuneration which provides all workers, as a minimum, with:

   (i) Fair wages and equal remuneration for work of equal value without distinction of any kind, in particular women being guaranteed conditions of work not inferior to those enjoyed by men, with equal pay for equal work;

   (ii) A decent living for themselves and their families in accordance with the provisions of the present Covenant;

(b) Safe and healthy working conditions;

(c) Equal opportunity for everyone to be promoted in his employment to an appropriate higher level, subject to no considerations other than those of seniority and competence;

(d) Rest, leisure and reasonable limitation of working hours and periodic holidays with pay, as well as remuneration for public holidays

Article 8

1. The States Parties to the present Covenant undertake to ensure:

(a) The right of everyone to form trade unions and join the trade union of his choice, subject only to the rules of the organization concerned, for the promotion and protection of his economic and social interests. No restrictions may be placed on the exercise of this right other than those prescribed by law and which are necessary in a democratic society in the interests of national security or public order or for the protection of the rights and freedoms of others;

[…]

(d) The right to strike, provided that it is exercised in conformity with the laws of the particular country.

2. This article shall not prevent the imposition of lawful restrictions on the exercise of these rights by members of the armed forces or of the police or of the administration of the State.

[…]

Article 9

The States Parties to the present Covenant recognize the right of everyone to social security, including social insurance.

[…]

Article 11

1. The States Parties to the present Covenant recognize the right of everyone to an adequate standard of living for himself and his family, including adequate food, clothing and housing, and to the continuous improvement of living conditions. The States Parties will take appropriate steps to ensure the realization of this right, recognizing to this effect the essential importance of international co-operation based on free consent.

2. The States Parties to the present Covenant, recognizing the fundamental right of everyone to be free from hunger, shall take, individually and through international co-operation, the measures, including specific programmes, which are needed.

Source: http://www2.ohchr.org/english/law/cescr.htm.

The current economic conditions in the United States draw urgency to the necessity of economic and social rights. Throughout history, individuals and communities in the United States have fought for their social and economic rights. I note the lessons we might learn from those examples of ordinary people standing up to authorities in defense of their economic and social rights.

Contemporary Social Conditions

In 2008, the New York Stock Exchange experienced a severe decline in the value of its stocks, leaving millions of people out of work. Economists have labeled this stock market crash as the worst in the United States since the Great Depression that began with the 1929 crash of the market. As most economic downturns operate, the financial sector recovered its profits far more quickly than the labor market began to accept new workers, and at press time, it was still not clear that the worst was over. The U.S. government has been defending the capitalist free market for many years. Yet, when this system failed in 2008, the government bailed out the financial industry with billions of dollars, while imposing austerity measures against workers and vulnerable populations at federal, state, and local levels across the country. This enormous intervention into the financial system illustrates that the financial industry has stronger leverage over the U.S. government than the citizens and workers that compose the country. Why were ordinary U.S. citizens and workers not protected? Why was there no economic bailout for the millions of workers who lost their jobs? Where was the relief for the millions of swindled homeowners?

The Grassroots Option

An effective human rights policy must be enforced by strong community organizations. While the government may pass legislation that may be to the liking of domestic human rights organizations, such gains may be eroded or not enforced if community organizations are not sufficiently engaged. Ultimately, it is up to these community organizations to monitor and enforce social and economic rights.

Citizens, and not the state, are also under the obligation to enforce public democracy and autonomous development. Community organizations are most effective when all stakeholders feel that their concerns have been heard and considered, if not implemented. The creation and strengthening of these local democratic spaces is the responsibility of common citizens. Development, a phenomenon that community organizations commonly consider to be an action undertaken by corporations, should also be primarily the responsibility of local community organizations. Small businesses are more accountable to local communities and, thus, better serve the needs and interests of those communities in which they are embedded.

In order to enhance the strength of local community groups so that such actions can be undertaken, more resources are needed for local community organizing initiatives, and more spaces for local civic dialogue must be established that create accountability and governance structures that serve local interests. Citizens must be willing to make time for public service, not as a charitable gesture but rather in their own interest as it is bound with their local community. The success of local priorities, such as increasing the availability of affordable housing for instance, depends on the strength of community organizations.

Everyone needs housing, and local community organizations can be most effective when they work to further these universal needs with other communities. One conduit for such community linkages has been the labor movement. Communities can establish strategic partnerships with local labor movements on common issues, particularly around the right to work. Many labor movements have organizations that have already established partnerships around labor issues. By further engaging these structures, community organizations can access new linkages, and labor organizations can also obtain new allies for the right to work for a living wage.

Some indigenous communities in the United States have strong community organizations. Bounded together by a common culture, language, and history, these community groups do so by necessity, both for the preservation of their own histories and to effectively resist challenges to their sovereignty. Just as these indigenous communities have formed such strong ties and have resisted external structures of authority from imposing new realities upon them, so too can other local communities learn from these successful strategies to increase the degree of control that they have over their jurisdictions.

Autonomous movements in the United States provide a source for inspiration. These are movements that defend community rights on their own terms. It is more difficult for private interests to corrupt disparate local communities and movements than it is for them to influence a central government. Also, each community is different and will adopt these programs and initiatives differently, according to its needs, so long as human rights are respected.

In 1965, Filipino and Mexican American farmworkers went on strike for the rights of migrant laborers in a California community. One of the demands was recognition of what became the United Farm Workers union. They also organized a consumer boycott of grapes, in protest over their treatment. Cesar Chavez played a pivotal role during the campaign, which lasted five years before the workers' demands were met. Migrant workers are a growing population in the United States, and Latinos are an increasingly growing demographic. Yet migrant workers continue to face problems, particularly with deportations and estrangement from their families. Indeed, Article 10 of ILO Social Policy Convention 82 states, "Where the circumstances under which workers are employed involve their living away from their homes, the terms and conditions of their employment shall take account of their normal family needs" (see Box 3.2). Local communities could use these and other important elements of this ILO convention to protect their local workers and local economies.

BOX 3.2: ILO SOCIAL POLICY CONVENTION 82

Article 11

Where the labour resources of one area of a non-metropolitan territory are used on a temporary basis for the benefit of another area, measures shall be taken to encourage the transfer of part of the workers' wages and savings from the area of labour utilisation to the area of labour supply.

[...]

Where workers and their families move from low-cost to higher-cost areas, account shall be taken of the increased cost of living resulting from the change.

Source: http://www.ilo.org/ilolex/english/convdisp1.htm.

Chavez's partner, Dolores Huerta, who was also integral to the boycott, has argued that one major hurdle for such grassroots mobilizing is the parochialism among social movements in the United States. Economic and social rights encompass a wide range of movement goals, and Huerta thinks that broad swaths of movements against economic and social domination should link together. The Dolores Huerta Foundation is one such organization that advocates such an approach.

Some issues may seem like they have nothing to do with each other. For instance, the "slow food" movement is one that supports local farmers and food that is grown locally. This is done through what are called Community Supported Agriculture (CSA) partnerships between consumers and farmers, or between local stores and farmers. This keeps the costs of transportation of food low, food that can sometimes come from thousands of miles away, consuming tons of carbon-emitting gases in the process.

What does the slow food movement have to do with other economic and social rights movements, such as the racial desegregation of neighborhoods? There are always connections between all of these movements that are not often acknowledged. Michelle Obama has brought attention to the issue of our food system in the United States. Obesity is a problem, particularly among youth, and this can be changed through a change in our eating cultures. Many of the people who are most obese are blacks and Latinos. However, the places with the highest concentration of CSA partnerships are mostly white. Because neighborhoods are often segregated, this exacerbates problems of both obesity and segregation.

There are more linkages between movements than we often allow ourselves to recognize. It is reasonable to organize around a single issue, focusing on accomplishing a single goal. However, the structures of society that oppress the most vulnerable remain intact after incremental changes to individual issues. Nevertheless, the rubric of economic and social human rights allows communities to link these issues and to develop a broader platform.

What does it mean to do grassroots organizing? This involves getting together with others in one's community to identify what the problems are. In the early years of the women's movement, women's groups formed to discuss mutual experiences of violence or mistreatment. These groups eventually formed the backbone of a vast grassroots movement. The issue that a local community might decide to intervene in could be unemployment, housing, environmental degradation, the quality of the drinking water, or low wages. Once a community group gathers information and decides what the problems are, group members can begin to brainstorm about what is to be done. Then, the community can identify allies and stakeholders. It is long and hard work, but it can be gratifying and rewarding.

Grassroots organizing has historically accomplished much, but sometimes communities might decide that they want to join with other communities in order to change a state or federal law. Laws cannot fix everything, but sometimes they can be tactically useful in the short term. That is where public policy can come in handy. Communities, however, are ultimately responsible for ensuring that laws are implemented, enforced, patrolled, and upheld.

Economic and social rights are urgently needed in the United States in order to emancipate workers and citizens from the financial industry that has come to dominate U.S. society. However, these rights have been understood primarily in litigious terms. It should be understood that meaningful economic and social rights will not be granted—they must be demanded. Communities ought not to wait for the "right" politician or leader to come along. We can do it ourselves. While the study of human rights law has been dominated by lawyers, the study of society and social change is done by sociologists.

In 2004, Arundhati Roy delivered the keynote address at the annual meeting of the American Sociological Association, reminding sociologists of what is at stake. Sociologists have studied economic and social inequality in the United States for decades, accumulating and analyzing reams of data. For this reason, sociology is uniquely poised to identify these levers of social change. The struggle for human rights in the United States cannot rely exclusively on government structures, structures that are resistant to acknowledge these rights. We must achieve these rights ourselves.

The current dominance of law in the field of human rights is useful because it identifies the legal strategies for implementing sound rights. It is limited in that it only focuses on the juridical process, without recognizing the sociological determination of how societies change. Laws alone do not create change. Grassroots movements must demand and advocate for these laws, and force structures of authority, such as governments, corporations, and armed groups, to enforce them and to prosecute those who violate them. There must be consequences to the violation of these rights if governments and other "authorities" do not uphold these rights, consequences that only grassroots pressure can give birth to.

Human rights are not limited to what the courts can arbitrate. Moreover, even law is rooted in the ethical character of society. As Robert Alexy (2010) has argued, even some constitutional provisions stem from ethical principles rather than from laws. While human rights should be sought through the legal code, its depth and strength depend on the ethical character of societies and communities. The cultural shifts on which laws depend are formed by communities through social change processes. As Kenneth Andrews (2004) argued, even in the U.S. African American civil rights movement, local laws changed to reflect the success of the social movement several years before the passage of the civil rights acts. These changes were strongest, Andrews argues, in communities in which the movement was most organized.

Human rights are a social phenomenon, developed through interactions between mobilized communities and legal and government institutions. While lawyers wield opinions related to nation-state discourses, sociologists can wield facts about such societies and the interactions within them.

Institutions deliver and mitigate rights, and cultures complicate them—dynamics better understood by sociologists.

Sociologists also have the advantage of having evidence and data for their positions on human rights. Because sociologists have long documented the structures that reproduce inequality, they know how immutable these structures can be in the absence of concerted and intentional effort on the part of ordinary people. Their command of data makes it more difficult to deny the inequality, leaving open to debate only what should be done about it.

Data

As Blau et al. (2008) argue in *The Leading Rogue State*, while most countries have made considerable advances in acknowledging the inalienable social and economic rights of all people, the United States has not. Several metrics show that where the United States was a leader in human rights measures, it has now fallen behind other industrialized nations.

The Gini coefficient[1] for the United States has grown steadily ever since 1950, showing a widening gap between the rich and the poor. This means that the United States was once one of the most equal countries in the world—having the smallest difference in income between the rich and the poor. Today, however, the United States is among the most unequal among the rich countries.

The Center for American Progress keeps track of the number of international charters ratified by different countries. The United States has the lowest number of ratified treaties among G20 nations (Schultz 2009). The United States has not even ratified one of the most important, the ICESCR. Although President Jimmy Carter signed the treaty, Congress has refused to ratify it, stating that its provisions are a social goal rather than an inalienable right.

The Global Peace Index compiles several indicators to show which countries are moving toward a more peaceful society. The United States ranks poorly. The 2009 ranking for the United States fell sharply due to Guantánamo Bay and the treatment of Arabs and Muslims in the United States (Institute for Economics and Peace 2010). This erosion of rights for those who are not valued by society undermines the rights of every citizen.

Human rights are often thought of as something that is needed in other countries, when in fact the need is urgent in the United States. The failure to recognize the right to housing, for instance, has led to severe homelessness in communities such as Camden, New Jersey, one of the poorest communities in the United States. Even the District of Columbia sees stark inequality and homelessness. According to the Center for Economic and Social Rights (2010), 20.6 percent of U.S. children were living in poverty in 2009. This is very high, over one in five children, when compared with countries in the same income bracket as the United States. This is unusual for a country in the highest economic income bracket. Additionally, according to 2010 World Bank data, the United States also has a very high infant mortality rate compared to other Organisation for Economic Co-operation and Development countries. As long as the United States is not investing in children, its future economic growth outlook is poor.

The Gender Equity Index, compiled by Social Watch (2009), measures inequality between men and women, placing the United States in 25th place. And although gender equity in the United States has improved, women continue to earn less than men for conducting the same work. The Happy Planet Index, which measures countries based on a composite of indicators indicating a high quality of life and happiness, also has consistently given the United States a low ranking (New Economics Foundation 2010).

When U.S. citizens are asked whether they support specific economic or social rights, they always say they do. In a public opinion poll in 2006, 75 percent of respondents thought that people should have the right to work. When U.S. citizens are asked more generally about human rights, most people are quite supportive of the main tenets of human rights. When asked where the following phrase comes from—"From each according to their ability, to each according to their need"—most citizens think that the phrase originates in the U.S. Constitution. They are right to believe that it should appear in the Constitution, but no such idea appears there; that statement belongs instead to philosopher Karl Marx.[2] Twenty-nine percent of Americans also have "a positive reaction to the word *socialism*," according to a May 2010 Pew Research Center poll. The percentage is even higher, 43 percent, among people under the age of 30, 48 percent of whom, by the same token, have a negative reaction to the word *capitalism*. In an April 2010 Rasmussen poll, only 53 percent of Americans said that capitalism is preferable to socialism. Those under 30 are split nearly equally: 37 percent preferring capitalism, 33 percent preferring socialism, and 30 percent undecided.

How could it be that people in the United States live in such poor economic and social conditions? People who live in the United States do not always realize that this is the case, because they are not as aware about conditions in other countries. Those in the United States often believe that because they live in the richest country in the world, they must live in the best conditions and enjoy the most freedoms in the world. There are many great things about U.S. culture and the stability of the political system. But as Blau and Moncada (2006) have argued, "Patriotism, like nationalism, impedes the comprehension of the human rights we all share" (p. 46). National reverie must be balanced with global awareness. The social conditions in which we find ourselves in the United States demand an intervention.

A New Bill of Rights

The United States once was a leader in human rights, having housed the United Nations since its inception. The Universal Declaration of Human Rights, the central treaty of the United Nations, was drafted by Eleanor Roosevelt, a U.S. First Lady. In the decades since then, the United States has lost its leadership. The country has lost its way to the extent that it has been referred to by some observers as the "leading rogue state" (Blau et al. 2008). In order to reverse this trend, ordinary citizens must organize around economic and social rights and demand them from the government.

A U.S. political philosopher and grassroots political leader in the Northeast, Malcolm X advocated for the right to work, the right to self-determination, and the freedom from discrimination. He believed in these principles so deeply that he took the United States to the United Nations over these demands. Box 3.3 illustrates how Malcolm X and his movement demanded exactly this. Malcolm X and many others like him have organized at the grassroots level on behalf of economic and social rights. Earlier in the twentieth century, and after decades of intense battle, workers finally achieved the 8-hour workday and 40-hour workweek. Today, even these basic gains have been eroded.

One amendment in a New Bill of Rights that might be considered is one that was introduced by President Franklin Delano Roosevelt in 1944. In what Roosevelt called the "Second Bill of Rights," he argued that Congress should pass a set of laws that protected social and economic rights in ways that had never been seen before. Eleanor Roosevelt, and the grassroots movements budding around the president's feet, forced his hand.

Some 80 years later, it is necessary that we codify these rights. But this will not occur without building the strength of community organizations to the levels at which they were in the 1930s and 1940s, or even the 1960s. These rights can be adopted and upheld in our own communities, spreading and growing at the grassroots level until they can no longer be ignored by the government.

It is possible for these rights to be advocated for from the very top of the government. Eleanor Roosevelt advocated for these rights and spent her focus on developing community action. Roosevelt (1948) was so effective in this advocacy work that black women all over the South founded community groups called "Eleanor Clubs" in her honor, which strove to adopt human rights provisions locally. The international human rights movement

BOX 3.3: ECONOMIC RIGHTS: THE RIGHT TO WORK

Malcolm X and the "Ballot or the Bullet" Speech

In 1964, Malcolm X delivered one of the most memorable speeches in American history before a Methodist congregation in Cleveland, Ohio. In "The Ballot or the Bullet," Malcolm X spoke of the necessity to expand the African American civil rights movement to the international stage:

> When you expand the civil-rights struggle to the level of human rights, you can then take the case of the black man in this country before the nations in the UN [United Nations]. You can take it before the General Assembly. You can take Uncle Sam before a world court. But the only level you can do it on is the level of human rights. Civil rights keeps you under his restrictions, under his jurisdiction. Civil rights keeps you in his pocket. Civil rights means you're asking Uncle Sam to treat you right. Human rights are something you were born with. Human rights are your God-given rights. Human rights are the rights that are recognized by all nations of this earth. And any time any one violates your human rights, you can take them to the world court.

Malcolm X understood that these rights could not be undertaken under U.S. law the way that the law is currently written. He emphasized the importance of people organizing themselves in order to ensure these rights.

Source: http://teachingamericanhistory.org/library/index.asp?document=1147

began with Roosevelt in the United States, and the democratic ideals of the United States were eventually embraced by other nations. Contemporaneously, not only have other countries caught up, but they have waged ahead. The United States should once again be motivated to play an active leadership role, in partnership with other countries, in the enforcement of economic and social rights.

Another club and community group founded was the Highlander Folk School (now the Highlander Research and Education Center), which trained and educated many of the people who went on to become leaders in the U.S. African American civil rights movement, including Martin Luther King Jr. Many local labor leaders were also trained here, who then went on to work in the South and the Midwest. In Chapter 12, Judith Blau discusses the Carrboro Human Rights Center, a similar endeavor to empower a local community, this one heavily Latino. There ought to be more such community schools as the Human Rights Center and the Highlander Folk School that address local issues and train people in addressing the problems that plague local communities through grassroots activism and empowerment.

To take an example from a nearby country, Colombia has one of the oldest democracies in the world. Inspired by George Washington and the American Revolution, General Simon Bolivar and his armies overthrew their Spanish colonizers to create the free country we now know as Colombia. Colombia has been a strong U.S. ally in South America for several decades. It is where we get much of our coffee and flowers and emeralds, and even some of our oil and coal. But even this country, which has a much lower gross domestic product than the United States, has stronger economic and social rights laws.

Just as Colombia has been influenced by us, so too can we learn from its legal advances. Colombia has made these advances because of pressure from grassroots social organizations. Eventually, the pressure from grassroots groups became so great that the government had to give in and rewrite the country's constitution in 1991, acknowledging social and economic rights, among others. Box 3.4 illustrates some of these victories.

BOX 3.4: EXCERPT FROM THE 1991 COLOMBIAN CONSTITUTION

The following are basic rights of children: life, physical integrity, health and social security, a balanced diet, their name and citizenship, to have a family and not be separated from it, care and love, instruction and culture, recreation, and the free expression of their opinions. They will be protected against all forms of abandonment, physical or moral violence, imprisonment, sale, sexual abuse, work or economic exploitation, and dangerous work. (Article 44)

Source: http://confinder.richmond.edu/admin/docs/colombia_const2.pdf.

How Others Have Done It

One hundred years ago, many U.S. citizens did not even have civil and political rights (such as the right to vote), let alone economic and social rights. The abolition movement set to change that by struggling for the rights of nonwhites. The NAACP (National Association for the Advancement of

Colored People) looks very different now than it did a century ago. Back then, local chapters across the country were rooted in strong communities that organized according to the needs that arose in local contexts. There was a branch of the NAACP that coordinated and created national policy, but there was often tension between the central office and the local chapters. This was because communities ran and held their local chapters accountable to the people of the communities, and if the central NAACP was not tending to those needs, then it was sometimes simply ignored. Communities today should hold the organizations to which they belong to similar standards.

All U.S. citizens learn about Martin Luther King Jr. and the civil rights movement of the 1960s in grammar school. However, even this movement was successful not because of its great leaders, but because of the strong local communities and visionary local organizers that played a catalytic role. These organizers included Ella Baker, who tirelessly traveled between communities to organize people and to have them registered to vote. Baker famously said, "Strong people don't need strong leaders" (Center for Constitutional Rights 2011). She encouraged autonomous community groups for the training of local organizers. It was efforts from Baker and the hundreds of other local organizers that helped give the civil rights movement backbone and kept the leadership from negotiating away too much too quickly. A simple idea, and the will of a community to follow that idea, is all that is needed in order to make change possible.

This is essential for *ensuring* economic and social rights because the regulatory mechanisms for ensuring these rights are strong communities. Even if the political structures in the United States were to pass—for instance, Roosevelt's Second Bill of Rights—economic pressures would ensure that these rights would be weakly enforced and quickly dissolved without the counterbalance that strong communities provide.

For instance, in the South during the late nineteenth century, an organization called the Farmers' Alliance formed an independent economic system in order to become independent from imposed inflated prices for jute (a kind of twine used to bundle hay). The Great Jute Boycott involved farmers in the South who banded together and even ran their own political candidates in order to obtain leverage over their competitors and to improve and invest in their own communities.

In the Tulsa, Oklahoma, of the early twentieth century, blacks banded together to form their own economic structures in order to not have to depend on whites. This "Black Wall Street," as it was called, diversified the control over economic structures in the community. This decentralization over the control of resources is imperative to reduce the potential for the abuse of power of any one group over another. The example shows that local communities construct economic and social rights, rather than economic and social rights being granted by governments.

Local communities are important in every successful movement. In the Flint Sit-Down Strike of 1936–1937, General Motors workers took over the automobile factories in order to protest cuts in wages. However, the strike would have never been successful without local community support. Local grocers extended credit to families who were affected by the strike, local bakers provided free or cheap bread, and workers from the surrounding area came to their aid. The relationship went both ways, with workers supporting local stores so that big bad chains would not put them out of business. However, these interdependent relationships cannot happen without strong communities that recognize the value of these relationships and how they help maintain local autonomy. This local autonomy is important for maintaining the decentralization of power that keeps authorities accountable.

Movements in other countries have already acknowledged that local autonomy across movements and linkages across movement issues are essential for ensuring economic and social rights. The alter-globalization movement, which took hold in 1999 in Seattle, Washington, has made people more aware that the decisions that we make about how we live our lives in the United States have impacts that we do not always see elsewhere. This insight has engendered transnational alliances across national boundaries on common issues for social rights and economic rights. Marriage equity is being implemented across the western hemisphere, in part due to these linkages. In 2010, Argentina became the first country in Latin America to allow gay marriage. The World Social Forum, which began in Brazil, comprises transnational collaborations that bring activists together to discuss ways in which grassroots movements can deepen human rights in the Global South. We can leverage these victories to push further, for instance, for the right for everyone to have a living wage.

None of these victories come easily. *Structures of authority* block these kinds of grassroots efforts in order to protect their private interests, rather than serving the public interest. This is unfortunate, but it has always been the case. Grassroots efforts obtain and defend laws and other gains in the public interest. Capitalism, and other such structures, can and do erode our rights when communities are not mobilized.

Intellectual Contributions

Several intellectual thinkers and movements have contributed to this emancipatory strategy to ensure economic and social rights. The Fabians were a group of British intellectuals who believed that society could be fixed, but to do so required respecting the rights of individuals. Even though equality was a founding principle of the U.S. Constitution in 1776, it was still a radical idea 125 years later in twentieth-century London! They were called the "Fabians" after the Roman general Fabius, who held off the invading Hannibal by simply not engaging his armies. Hannibal relied on mercenaries who were not loyal to him unless they had the ability to plunder localities. But once they had exhausted the resources surrounding Rome, these mercenaries became restless and would mutiny. It was a war of attrition, with Fabius simply waiting, strategically exploiting Hannibal's weakness.

The British Fabians used indirect methods to influence politics, using education, traveling public lectures, and literature. They fundamentally believed that it was possible for civil society to demand such rights from the government and, over the course of many years, contributed to the movement that secured these rights for Britons.

Economic rights without social rights are not acceptable—they cannot be separately advocated for, since ensuring one depends on the relative strength of the other. As Nancy Fraser (1997), a contemporary political philosopher, argues, economic remuneration is not enough: People also seek recognition. Economic equality cannot be achieved unless all groups are protected and are recognized as legitimate and valued by society. Likewise, economic parity depends on our mutual recognition of each other's intrinsic value. For instance, the right to work cannot be ensured if Latinos do not have equal civil rights.

The interconnectedness of economic and social rights, as evidenced by international movements, is also consistent with what Emmanuel Levinas (1998), a twentieth-century philosopher, argued: People have an intrinsic responsibility to each other, and actions that do not reflect this reality are not only unethical because they do not recognize this value, but they are even *irrational*! Indeed, as our society becomes increasingly interdependent, this reality becomes ever truer.

Moving Forward

One important distinction between the domestic and international human rights movements is that movements abroad tend to be united on a slate of issues, recognizing this interconnectedness between economic and social rights. In the United States, movements and organizations tend to focus on one issue at a time—for instance, banning the use of land mines or campaigning against female genital mutilation. In grassroots movements abroad, these issues are linked and striven for according to a broader plank of human rights.

Movement parochialism in the United States unnecessarily sacrifices the networked relationships that so often lead to success in similar movements abroad. This is due to the funding structure in the United States. Foundations often are very specific about the kinds of issues that they would like to see addressed, itemizing exactly how monies are to be spent. These funding practices are often undemocratic. Movements need to create distance from these systems, communities must demand that grant-making agencies be held accountable for their decisions, and the federal government should regulate this industry, which acts without abandon. Undemocratic and unaccountable grant-making institutions are neither necessary nor sufficient for ensuring economic and social rights. They centralize authority among elites rather than enabling local communities to work on local priorities.

How is this to be accomplished? These can seem like insurmountable tasks. However, no structures of authority last forever. Persistent activists have constantly claimed victory over seemingly immutable realities.

A multipronged approach that attacks at different structural points in society may be promising. Lobbying at the federal, state, and local levels is necessary to create pressure for change. But I have emphasized in this chapter local action for a reason: It has been the case in the last 40 years in the United States that social movement activists have increasingly focused on federal and state action. However, we forget that these government structures rely on local communities to validate them. This power has been underutilized, at our own peril.

At the local level, there are Human Rights Cities, municipalities that pass human rights ordinances that recognize enforcement mechanisms for pieces of the Universal Declaration of Human Rights. They also put funding into human rights centers that help to reduce inequality in localities. They provide public spaces for community events and meetings to identify needs in the community.

Communities can also make specific legislative demands, such as rent control. If it is not possible to issue these laws, then communities should look at creating solutions, such as forming joint ventures for cooperative apartment complexes with a board of directors that is locally accountable and that will adjust graduated rents according to community needs. Development initiatives, such as New Urbanism, with increased green spaces and town squares, are important trends. This movement should be made appropriate to local spaces with community needs so as not to create gentrification. The best way to do that is to make sure that local, grassroots stakeholders are central in the planning. The only way to make this happen is for movements to insist upon it.

Some communities in the United States and elsewhere have "local currencies," which are attempts to keep money circulating in the community.

Usually, people can spend money at a store, and then that store can use that money in whichever way it sees fit—usually extracting the money from the community. When a store gives a consumer change after a purchase, that money can be taken by the consumer and used wherever he or she likes. The problem this creates is that sometimes money can be extracted from a community in the form of profits, without investing in the community. Local currencies attempt to circumvent this problem by having legal tender that is only valuable in a particular geographic zone. They have exchange rates, if one needs to convert dollars into the local currency, or vice versa. Some communities even have a community bank that specializes in this currency. Another advantage is that this strategy can insulate communities from the "boom and bust" cycles of Washington and Wall Street, bringing control of the local economy to the local community.

One other advantage of local currencies is that communities can give people who might not otherwise be productive something to do. This can create alternative and flexible employment for the currently unemployed. This can be expanded during times of crisis. It keeps people busy and creates bonds between people locally. Such jobs can include running errands for people in need or cleaning up public places or finding creative ways to match individuals' trained skills with something the community could use. There is no need for communities to waste talent because of an externally controlled economic pressure. This control can be wielded locally.

At the federal level, communities should advocate for change to federal wage regulations. The current minimum wage is not sufficient for families. When the minimum wage was created, it was meant to be used for someone to be able to live on that salary. However, because this was never pegged to the rate of inflation of the price of consumer goods, the minimum wage has fallen drastically below what a person needs in order to subsist. The minimum wage needs to become a living wage, so that people can actually depend on their jobs.

Welfare reform under the Clinton administration was motivated by a desire to make people work for the payments they receive. For this reason, many places, including New York, created workfare programs for people to get paid in return for doing work for the city. But there were many labor mobilizations against these efforts. Workfare did not work for most people. Instead, the city wielded workfare as a mechanism with which to cut costs (Krinsky 2007).

Instead of workfare, the role of civil servants could be expanded to create a development corps. These civil servants, paid by tax dollars, would create grassroots development projects. These projects would be funded by the state but planned and undertaken by local communities, according to the needs that they feel address their communities and with the assistance of members of the development corps.

A strengthening of regulatory agencies that control the size and authority of corporate entities is also an important goal that communities may consider when looking toward federal policy. Because such a campaign would meet strong opposition from private interests, it is important for local communities to be organized and ready for the potential disruption that this may entail. As Piven and Cloward (1977) argue, it is grassroots organizations that disrupt structures that are the agents of economic change. With the help of federal regulators, these communities may be more successful.

So long as communities support the government, they should also advocate for increased government transparency, so that communities are better able to do their work of holding government accountable. If communities do not have access to information, then they cannot act upon that information. As Javier Auyero and Debora Swistun (2008) showed how, in an environmentally devastated neighborhood in Buenos Aires, Argentina, members of the local community did not mobilize against pollution because they did not have access to the correct information about the environmental pollutants in their community. This "toxic uncertainty" paralyzed potential movements. Communities in the United States can overcome this by insisting on transparency and disclosure of environmental or other effects of government and corporate activity.

In the global economy, the free market has led to the opening up of borders for capital markets. People can trade money and goods across borders without fees and without restrictions. The problem with this is that people do not have these same freedoms, so capital can move from one place to another, moving jobs to other countries. However, people are stuck. Money is free to move around the world, but people are not. This is why we need to globalize people, granting everyone the ability to move freely around the world for work and livelihood, just as capital can. Also, because communities have roots, and people have roots, capital should also be given roots and be restricted through local currencies and other initiatives to reflect the extent to which people are limited in their willingness to chase jobs around the world. The democratic solution could emerge as something akin to the United Nations, but with delegates that are democratically elected from different regions in the world, rather than appointed by and beholden to government structures of authority.

Conclusion

Ensuring economic and social rights requires the development of a strategic agenda. Too often, single-issue movements arise as a reaction to an acute injustice. Strong communities are essential for instilling the values of economic and social justice from the ground up. This way, communities can vet and judge the proposals and initiatives that arise according to already existing values that uphold economic and social rights.

Not all of these strategies need to be taken on at the same time or by any one individual or community. Individuals and groups will gravitate toward certain ideas that are the most compelling at a particular time and place. Some of the specific ideas discussed here may not speak to certain communities at all. This reflects the diversity of individuals and communities in the United States, each of which has important gifts that can be used in some way in service of protecting our fellow residents by obtaining economic and social rights. What is important is that we do something, anything, to make this a reality.

Discussion Questions

1. Why can't communities rely on governments to ensure economic and social rights?

2. Why do communities need economic and social rights?

3. How do social movements help to ensure economic and social rights?

4. Do you think Franklin Delano Roosevelt or Eleanor Roosevelt had more impact on ensuring economic and social rights? Why?

5. What does the author mean by "structures of authority" blocking grassroots initiatives for economic and social rights?

6. What else can communities do to ensure economic and social rights that the author failed to mention?

Notes

1. The Gini coefficient is a measure of inequality that sociologists and economists commonly use in studies of inequality.

2. Poll on Constitution, *Boston Globe Magazine*, September 13, 1987, cited by Julius Lobel, in Julius Lobel, ed., "A Less than Perfect Union" (*Monthly Review*, 1988, p. 3).

References

Alexy, Robert. 2010. "The Construction of Constitutional Rights." *Law & Ethics of Human Rights* 4(1). Retrieved January 16, 2011 (http://www.bepress.com/lehr/vol4/iss1/art2).

Andrews, Kenneth T. 2004. *Freedom Is a Constant Struggle: The Mississippi Civil Rights Movement and Its Legacy.* Chicago: University of Chicago Press.

Auyero, Javier, and Debora Swistun. 2008. "The Social Production of Toxic Uncertainty." *American Sociological Review* 73:357–79.

Blau, Judith R., David L. Brunsma, Alberto Moncada, and Catherine Zimmerman, eds. 2008. *The Leading Rogue State: The United States and Human Rights.* Boulder, CO: Paradigm.

Blau, Judith R. and Alberto Moncada. 2006. *Justice in the United States: Human Rights and the U.S. Constitution.* Lanham, MD: Rowman & Littlefield.

Center for Constitutional Rights. 2011. "Ella Baker Summer Internship Program." Retrieved January 2, 2011 (http://ccrjustice.org/ella-baker-fellowship).

Center for Economic and Social Rights. 2010. "Fact Sheet No. 11: United States of America." Brooklyn, NY: Center for Economic and Social Rights.

Democracy Now! 2004. "Arundhati Roy Addresses Tens of Thousands at World Social Forum Opening in Bombay." Retrieved January 2, 2011 (http://www .democracynow.org/2004/1/20/arundhati_roy_addresses_tens_of_thousands).

Fraser, Nancy. (1997). *Justice Interruptus: Critical Reflections on the "Postsocialist" Condition.* New York: Routledge.

Institute for Economics and Peace. 2010. "Global Peace Index: Methodology, Results and Findings." Sydney, Australia: Institute for Economics and Peace.

International Labour Organization. N.d. "Database of International Labour Standards." Retrieved January 2, 2011 (http://www.ilo.org/ilolex/english/con vdisp2.htm).

Krinsky, John. 2007. *Free Labor: Workfare and the Contested Language of Neoliberalism.* Chicago: University of Chicago Press.

Levinas, E. (1998). *Entre Nous: On Thinking-of-the-Other.* New York: Columbia University Press.

New Economics Foundation. 2010. "The Happy Planet Index 2.0." London: New Economics Foundation.

Piven, Frances Fox and Richard A. Cloward. 1977. *Poor People's Movements: Why They Succeed, How They Fail.* New York: Pantheon Books.

Roosevelt, Eleanor. 1948. *If You Ask Me.* London: Hutchinson.

Schultz, William F. 2009. *The Power of Justice: Applying International Human Rights Standards to American Domestic Practices.* Washington, DC: Center for American Progress.

Social Watch. 2009. "Gender Equity Index." Montevideo, Uruguay: Author.

World Bank. 2010. "World Development Indicators." Retrieved January 6, 2011 (http://data.worldbank.org/data-catalog/world-development-indicators/wdi-2010).

4

Promoting Cultural Rights

Laura Toussaint

"Cultural diversity is as necessary for humankind as biodiversity is for nature."

—UNESCO Universal Declaration on
Cultural Diversity, Article 1

When you think of human rights, culture is probably not the first thing that comes to mind. In the United States, needs and rights tend to be emphasized at the individual rather than the group level. For example, people raised in individualistic cultures like the United States are likely to understand the need for food as a human right, but they might have a more difficult time imagining the right of a group to eat a particular type of food.[1]

Culture is "the totality of learned, socially transmitted customs, knowledge, material objects and behavior" (Schaefer 2009:57) and includes both material and nonmaterial elements. Material culture refers to tangible aspects of daily life, such as food, technology, and architecture. Examples of nonmaterial culture include religion, ceremonies, rituals, holidays, language, and artistic expressions. The preamble to the United Nations Educational, Scientific, and Cultural Organization (UNESCO; 2001) Universal Declaration on Cultural Diversity states that "culture should be regarded as the set of distinctive spiritual, material, intellectual, and emotional features of society or a social group, and that it encompasses, in addition to art and literature, lifestyles, ways of living together, value systems, traditions and beliefs."

Of the main categories of rights espoused in international documents (civil and political, economic and social, and cultural), culture has been the least addressed (United Nations Development Programme 2004). However, in recent years, the notion of human rights has expanded to encompass Howard and Donnelly's (1987) definition of human rights as rights people have simply by virtue of being human. The need for recognizing cultural rights has become more apparent as virtually all nations are increasingly influenced by multiculturalism. There are approximately 5,000 ethnic groups and nearly 200 countries in the world today, two thirds of which have at least one ethnic or religious minority group that comprises at least 10 percent of the population. Migration has also shifted cultural demographics (e.g., almost 50 percent of Toronto's population was born outside of Canada), and today's migrants are maintaining closer ties to their home countries than previous generations did. As Turner's (2006) theory of cultural recognition asserts, human rights extend beyond citizenship, and recognizing cultural rights is a critical component of this contemporary human rights perspective. Alarming information, such as the fact that approximately 900 million people belong to groups that experience some type of cultural marginalization (United Nations Development Programme 2004), every 14 days a language dies, and more than half of the 7,000 languages spoken today could disappear by 2100 (National Geographic 2010), suggests that much work is yet to be done in firmly securing a place at the human rights table for culture.

Theories and Applications

Social scientists have long tried to interpret the impact of cultural diversity, the results of which have been as varied as culture itself depending on factors such as how different groups initially come into contact, power dimensions, economic relations, and communication. However, a general continuum for analyzing intercultural contact ranges from ethnocentrism to cultural relativism. Ethnocentrism is the perception that one's own culture is the norm and provides the standard by which all other cultures should be measured. *Cultural relativism* is the view that each culture should be evaluated by its own standards, and that varying social contexts produce different values and norms.

Assimilation, or the blending of cultures, is what most American children are taught in school about intergroup relations. While Marger (2009) suggests this theory can generally be applied to multiethnic societies where people have entered as voluntary immigrants, he cautions there are many factors involved regarding if, how, or when groups assimilate. Groups that enter a society voluntarily and are culturally similar to the dominant group tend to be assimilated the furthest, such as those culturally closest to Anglo Protestants in the United States. Visibility is the factor Marger identifies as most crucial in assimilation. When groups have overt physical differences from the dominant group such as a different skin tone, separation is more pervasive. Marger notes it is not the physical characteristics of ethnic groups themselves that determine assimilation, but the beliefs attached to such distinctions, illustrating the interconnectedness of racial, ethnic, and cultural discrimination.

The "melting pot" analogy is often used in textbooks to describe assimilation as the history of immigrants coming to the United States to build a new life and blend into one culture, which often makes contributions of specific groups invisible. If multiple cultures are melted into one pot, it is all too easy for the dominant cultural group in control of the pot to absorb the credit. Mander (1991) notes the U.S. Constitution was likely modeled after the Great Binding Law of the Iroquois Confederacy, but this information is not presented during the course of American citizens learning the history of their country. He describes how dependent the English colonists were on the Iroquois for day-to-day dealings as well as military alliances against the French. Many of those negotiations occurred as part of Indian councils, following their rules and procedures. As the colonists were struggling to create a new democracy and did not have a model from their home country, they were heavily influenced by the Iroquois model that had successfully functioned for centuries. The Great Binding Law of the Iroquois Confederacy specified many elements that the colonists incorporated into what eventually became the U.S. Constitution, such as states' rights and a system for democratically electing representatives (Mander 1991). All cultures have been influenced by others whether or not proper credit is given, as Mander notes and Ralph Linton observed (see Figure 4.1) long before *globalization* became a buzzword.

While assimilation stresses cohesion, pluralism emphasizes differences and encourages the maintenance of group boundaries. The metaphor for pluralism is the salad, in which different ingredients coexist in one bowl and contribute a unique flavor to the final product. In the equalitarian form of pluralism, groups adhere to a common political and economic system while maintaining cultural differences. One indication of a pluralistic society is the degree to which multilingualism is not only accepted, but also respected. Switzerland, for example, has four national languages used in both official and unofficial forms of communication.

Figure 4.1   One Hundred Percent American

There can be no question about the average American's Americanism or his desire to preserve this precious heritage at all costs. Nevertheless, some insidious foreign ideas have already wormed their way into his civilization without his realizing what was going on. Thus dawn finds the unsuspecting patriot garbed in pajamas, a garment of East Indian origin; and lying in a bed built on a pattern which originated in either Persia or Asia Minor. He is muffled to the ears in un-American materials: cotton, first domesticated in India; linen, domesticated in the Near East; wool from an animal native to Asia Minor; or silk whose uses were first discovered by the Chinese. All these substances have been transformed into cloth by methods invented in Southwestern Asia. If the weather is cold enough he may even be sleeping under an eiderdown quilt invented in Scandinavia.

On awakening he glances at the clock, a medieval European invention; uses one potent Latin word in abbreviated form, rises in haste, and goes to the bathroom. Here, if he stops to think about it, he must feel himself in the presence of a great American institution; he will have heard stories of both the quality and frequency of foreign plumbing and will know that in no other country does the average man perform his ablutions in the midst of such splendor. But the insidious foreign influence pursues him even here. Glass was invented by the ancient Egyptians, the use of glazed tiles for floors and walls in the Near East, porcelain in China, and the art of enameling on metal by Mediterranean artisans of the Bronze Age. Even his bathtub and toilet are but slightly modified copies of Roman originals. The only purely American contribution to the ensemble is the steam radiator, against which our patriot very briefly and unintentionally places his posterior.

In this bathroom the American washes with soap invented by the ancient Gauls. Next he cleans his teeth, a subversive European practice which did not invade America until the latter part of the eighteenth century. He then shaves, a masochistic rite first developed by the heathen priests of ancient Egypt and Sumer. The process is made less of a penance by the fact that his razor is of steel, an iron-carbon alloy discovered in either India or Turkestan. Lastly, he dries himself on a Turkish towel.

Returning to the bedroom, the unconscious victim of un-American practices removes his clothes from a chair, invented in the Near East, and proceeds to dress. He puts on close-fitting tailored garments whose form derives from the skin clothing of the ancient nomads of the Asiatic steppes and fastens them with buttons whose prototypes appeared in Europe at the Close of the Stone Age. This costume is appropriate enough for outdoor exercise in a cold climate, but is quite unsuited to American summers, steam-heated houses, and Pullmans. Nevertheless, foreign ideas and habits hold the unfortunate man in thrall even when common sense tells him that the authentically American costume of gee string and moccasins would be far more comfortable. He puts on his feet stiff coverings made from hide prepared by a process invented in ancient Egypt and cut to a pattern which can be traced back to ancient Greece, and makes sure that they are properly polished, also a Greek idea. Lastly, he ties about his neck a strip of bright-colored cloth which is a vestigial survival of the shoulder shawls worn by seventeenth century Croats. He gives himself a final appraisal in the mirror, an old Mediterranean invention, and goes downstairs to breakfast.

Here a whole new series of foreign things confronts him. His food and drink are placed before him in pottery vessels, the proper name of which—china—is sufficient evidence of their origin. His fork is a medieval Italian invention and his spoon a copy of a Roman original. He will usually begin the meal with coffee, an Abyssinian plant first discovered by the Arabs. The American is quite likely to need it to dispel the morning-after effects of over-indulgence in fermented drinks, invented in the Near East; or distilled ones, invented by the alchemists of medieval Europe.

Whereas the Arabs took their coffee straight, he will probably sweeten it with sugar, discovered in India; and dilute it with cream, both the domestication of cattle and the technique of milking having originated in Asia Minor.

If our patriot is old-fashioned enough to adhere to the so-called American breakfast, his coffee will be accompanied by an orange, domesticated in the Mediterranean region, a cantaloupe domesticated in Persia, or grapes domesticated in Asia Minor. He will follow this with a bowl of cereal made from grain domesticated in the Near East and prepared by methods also invented there. From this he will go on to waffles, a Scandinavian invention, with plenty of butter, originally a Near Eastern cosmetic. As a side dish he may have the egg of a bird domesticated in Southeastern Asia or strips of the flesh of an animal domesticated in the same region, which has been salted and smoked by a process invented in Northern Europe.

Breakfast over, he places upon his head a molded piece of felt, invented by the nomads of Eastern Asia, and, if it looks like rain, puts on outer shoes of rubber, discovered by the ancient Mexicans, and takes an umbrella, invented in India. He then sprints for his train—the train, not sprinting, being an English invention. At the station he pauses for a moment to buy a newspaper, paying for it with coins invented in ancient Lydia. Once on board he settles back to inhale the fumes of a cigarette invented in Mexico, or a cigar invented in Brazil. Meanwhile, he reads the news of the day, imprinted in characters invented by the ancient Semites by a process invented in Germany upon a material invented in China. As he scans the latest editorial pointing out the dire results to our institutions of accepting foreign ideas, he will not fail to thank a Hebrew God in an Indo-European language that he is a one hundred percent (decimal system invented by the Greeks) American (from Americus Vespucci, Italian geographer).

Source: Linton, R. 1937. "One Hundred Percent American." *The American Mercury* 40:427–29. (Available from http://theamericanmercury.org/.) Courtesy of *The American Mercury*.

While pluralism is often presented as the opposite perspective of assimilation, both theories lack an analysis of power. For instance, not all groups came to the United States voluntarily or had the same opportunities as immigrants who were culturally similar to the dominant group. Colonialism theories contribute an analysis of power relations among groups. While those frameworks generally examine foreign domination and control, internal colonialism theory is useful for incorporating a power dimension in analyses of intergroup relations within the same country. Blauner (1972) developed internal colonialism theory to describe the different experiences of Europe-born immigrants and those who became "racialized" (African Americans, Asian Americans, Native Americans, and Latinos) and systematically disadvantaged in the socioeconomic-cultural power structure. The elements of internal colonialism include labor exploitation, land theft, and suppression of political and cultural rights (Blauner 1972).

Blauner's (1972) theory remains relevant today, particularly as assertions of minority cultural rights are met with a backlash by those claiming to represent the dominant culture. For example, a 2004 city council–approved right of Muslim residents in Hamtramck, Michigan, to broadcast their call to prayer sparked protests, petitions, and even death threats. The current protest over the proposed community center that includes a mosque and is located two blocks from the New York site of the *9/11 terrorist attacks* has also sparked intense debate. Imam Feisal Abdul Rauf, the leader of the project, asserts the center will only promote moderate Islam, but opponents have initiated legal action by attempting to void the ruling that allows construction of the mosque to proceed. President Barack Obama and New York City Mayor Michael Bloomberg have defended the project as constitutionally protected by the First Amendment, while other politicians including Sarah Palin have spoken out against it. One of the protests that particularly attacked culture was described in this way: "A man wearing a keffiyeh, a traditional Arab headdress, mounted one of two mock missiles that were part of an anti-mosque installation. One missile was inscribed with the words: 'Again? Freedom Targeted by Religion'; the other with 'Obama: With a middle name Hussein. We understand. Bloomberg: What is your excuse?'" (Dobnik 2010).

There has also been backlash against linguistic diversity in the United States. From 1980 to 2007, the percentage of people who speak non-English languages increased by 140 percent; there are currently 303 languages spoken at home other than English, and 20 percent of the U.S. population speaks a non-English language at home (U.S. Census Bureau 2010). Although the U.S. Constitution does not specify an official language, there have been attempts at a constitutional federal amendment to make English the official U.S. language. Thirty states have some form of an "Official English" law, and nearly 50 percent of them have been passed in the last 20 years (U.S. English 2010).

Language repression particularly has an impact on how children experience the education system. Studies have shown that children educated in their mother tongue during the first six years of school have much better academic performance as compared to those immediately immersed in an English-only academic environment (United Nations Development Programme 2004). Such barriers in early education often lead to challenges in later years. For example, only around 50 percent of Mexican American youth graduate from high school (Adalberto and Turner 2011), which in turn hinders their ability to find living wage jobs, purchase a home, and provide a stable economic environment for their families. As societies composed of people who are educated, healthy, and economically stable set the foundation for stronger, safer countries, it is in the interest of the collective good to promote rights that facilitate such conditions. See Figure 4.2 for another example of how the benefits of cultural rights extend beyond particular groups.

Figure 4.2   Who Were the Code Talkers?

"Were it not for the Navajos, the Marines would never have taken Iwo Jima."

—Major Howard Connor,
U.S. Marine Corps 5th Division Signal Officer

The Code Talkers were American Indians who used their native language in U.S. military service. They were recruited to communicate radio commands that the Japanese could not intercept, as the United States was faced with Japanese intelligence experts who were highly skilled at breaking codes sent in English and thus able to sabotage American military communication, a situation so dire that it could have cost the United States the war. While other native languages were used in code talking, the Navajos were the largest group to serve as Code Talkers. The military instituted the Code Talker program after Philip Johnston proposed using the Navajo language to send codes. Johnston was the son of a Protestant missionary who had grown up on the Navajo reservation. He reasoned that since the language had no alphabet and was difficult to master without early exposure, it could serve as an indecipherable code.

Often referred to as the "original 29," the first unit of Code Talkers was formed in 1942. Most of them were young men; some were even boys. Without birth certificates, their ages could not be verified at the time, but after the war it was discovered that some recruits had been as young as 15.

(Continued)

(Continued)

Ironically, the very languages that helped secure U.S. military victories were targeted for repression through Indian boarding schools. Some Code Talkers communicated radio messages using their native language, while others developed their own code based on words from their language. The Navajo Code Talkers created a written code dictionary. Made public in 1968, it is now available for viewing on the Naval History and Heritage Command's website. In 2001, the Code Talkers were finally awarded their long overdue Congressional Medals of Honor. To honor the veterans, help advance understanding of the Navajo culture, and keep this important but often neglected part of American history alive, a Navajo Code Talker museum is scheduled to be built by 2012 in Arizona.

Sources: http://www.navajocodetalkers.org/; http://www.history.navy.mil/faqs/faq61-4.htm; http://www.nmai.si.edu/education/codetalkers/html/chapter2.html; http://www.hmdb.org/marker .asp?marker=27909.

Native American *boarding schools* are another example of attempts at linguistic repression.[2] This method of education was an attempt to "convert" American Indians to European culture. In the early 1600s, both French and Spanish missionaries established schools for the purpose of teaching American Indians the language and culture of the missionaries' home country (Adalberto and Turner 2011). Starting in 1879 with the Carlisle Indian School, the Bureau of Indian Affairs (BIA) promoted boarding schools as the best vehicle for assimilating young Indians into the dominant U.S. culture. Indian children were typically taken from their homes at age 6 and placed in boarding schools, where they were punished for speaking their language and forced to change their hair and clothing. They were rarely allowed home to visit, and returned when they were 18 to their original culture, which in most cases had become unfamiliar to them.

Marder (2004) suggests that Indian boarding schools fit one of the criteria for being a crime against humanity (the forced transfer of children from a targeted racial, ethnic, national, or religious group to be reared and absorbed by a physically dominating group) under the United Nations Convention on the Prevention and Punishment of the Crime of Genocide.

Due to differences in resources, location, and contact with the U.S. government, not all tribes experienced this type of forced assimilation, and some resisted. Benjamin Franklin recalled the commissioners of Virginia sending the Iroquois an offer to educate their children in "All the Learning of the White People." The Iroquois responded by stating that in their previous experience with this kind of education, their youth returned "totally good for nothing." However, they returned this offer to the commissioners: "If the Gentlemen of Virginia will send us a Dozen of their Sons, we will take great Care of their Education, instruct them in all we know, and make Men of them" (Jorgenson and Mott 1962:52).

Asserting Cultural Rights Via Constitutions and International Agreements

Constitutions

Table 4.1 Examples of Cultural Rights in National Constitutions

Nation and Year	Section	Rights Referenced
Andorra, 1993	Articles 5 and 34	UDHR binding; cultural and artistic heritage.
Brazil, 1988	Articles 67, 210, 215, 216, 231, and 232	Education curricula that promote cultural, artistic, and mother tongue; forms of expression; material creations; indigenous land rights.
India, 1950	Articles 15, 16, 25–30, and 350	Religion; place of birth; cultural and linguistic minority group interests, including the establishment of educational institutions; provision of facilities for mother tongue instruction; presidential appointment of a special officer for linguistic minorities.
Kenya, 2010	Articles 7, 11, and 56	Language; culture; establishment of affirmative action programs to promote the interests of minorities and marginalized groups.
Switzerland, 1999	Articles 4, 69, and 70	Multiple national languages; support for cultural activities that consider national diversity.
United States, 1788 (1791)	Bill of Rights: Amendment I	Religion.
Venezuela, 1999	Articles 9, 98–101, and 119–126	Linguistic and cultural heritage; intellectual property; provision of support for cultural activities within the culture and promotion of Venezuelan culture abroad; indigenous land rights.

As the small sample of constitutions displayed in Table 4.1 demonstrates, they vary widely in terms of references to cultural rights. The U.S. Constitution does recognize religious freedom, but other cultural differences are not affirmed, nor are institutional inequalities acknowledged or attempted to be rectified. Blau and Moncada (2006) refer to the U.S. constitutional approach as singularism, in which assimilation is established as the standard. Constitutions that go beyond prohibiting discrimination to affirming cultural rights are operating from a framework of pluralism (Blau and Moncada 2006). Such constitutions offer positive rights in the sense that they promote conditions by which people might engage in such rights, rather than only protecting against violations. Examples of pluralism in constitutions include recognition and promotion of language rights (including the right to mother tongue instruction and culturally relevant educational curricula), support for cultural activities and artistic expressions, and indigenous land rights. Most of the constitutions cited in Table 4.1 reference at least one of those rights. Some nations even display support through formal recognition of multiple languages spoken within their borders. Switzerland has four national languages to reflect its linguistic diversity, while India's constitution recognizes 15 national languages that are spoken in over 1,600 dialects.

Of course, since every country has different circumstances, across-the-board comparisons of constitutional rights are not feasible. As acknowledged in the 2004 Human Development Report, "It will never be fully possible to compare homogenous Japan with diverse India, or how Europe is dealing with issues posed by immigration with how Latin America is meeting the demands of indigenous people for land and self-rule" (United Nations Development Programme 2004:31). Thus, exploring specific rights promoted by different countries is not to suggest there should be a one-size-fits-all approach to establishing national standards, but rather is to emphasize that as nations' global interdependence grows, so does the need for dialogue about the challenges and opportunities involved in promoting cultural rights. As constitutions are the supreme law of the land for nations, they offer an important point of entry for such conversations. Something as simple as recognizing that constitutions are living documents and many countries update them periodically to reflect new realities of citizens can be inspiring for countries that have not done so.

Since indigenous communities all over the world have been targets of cultural rights violations, the following discussion of indigenous rights from selected constitutions in Table 4.1 illustrates the various ways such rights are recognized and promoted, as well as the barriers for some communities in the full protection of their rights. Kenya's new constitution is a hopeful sign that indigenous rights are increasingly recognized at both the individual and the collective level. Examples include recognizing the right of marginalized communities to cultural self-determination, promotion and protection of indigenous languages and technologies, and land rights held by communities identified on the basis of ethnicity or culture. Dual citizenship is also acknowledged, which benefits groups such as the Maasai that live across boundaries (International Work Group for Indigenous Affairs 2010).

Brazil's 1988 constitution also generated high hopes for indigenous rights. It states that "Indians shall have their social organization, customs, languages, creeds and traditions recognized, as well as their original rights to the lands they traditionally occupy, it being incumbent upon the Union to demarcate them, protect and ensure respect for all of their property" (Article 231). Although Article 67 further specifies that Brazil demarcate Indian lands within five years, progress has been slow, and there are territories still waiting for formal demarcation. Borges and Combrisson (1998) note that the demarcation delay is due in part to Decree #1775 that was signed into law in 1996. The decree introduced the "principle of contradictory" within the procedure for land demarcation, which provides a legal mechanism for competing interests to claim land access and appeal against demarcation for indigenous communities. As powerful monetary interests are often behind appeals of ranchers, miners, and loggers claiming land access, their ability to contest demarcation has prevented some indigenous communities from experiencing their constitutional rights and has set the stage for escalating violence against tribal groups (Borges and Combrisson 1998).

Indigenous communities hold 22 percent of the land in the Amazon, which has become increasingly sought after by farmers who produce beef and soy, two of Brazil's largest exports (Associated Press 2009). Supported by local politicians, a group of farmers who wanted claim to Raposa Serra do Sol petitioned the Brazilian Supreme Court to overturn the legal recognition of that territory as indigenous land. In 2008, the Court ultimately ruled in favor of indigenous land rights, affirming that Raposa Serra do Sol had been demarcated according to the constitution and that Indian territories should be maintained as single areas (i.e., not carved up among competing interests). The Court also ordered the farmers to leave (Survival International 2008). Although the decision was hailed as a victory for indigenous rights, such attempts at overturning legal recognition of Indian territory illustrates the importance of vigilance in upholding constitutional protections of groups whose resources are continually targeted by competing powerful interests.

In the United States, constitutional protection of indigenous cultural rights has primarily been asserted via the freedom of religion clause in the First Amendment. As American Indian religious practices are tied to the natural environment and many sacred sites are on land managed by the U.S. federal government rather than under tribal control (Albert 2009), the American Indian right to worship exposes the challenges of applying the right to religion within the current constitutional framework. The First Amendment states "Congress shall make no law respecting an establishment of religion, or prohibiting the free exercise thereof."[3] The former is known as the Establishment Clause, while the latter is referred to as the Free Exercise Clause. As applied to Native Americans, the first challenge is the constitutional framework itself because the administration of public lands on which there are American Indian sacred sites often involves decisions about competing uses that are *both* protected under the constitution. Typically, such situations force courts to decide if a group's right to its religious practices overrules other claims of those using public land or if protecting religious practices violates the Establishment Clause. Other challenges of applying the First Amendment to native religious practices include the amount of diversity within indigenous nations and cultures, the different views of sites they consider sacred, and the fact that religion is not separated from other aspects of life in American Indian spiritual beliefs. Since the U.S. Constitution theoretically separates church and state, judges have not often viewed the accommodation of Indian practitioners' ability to hunt or fish as religious protection (Albert 2009).

Given the challenges involved in constitutional protection, other measures have been pursued for asserting native rights[4] including the American Indian Religious Freedom Act (AIRFA) of 1978. It was a policy statement intended to protect Native American spiritual expressions and practices, but it lacked institutional enforcement and did not hold up in court. For example, the 1988 Supreme Court ruling in *Lyng v. Northwest Indian Cemetery Protective Association* was an especially hard blow for Native American religious rights, as it demonstrated the Court's reluctance to invoke AIRFA and practitioners' constitutional Free Exercise claims to sacred sites. The Court stated that even if the Forest Service's decision to build a road through an area sacred to Native Americans would "virtually destroy" their ability to practice their religion, "the Constitution simply does not provide a principle that could justify upholding respondent's legal claims." The Court concluded that the Free Exercise Clause was not invoked because the road's location did not violate practitioners' religious beliefs or penalize their activities and concluded that "whatever rights the Indians may have to the use of the area . . . those rights do not divest the government of its right to use what is, after all, *its* land" (Albert 2009:472). The Court's conclusion reinforces that the U.S. government's political notion of land ownership is at the heart of struggles over sacred sites.

The Devils Tower case is an example of a legal struggle that did favor native rights. The Devils Tower National Monument in Wyoming (also known as Bear Lodge) is considered a sacred site by several American Indian groups. The monument is part of the Black Hills lands originally ceded to Native Americans as part of a reservation, but was seized by the federal government in 1875 after gold was discovered there. Today, there are over 20 tribes for which the monument holds cultural significance (Usborne 1996). In addition to sacred narratives about cultural heroes, rituals, and objects, traditional ceremonies performed at Devils Tower include sweat lodges, vision quests, and sun dances (San Miguel 1994).

The monument is also popular for rock climbing and other recreational activities. Tribes have been voicing their concerns for years over climbers disturbing their place of worship. A 1993 resolution by the Dakota, Nakota, and Lakota nations identified Devils Tower as a "primary and significant" site for their religion. The resolution described the damage done to Devils Tower by rock climbers, asserted it was the Indian nations' duty to protect sacred sites for future generations, and stated the nations did not support federal agencies allowing the continued destruction of the monument (Dussias 2001). Holy Rock, former president of the Oglala Sioux, explained it this way: "It would be like someone going to England with their climbing equipment and proceeding to scale your great cathedrals on a Sunday" (Usborne 1996).

In response to tribal concerns, the National Park Service (NPS) insti-tuted a new plan in 1996 under which licenses for commercially led climb-ing would not be given during the month of June (a time of special significance to Native Americans for ceremonies and rituals), and a vol-untary ban on casual climbing during the same period would be enacted along with other activities to educate the public about the spiritual and cultural significance of Devils Tower for Native Americans. A group of climbing guides sued the NPS, claiming the ban violated their constitu-tional rights. In mid-June 1996, a district court ruling issued an injunction against the ban on commercial climbing, arguing the NPS policy violated the constitution by promoting a religious practice at the expense of other rights and entangling government involvement in religious affairs. In November 1996, the NPS adopted an addendum to the management plan that removed the ban on commercial climbing licenses, but the voluntary ban on casual climbing remained (Dussias 2001). Ultimately, the U.S. district court's 1998 decision concerning Devils Tower (*Bear Lodge Multiple Use Association v. Babbitt*) affirmed the NPS's voluntary ban on climbing during the month of June. The court reasoned the NPS's stated purposes of the ban (removing barriers to worship and helping to preserve

Native American cultural practices that are intertwined with Native American religious methods of worship) did not violate the Establishment Clause and thus were a permissible accommodation of religious worship (Albert 2009). However, the victory was incomplete for tribes who consider the monument a sacred space, since some climbers chose to disregard the voluntary ban.

Given the difficulties of protecting cultural rights in general and native rights in particular under the current U.S. Constitution, any serious agenda for truly advancing cultural rights should consider proposed amendments to the Bill of Rights. As a point of departure, specifying aspects of collective social life would provide a more supportive legal framework for groups that are consistently denied the right to full expression of their rights. Such aspects might include language rights, including provision of mother tongue education; indigenous land rights, including protection of sacred sites; intellectual property rights; and allocation of government funds and personnel to support such efforts.

International Agreements

Using selected examples from documents in Table 4.2, this section addresses the challenges and opportunities related to asserting cultural rights via agreements between countries.

Declarations

Arguably the most well-known international human rights instrument, the Universal Declaration of Human Rights (UDHR) is referenced by many documents devoted to cultural rights that seek to build on UDHR Article 22. The Declaration on the Rights of Indigenous Peoples is another important step for cultural rights, as it is the first comprehensive human rights document entirely devoted to the rights of indigenous peoples. It was adopted in 2007 by the General Assembly with 144 states in favor, 4 votes against (Australia, Canada, New Zealand, and the United States), and 11 abstentions. In March 2010, Canada stated it would take steps to endorse the Declaration on the Rights of Indigenous Peoples, while in April 2010, the United States indicated it will review its position on the declaration. The Indian Law Resource Center has started a campaign urging citizens and organizations to write letters to President Obama during the period of review encouraging him to endorse the Declaration on the Rights of Indigenous Peoples, which he did in 2010. The declaration will be another tool for asserting cultural rights of Native Americans in that it provides

Table 4.2   Examples of Cultural Rights in International Human Rights Documents

Document and Year Adopted	Section	Excerpts
Universal Declaration of Human Rights, 1948	Article 22	Everyone . . . is entitled to realization . . . of the economic, social and cultural rights indispensable for his dignity and the free development of his personality.
European Social Charter, 1961	Preamble	The enjoyment of social rights should be secured without discrimination on grounds of race, colour, sex, religion, political opinion, national extraction or social origin.
International Convention on the Elimination of All Forms of Racial Discrimination, 1965	Article 7	States Parties undertake to adopt immediate and effective measures, particularly in the fields of teaching, education, culture and information, with a view to combating prejudices which lead to racial discrimination and to promoting understanding, tolerance and friendship among nations and racial or ethnical groups.
International Covenant on Economic, Social, and Cultural Rights, 1966	Article 15(1a)	The States Parties to the present Covenant recognize the right of everyone to take part in cultural life.
American Convention on Human Rights, 1969	Article 26	The States Parties undertake to adopt measures . . . with a view to achieving progressively . . . the full realization of the rights implicit in the economic, social, educational, scientific, and cultural standards set forth in the Charter of the Organization of American States as amended by the Protocol of Buenos Aires.
African Charter on Human and Peoples' Rights, 1981	Article 22(1)	All peoples shall have the right to their economic, social and cultural development with due regard to their freedom and identity and in the equal enjoyment of the common heritage of mankind.

(Continued)

(Continued)

Document and Year Adopted	Section	Excerpts
C169 Indigenous and Tribal Peoples Convention, 1989	Article 2 (2b)	Governments shall have the responsibility for . . . promoting the full realisation of the social, economic and cultural rights of these peoples with respect for their social and cultural identity, their customs and traditions and their institutions.
Declaration on the Rights of Persons Belonging to National or Ethnic, Religious, and Linguistic Minorities, 1992	Preamble	The promotion and protection of the rights of persons belonging to national or ethnic, religious and linguistic minorities contribute to political and social stability and peace and enrich the cultural diversity and heritage of society.
Universal Declaration on Cultural Diversity, 2001	Article 4	The defence of cultural diversity is an ethical imperative, inseparable from respect for human dignity. It implies a commitment to human rights and fundamental freedoms, in particular the rights of persons belonging to minorities and those of indigenous peoples.
Convention on the Protection and Promotion of the Diversity of Cultural Expressions, 2005	Article 13	Parties shall endeavour to integrate culture in their development policies at all levels for the creation of conditions conducive to sustainable development and, within this framework, foster aspects relating to the protection and promotion of the diversity of cultural expressions.
Declaration on the Rights of Indigenous Peoples, 2007	Article 8(1)	Indigenous peoples and individuals have the right not to be subjected to forced assimilation or destruction of their culture.

international baselines for indigenous rights and can help proactively formulate national laws that protect such rights.

While promoting the recognition of differences, cultural rights are not about rehashing the "clash of civilizations" argument. In fact, the first major

UN standard-setting instrument on cultural diversity (UNESCO Universal Declaration on Cultural Diversity) was adopted unanimously by the General Assembly in November 2001, in the wake of the September 11, 2001, terrorist attacks. Although the declaration had been a work in progress for years prior to its adoption, 9/11 was cited as an example of the need for intercultural understanding and dialogue as components of a comprehensive, proactive framework for cultural rights. Koïchiro Matsuura, UNESCO's director-general at the time of the declaration's adoption, said he hopes the Universal Declaration on Cultural Diversity will eventually "acquire as much force as the Universal Declaration of Human Rights" (UNESCO 2001).

The Universal Declaration on Cultural Diversity identifies multiple areas that could be strengthened by protecting and promoting diversity. For instance, Article 2 states the importance of public policies that respect diversity: "Policies for the inclusion and participation of all citizens are guarantees of social cohesion, the vitality of civil society and peace. Thus defined, cultural pluralism gives policy expression to the reality of cultural diversity." Article 3 solidly connects diversity to development, a theme increasingly addressed in contemporary debates about the ethics of economic globalization: "Cultural diversity widens the range of options open to everyone; it is one of the roots of development, understood not simply in terms of economic growth, but also as a means to achieve a more satisfactory intellectual, emotional, moral and spiritual existence." Article 5 addresses the importance of a social environment that sustains cultural rights: "All persons have the right to express themselves and to create and disseminate their work in the language of their choice, and particularly in their mother tongue; all persons are entitled to quality education and training that fully respect their cultural identity; and all persons have the right to participate in the cultural life of their choice and conduct their own cultural practices."[5] In its "Main Lines of an Action Plan," the declaration outlines several specific objectives for member states, including encouraging linguistic diversity and incorporating cultural diversity into international debates on development and policymaking.

Conventions

The International Covenant on Economic, Social, and Cultural Rights (ICESCR) helped broaden the global human rights framework by including aspects commonly left out of human rights discussions, such as the rights to food, health care, housing, and self-determination. There are currently 69 signatories and 160 parties to the covenant. The United States signed the document in 1979, but has not yet ratified it. As a binding agreement, ratification would mean that the United States would be required to submit reports to the UN Committee on Economic, Social, and Cultural Rights on steps it has taken to achieve the rights outlined in the covenant. If ratified, judges would be bound to recognize the covenant as part of the law, enacting the possibility that cases of rights violations under the covenant could be brought before U.S. courts.

An *Optional Protocol to the International Covenant on Economic, Social, and Cultural Rights* was adopted in 2008 but has not yet been entered into force. Enforcement is key to bridging the gap between the rights enshrined in international documents and the actual experiences of individuals and groups whose rights are still not fully realized. The optional protocol is an important step in that direction, as it is the first instrument that would allow individuals to seek justice at the international level for violations of rights protected under the ICESCR. The optional protocol has been signed thus far by 32 countries. Ecuador and Mongolia are currently the only two countries that have ratified the protocol, although the Portuguese Parliament has adopted a recommendation to the government for ratification. When 10 parties ratify it, the protocol will enter into force.

There are currently 85 signatories and 173 parties to the International Convention on the Elimination of All Forms of Racial Discrimination (ICERD), a document that includes upholding cultural rights as part of a legally binding agreement to eliminate racial discrimination. The United States ratified it in 1994 with several reservations asserting circumstances under which the United States does not accept certain obligations of the ICERD. As part of the ICERD committee's review process for countries that have ratified it, nonprofit organizations can submit their information (also called "shadow reports") alongside the required government reports. For example, Survival International's report[6] outlined Brazil's ICERD violations against the Guarani people, while the Western Shoshone Defense's report[7] documented how the U.S. government is in violation of the ICERD in its dealings with the Western Shoshones.

Another important instrument for cultural rights is the ILO 169 Indigenous and Tribal Peoples Convention, established by the International Labour Organization as an international convention that emphasizes the connections between cultural rights, land ownership, and self-determination. Thus far, only 20 countries have ratified it: Argentina, Bolivia, Brazil, Chile, Colombia, Costa Rica, Denmark, Dominica, Ecuador, Fiji, Guatemala, Honduras, Mexico, Nepal, the Netherlands, Norway, Paraguay, Peru, Spain, and Venezuela. The ILO 169 promotes land ownership rights, equality, freedom, and self-determination of indigenous communities. As governments that ratify the convention are legally bound by it, the ILO 169 has more enforcement power than the UN Declaration on the Rights of Indigenous Peoples.

Other Methods of Advancing Cultural Rights

To draw attention to cultural rights and encourage their promotion at all levels, the UN sponsors themes around which awareness-raising activities are planned such as the International Year for the Rapprochement of Cultures (2010), the International Day of the World's Indigenous People (August 9), and the World Day for Cultural Diversity for Dialogue and Development (May 21). The institutional designation of such themes reaffirms grassroots organizations that have been working on these issues for years and connects local struggles to global processes. The participation of activist organizations in the ICERD committee review process is another particularly tangible avenue of collaboration among multiple stakeholders in documenting cultural rights violations and creating recommendations for holding states accountable to the ICERD.

Many of the grassroots efforts to assert cultural rights happen outside the international spotlight. The following examples provide just a small sample of the countless ways those rights are advocated. The American-Arab Anti-Discrimination Committee has been working for over 30 years to improve conditions for Arab and Muslim Americans. The Native Resource Coalition is one of many organizations fighting against environmental racism and corporate takeover of sacred sites. Native women are often at the forefront of such struggles (Taliman 2009). Alto Arizona was formed in protest of the recent Arizona laws SB 1070 and HB 2281 that respectively legalize racial profiling and prohibit ethnic studies courses in public schools. African American and Native American groups have also lent their support to the immigrant rights movement and spoke out against the Arizona laws.[8] Protecting language has been an important area of cultural rights, particularly for indigenous groups. Native immersion language programs provide a tangible way of keeping this aspect of culture alive and have been correlated with increased academic achievement.[9]

Linguistic diversity is one of many areas in which groups are asserting their cultural rights. As discussed throughout this chapter, people were resisting cultural repression in various ways long before constitutions and international agreements recognized it. Now, as institutional dialogue is slowly catching up, there are multiple opportunities to meet the serious global cultural rights crisis with an equally serious movement that builds on grassroots momentum in advancing cultural rights as an expression of what it means to be fully human.

Sample of Websites Providing Information on Cultural Rights

- Center for World Indigenous Studies: http://cwis.org/
- Enduring Voices Project: http://www.nationalgeographic.com/mission/enduringvoices/
- First Peoples Scholarly Publishing: http://www.firstpeoplesnewdirections.org/
- International Work Group for Indigenous Affairs: http://www.iwgia.org/
- Living Tongues Institute for Endangered Languages: http://www.livingtongues.org/hotspots.html#NGmagmap
- The Pluralism Project: http://pluralism.org/
- Sacred Land Film Project: http://www.sacredland.org/
- UNESCO World Report: Investing in Cultural Diversity and Intercultural Dialogue: http://unesdoc.unesco.org/images/0018/001852/185202e.pdf
- World Values Survey: http://www.worldvaluessurvey.org/

Discussion Questions

1. How do you think UNESCO and other international bodies working to promote cultural rights can protect such rights *and* have an international standard of treatment? What about practices like female genital mutilation that some view as a cultural right and others view as morally abhorrent? What are some other dimensions involved in those issues that are often hidden in *cultural relativism* versus international standards debates (e.g., poverty, education, women's status)?

2. Why do you suppose, when an event like 9/11 occurs, specific elements of culture such as language and religion become the focus of an individual or a small group's actions when it belongs to a minority group but, when such an act occurs at the hands of someone from the dominant group (such as Timothy McVeigh), those actions are written off as the result of a sick individual and not tied directly to its culture?

3. Education has been promoted as an important method of social mobility in the United States. After learning about the *boarding school* experiences of Native American children, how do you think increasing access to education should be balanced with culturally relevant and respectful curricula?

4. Look at several constitutions (including Brazil's) to compare them with one another and to the U.S. Constitution. You will find most of them here: http://confinder.richmond.edu/

Notes

1. Thanks to Keri Iyall Smith for using this example to illustrate individual versus collective rights as well as her guidance in early discussions of this project.

2. For a description of boarding schools from first-person alumni accounts, see http://www.heard.org/currentexhibits/hmm/BoardingSchoolExperience.html.

3. See http://www.usconstitution.net/xconst_Am1.html.

4. See Executive Order 13007 (http://www.gsa.gov/portal/content/101585) and the Memorandum Opinion for the Secretary of the Interior: http://www.justice.gov/olc/sacredsites.htm.

5. See http://portal.unesco.org/en/ev.php-URL_ID=13179&URL_DO=DO_TOPIC&URL_SECTION=201.html.

6. See http://www.scribd.com/doc/29404466/Violations-of-the-Rights-of-the-Guarani-of-Mato-Grosso-Do-Sul-State-BRAZIL.

7. See http://www.wsdp.org/shadowreport75th.pdf.

8. See http://sfbayview.com/2010/latinos-blacks-join-fight-for-civil-rights-in-arizona/ and http://deletetheborder.org/node/2565.

9. See http://www.culturalsurvival.org/publications/cultural-survival-quarterly/united-states/language-success and http://www.aihec.org/resources/documents/NativeLangugageImmersion.pdf.

References

Adalberto, Aguirre, and Jonathan Turner. 2011. *American Ethnicity: The Dynamics and Consequences of Discrimination.* New York: McGraw-Hill.

Albert, Michelle Kay. 2009. "Obligations and Opportunities to Protect Native American Sacred Sites Located on Public Lands." *The Columbia Human Rights Law Review* 40(2):471–521.

Associated Press. 2009. *Brazilian Court Ruling Backs Indian Reservation.* March 19. Retrieved August 6, 2010 (http://www.msnbc.msn.com/id/29779273/).

Blau, Judith and Alberto Moncada. 2006. *Justice in the United States: Human Rights and the U.S. Constitution.* Lanham, MD: Rowman and Littlefield.

Blauner, Robert. 1972. *Racial Oppression in America.* New York: Harper and Row.

Borges, Beto and Gilles Combrisson. 1998. "Indigenous Rights in Brazil: Stagnation to Political Impasse." Retrieved July 28, 2010 (http://saiic.nativeweb.org/brazil.html).

Dobnik, Verena. 2010. "Muslim Center Dispute Sparks New York Rallies." August 22. Retrieved August 23, 2010 (http://www.msnbc.msn.com/id/38807231/ns/us_news-life).

Dussias, Allison. 2001. "Cultural Conflicts Regarding Land Use: The Conflict Between Recreational Users at Devil's Tower and Native American Ceremonial Users." *Vermont Journal of Environmental Law* 2(1). Retrieved July 28, 2010 (http://www.vjel.org/journal/VJEL10005.html).

Howard, Rhonda E., and Jack Donnelly. 1987. *International Handbook of Human Rights*. Westport, CT: Greenwood Press.

International Work Group for Indigenous Affairs. 2010. "New Constitution in Kenya." Retrieved August 16, 2010 (http://www.iwgia.org/sw42636.asp).

Jorgenson, Chester E. and Luther Frank Mott, eds. 1962. *Benjamin Franklin*. New York: Hill and Wang.

Mander, Jerry. 1991. *In the Absence of the Sacred: The Failure of Technology and the Survival of the Indian Nations*. San Francisco: Sierra Club Books.

Marder, William. 2004. *Indians in the Americas: The Untold Story*. San Diego, CA: Book Tree.

Marger, Martin N. 2009. *Race and Ethnic Relations: American and Global Perspectives*. Belmont, CA: Wadsworth.

National Geographic. 2010. "Disappearing Languages." accessed July 20, 2010 (http://www.nationalgeographic.com/mission/enduringvoices/).

San Miguel, George L. 1994. "How Is Devils Tower a Sacred Site to American Indians?" National Park Service. Retrieved July 28, 2010 (http://www.nps.gov/deto/historyculture/sacredsite.htm).

Schaefer, Richard T. 2009. *Sociology: A Brief Introduction*. New York: McGraw-Hill.

Survival International. 2008. "Indians Rejoice as Supreme Court Affirms Land Rights." Retrieved July 4, 2010 (http://www.survivalinternational.org/news/4021).

Taliman, Valerie. 2009. "Saving Native Lands." Pp. 478–80 in *Experiencing Race, Class, and Gender in the United States*, edited by Roberta Fiske-Rusciano. Boston: McGraw-Hill.

Turner, Bryan S. 2006. *Vulnerability and Human Rights*. University Park: Pennsylvania State University Press.

United Nations Development Programme. 2004. "Human Development Report 2004: Cultural Liberty in Today's Diverse World." Retrieved July 2, 2010 (http://hdr.undp.org/en/reports/global/hdr2004/).

United Nations Educational, Scientific, and Cultural Organization. 2001. "General Conference Adopts Universal Declaration on Cultural Diversity." Retrieved July 2, 2010 (http://www.unesco.org/confgen/press_rel/021101_clt_diversity.shtml).

U.S. Census Bureau. 2010. "New Census Bureau Report Analyzes Nation's Linguistic Diversity." Retrieved July 28, 2010 (http://www.census.gov/newsroom/releases/archives/american_community_survey_acs/).

U.S. English. 2010. "Official English: States with Official English Laws." Retrieved August 16, 2010 (http://www.usenglish.org/view/13).

Usborne, David. 1996. "Battle for the Spirit of Devil's Tower." Retrieved August 4, 2010 (http://www.independent.co.uk/news/world/battle-for-the-spirit-of-devils-tower-1308105.html).

5

Globalizing the
Human Rights Perspective

Bruce K. Friesen

Sociologists have long been interested in studying the nature of social change. Indeed, the rapid industrialization of Western countries in the nineteenth century spawned new questions regarding social cohesion and inequality in mass, complex societies. Theorists such as Auguste Comte, Herbert Spencer, and William Graham Sumner developed sociocultural theories of social change that conceived of social change moving in a linear direction from primitive to complex, largely determined by factors unnoticed by the general population. Emile Durkheim ([1933] 1984), for example, argued that the nature of social cohesion undergoes a fundamental change from organic to mechanical solidarity during the process of modernization. Socioevolutionary theories developed prior to and apart from biological theories of evolution, but some recognize innate human tendencies such as sociability. Such theories typically identify a series of evolutionary stages that are characterized by an overall progression.

Classical socioevolutionary theories have a number of shortcomings. They imply that social change is necessarily linear, despite historical examples to the contrary. Europe, for example, existed for centuries in the Dark Ages, a time when societies lived in the shadow of the larger and technologically superior Roman Empire. The claim that modern societies are necessarily superior has been criticized as being ethnocentric since it generally implies progress. Measuring progress first requires the adoption of some type of objective criteria, and not all social change can be considered progress. Increasing environmental degradation is but one example. Classical socioevolutionary theories are also deterministic, suggesting that certain types of change are inevitable and impervious to human intervention. This runs counter to the many examples where a strategic, concerted effort makes huge changes in the way people live, act, and think.

Modern theories of sociocultural evolution have attempted to correct these weaknesses. In his own theory of social change, Tonnies ([1887] 2001) noted that societies are moving from simple, informal societies to those in which personal movement is more restricted by means of formal laws and rules. Unlike his predecessors, Tonnies rejected the notion of progress. He suggested that social change does not necessarily imply improvement, and that the cost of maintaining fairness in modern societies through a formal system of justice can reduce the amount of individual satisfaction and freedom. Theorists writing in the tradition of Tonnies are often referred to as *neoevolutionists*. Neoevolutionary perspectives generally acknowledge that certain types of innate tendencies exist in human social behavior but reject the determinism inherent in classical theories. Forces such as technological change can increase environmental pressure for systemic change without determining it or setting the direction in which change will occur. Other factors, human agency foremost among them, can ultimately influence the nature of any change. While identifying certain forces that may drive social change, neoevolutionists reject the notion that change is necessarily progress. Tying their perspectives more specifically to empirical evidence, neoevolutionists attempt to avoid ethnocentric biases. Thus, they rely on both natural and social scientific evidence to inform their theories.

This chapter adopts a neoevolutionary approach to understanding the nature of change in *moral systems*. Moral systems are advantageous in that they increase cohesion and commitment in a social unit, by dividing beliefs and behaviors into those that are valued and those that are despised. This in turn motivates individuals to adopt beliefs and actions that promote the general safety and welfare of the group, ultimately increasing the likelihood that the group will survive. Historically, the disadvantage of this system is that commitment to one particular group and its ethnocentric moral system may motivate groups to engage in warfare and genocide if it is perceived to be advantageous. Unchecked intergroup warfare, especially when equipped by sophisticated killing technology such as nuclear weaponry, can ultimately threaten the survival of the human species.

Among other factors, *population growth* places stress on moral systems. As populations increase, greater human diversity and intercultural contact challenge limited moral systems to account for the full diversity of human experience. Increasing diversity, of individual experiences, cultures, and peoples, places stress on the moral systems to account for the diversity and develop new morals that satisfy and integrate new members into a cohesive social system. This tension may eventually give way to the introduction of a more abstract and universal moral system than that which preceded it, making it a better fit with the changing demographics of the environment.

Seen in this light, the development of international human rights is an adaptive response to the processes of globalization. More than any other, the establishment of institutionalized genocide at the national level in Germany, a populous and supposedly civilized Western nation, caught the attention of countries and citizens of the world. It challenged the dominant secularized moral system of thought privileging the inherent rightness of the sovereign nation-state, leading to a moral crisis of international proportions. In its wake, citizens, nongovernmental organizations (NGOs), political leaders, and others responded to the crisis by advocating for a declaration of a universal moral standard in the form of human rights.

As a formal articulation of human rights, the resultant Universal Declaration of Human Rights is surprisingly universal. It incorporates humankind's sense of fairness, provides a greater sense of security of person, and focuses a new morality upon Amartya Sen's (1995) notions of *capabilities* of a society's citizens. Providing individuals and groups with structural opportunities and resources that will free and empower them to achieve their full potential is the ultimate expression of rights—a great improvement over the human species than previously. The human rights movement defines one *collective good* that transcends all others: humanity, as both a means to an end and an end in and of itself. Human potential is unlocked only as fast as nation-states embrace and formalize a commitment to a full range of human rights.

The Evolution of Moral Systems

For the purposes of this chapter, I define moral systems as the components of culture that provide (1) a metaphysic, or explanation of the meaning of life and one's place in the universe; (2) a moral code, or list of behavioral expectations; and (3) a creation myth explaining the manner in which the physical universe known to the social group originated. Taken together, these components of a moral system are self-reinforcing. They motivate societal members to work for the good of the group and endow each member with a sense of the inherent morality of the group and a spiritual connection with other members.

In and of themselves, moral systems are closed. That is, they apply only to members of the tribe or group who share the same moral system. Population growth, however, can tax the credulity of a moral system in a number of ways. *Internal population growth* provides a diversity of experience within the group by producing group members with a wider array of personalities, experiences, and behaviors. In large societies, social strata emerge in which the rights and privileges of some are denied to others. Subcultures and countercultures can emerge that test the limits of moral tolerance and understanding. Internal population growth is often facilitated by technological innovations that make it possible to sustain larger populations.

External population growth occurs as a group comes into contact with populations different from its own. Historically, external population growth has occurred through activities such as trade, conquest, and immigration. New populations are subsumed or amalgamated into political systems of increasing size, such as city-states, nations, and nation-states. Though increasing inequality and social stratification is a result of increasing size, questions of fairness and equality often fare prominently in public discourse. Mechanisms of redistribution are often implemented, even in societies with great amounts of inequality. Real or symbolic, these mechanisms indicate an ongoing concern with inequality.

In realizing growth and greater diversity, cultures can respond by demanding conformity and punishing the perceived moral violators, revise the moral system so as to become more inclusive, or eventually replace the outdated moral system with something that better accounts for the diversity of behavior and expands definitions of the group so as to include a greater number of people, views, and behaviors previously defined as aberrant. While changes to moral systems often occur gradually over a long period, ongoing questions of integration and stability motivate more open group members to be receptive to notions of morality that are more inclusive and universal. This is because the primary function of moral systems is integrative. Change in moral systems can at times occur relatively quickly, through social revolution. In traditional societies, conquerors often superimpose their moral system on the vanquished. In modern societies a plurality of moral systems can exist, but those that provide the most opportunity to integrate the population come to dominate over time.

To most neoevolutionists, human history can be demarcated by a series of stages that mark a shift in economic cooperation. Across the globe, this change has been uneven and unsteady, and rarely linear (Steward [1955] 1972). Conditions of geography, economics, and technology can push any society in a multitude of directions. Secondary factors like political systems, ideologies, and religion also have important, but indeterminate, influences. Still, in the course of the evolution of human societies, one finds a general move from hunting and gathering societies to advanced industrial societies.

Increasing societal growth and complexity can place stress on moral systems to change. Population growth can cause changes to traditional systems of social stratification, bringing to the fore new questions related to the equality of peoples. Changes in economic arrangements can similarly draw new moral questions about the distribution of resources. Old answers provide limited or undesirable answers to moral questions and the nature of the universe. Consequently, answers to moral questions become increasingly abstract and general so as to account for a greater array of social and economic experiences. At other times, an older moral system may simply be replaced by one that appears to be more relevant to the lives of people in a particular society.

The Expansion of Moral Systems

In traditional societies, most moral systems come to be organized in the form of a religion. As individuals are born into a society with norms and values existing outside of the person, Durkheim ([1912] 1962) argued that this transcendent, external moral force is eventually identified as a deity. Following this logic, deities of larger, more complex societies should be understood to have more powerful and abstract (incomprehensible) attributes, presumably because members of a large, complex society need to conceive of a more powerful and complex god than members of small, less complex societies in order to believe the deity has the ability to control all things. More powerful attributes of god are needed in larger, more complex societies. Religion thus offers an organized system of encouraging members of society to give themselves to the society and internalize its values and norms.

Research has demonstrated a correlation between the increasing structural complexity of social systems and the perceived attributes of a supreme being. Underhill (1975) found both economic and political complexity to have an impact on the development of monotheism, with the former having a greater influence. Underhill also found a positive relationship between increasingly powerful attributes of a supreme creator and increasing economic complexity.

Rowes and Raymond (2003) found a positive relationship between society size and belief in a moralizing god, theorizing that conflict with other groups results in an emphasis on adherence to moral rules and social cohesion in larger societies so as to avoid the costs associated with splitting the society into smaller groups.

Research reported in Lenski and Lenski's (1970) work illustrates the basic hypothesis. Population growth increases as economic systems change from hunting and gathering to simple horticultural, to advanced agrarian, and then on to industrialized. To measure the increasing power of a deity under monotheism, Lenski and Lenski conceptualized three categories of increasing power: (1) a god who created the world and left, (2) a god who created the world and holds it together, and (3) a god who created the world, holds it together, and is interested in moral behavior. Lenski and Lenski found a strong correlation between the type of society (i.e., hunting and gathering, simple horticultural, or advanced agrarian) and the perceived power of a supreme being. Lenski and Lenski attribute this correlation to changes in technology and communication, which in turn impact political organization, but increasing diversity as a result of internal and external population growth can also create pressure on moral systems to become increasingly universal so as to account for the diversity within society and to integrate members into a single moral system.

Human beings survived together by hunting and gathering for more than 100,000 years. These largely nomadic groups, generally numbering between 15 and 25, developed indigenous moral systems essentially tied to their natural environment. Moral systems were largely egalitarian, inclusive, and universal insomuch as the rules applied to each member of the group. Creation myths provided a meaningful metaphysic for group members. Because societal membership was primarily ascriptive through birth, less energy was needed to maintain the legitimacy or logical consistency of the moral code. As such, the moral system was largely closed, applicable only to group members. Others might be grafted in through marriage or enslavement, but trading with outsiders meant the development of new standards of behavior for the purposes of trading. Because other groups existed outside of the moral universe, enslavement, subjugation, and even cannibalization were possible outcomes of interaction, especially if one group was perceived to be a threat to another.

Technological innovations such as the domestication of plants and animals and the invention of digging sticks first appeared around 10,000 B.C.E., in a place in the Middle East known today as the Fertile Crescent. Diamond (2005) credits this revolution largely to geographical accident as humans in the area used rich resources at their disposal to innovate new techniques of economic cooperation. Group size increased into the hundreds as a more stable food supply brought about increased longevity and a decline in disease and death due to starvation. In fact, human groups began producing a surplus, used in trade or stored in anticipation of times of drought or throughout the seasons. Moral systems became more elaborate, formal, and ritualistic, as some societal members, freed from the work needed to survive by an increasing division of labor, became full-time religious figureheads and/or political leaders.

New religions spawned as some human societies evolved from simple horticultural and pastoral societies into advanced agrarian states around 3500 B.C.E. It is during this period that each of the major world religions had its beginnings. As illustrated above, new religions offered new and increasingly universal claims that carried the potential to unite diverse peoples. Each began as a cult, a religious movement set apart from the rest of society by its unique beliefs and proposed way of life. Over time, however, the religions gained both adherents and societal legitimacy.

In her sweeping history of the development of human rights, Ishay (2008) notes that several moral codes of antiquity contained within them universal altruistic guidelines applicable to a substantial portion of the human family. Hammurabi's code, the oldest surviving collection of laws, sanctioned punishments for those who transgressed the law, and discussed how marriages and divorces should be conducted. Likely influenced by other moral codes, the Cyrus Cylinder of ancient Persia contained elements of religious tolerance and humane principles. Ishay notes that such moral codes fell short of true universalism as they were applied only to certain segments of the population. Slaves and women, for example, were often not accorded the same rights and privileges as others. Nor were the same rights or processes of law granted to people outside of the empire or other political entity.

Nonetheless, populations expanded as city-states amalgamated into nations and eventually into empires. Moral codes were expanded so as to integrate increasingly diverse populations into a larger social system. Although Judaism, a religion with its origins in hunting and gathering societies, contained stipulations under which gentiles could be "grafted in" to the religion, its emphasis on ascription through birth was eventually superseded by the broader Christian claim of inclusion through (achieved) conversion. At times, older moral codes were replaced by newer ones. In 313 C.E., for example, the Roman emperor Constantine made Christianity the official religion of the empire. In the sixth century, the development of Islam had the effect of uniting different warring tribes, each with its own god, under the Shahada claim that there is no God but Allah (and Mohammed is the messenger of Allah). Some rulers fostered a good deal of tolerance for diversity while others insisted on strict adherence to the politically sanctioned moral code. Strict regimes generally ran the risk of dividing, rather than uniting, their minions.

The rise of a surplus in more complex social systems inevitably gave rise to questions of distribution. More powerful individuals or groups choose to hoard, rather than redistribute, goods, thus accruing greater wealth, prestige, and power in the process. While material inequality did increase in simple horticultural and advanced agrarian societies, it is important to note that many societies also institutionalized redistributive mechanisms. Two such examples are the potlatch among indigenous populations of the northwestern coast in North America and the year of Jubilee among Jews as described in the book of Leviticus. In the former, wealthier members of the tribe gave lavish gifts to others in a sacred ceremony, sometimes to the point of personal impoverishment. In the latter, debts would be forgiven and slaves freed roughly every 50 years. While formal religions more often accepted than challenged systemic inequality, most encouraged a sense of compassion, responsibility, and generosity toward society's most vulnerable.

Many modern societies implement redistributive mechanisms in the form of progressive taxation and redistribution through either universal or targeted social programs. Of interest are also the apparently volitional initiatives by some wealthy individuals to redistribute their wealth. In 2001, several dozen millionaires in the United States signed a petition requesting that then President George W. Bush not repeal an inheritance tax that taxed the estates of the wealthy more heavily than others upon their death (Johnson 2001). Even amid budgetary shortfalls in tax-heavy Germany in 2010, German businessmen petitioned the government to more heavily tax their income to help balance the national budget (BBC 2009). Among billionaires worldwide is a voluntary movement to donate at least 50 percent of their assets to charity upon their death (MSNBC 2010). At the time of this writing, more than 40 wealthy individuals had signed the pledge at http://givingpledge.org. While questions regarding sincerity of motives or follow-through abound, discomfort with large amounts of inequality appear to be an important motivator.

Designing Moral Systems: Modern Societies

If moral systems usually take the form of religious systems in traditional societies, the rise of a secular moral system is the purview of modern societies. Precursors of this secularizing trend included preindustrial merchant societies of the world. The Golden Age of Islam in the eighth to thirteenth centuries saw the encouragement and expression of humanistic, rational, and scientific thought, which at times included religious tolerance and occasional secularism (Goodman 2003; Kraemer 1992). These developments eventually found their way to the West. Using reason to question the legitimacy of exploitative and unequal practices of the Christian church led to the Protestant Reformation of the 1500s. Simultaneous social, economic, and technological changes in the seventeenth and eighteenth centuries combined in Europe to give eventual primacy to the use of reason and science over authority and tradition as ways of knowing. To be sure, increasing intercultural contact through world exploration and colonization efforts helped fuel this secular moral shift. Discussions in European circles abounded regarding the morals and manners of the indigenous peoples of the Americas, beginning with the conquistadors' harsh treatment of them (Pagden 1982). Once reason had been freed, universal ideas such as egalitarianism and democracy found fuller expression in the Enlightenment.

This connection between the rise of reason and the envisioning of universal fairness and democracy may not be coincidental. Imagine an experiment conducted with two volunteers. One person, designated as the "Proposer," is given a sum of money. The Proposer has one opportunity to make a cash offer to the second person. If accepted, both volunteers keep the cash they have received. If the offer is rejected, neither person is allowed to keep any of the money. Classic economic theory predicts that the second person would accept *any* cash offer from the Proposer, since it is logical that by accepting the offer, the second person would have more money than before the experiment began. In reality, however, this rarely happens. Offers of 20 percent or less of the total cash allotment are almost universally rejected, while offers approaching 50 percent are almost universally accepted. Of greater importance to the participants than economic gain, then, is a sense of fairness or social equality. People would sooner reject an offer perceived to be unfair and receive nothing than accept an offer seen to be decidedly unequal.

A substantial body of research in experimental economics using this situation has emerged in recent years (Davis and Holt 1993; Dawes et al. 2007; Fehr and Schmidt 1999; Lowenstein, Thompson, and Baserman 1989). Sometimes called the Ultimatum Bargaining Game, these results have been replicated in a variety of cultures and under a variety of conditions (Bolton and Zwick 1995; Cameron 1999; Tompkinson and Bethwaite 1995). Recent research provides evidence of a neuropsychological basis for such behavior in humans (Tricomi et al. 2010). Similar behavior has been noted in other cooperative species such as dogs (Range et al. 2009) and nonhuman primates (Bryner 2007).

Such an aversion to inequality may well be a powerful evolved tendency in humans to reinforce cooperation. This tendency facilitates the development of cultural norms based on an overall sense of equality and fairness. Over time, a social group develops a moral system that reinforces basic notions of equality and cooperation in the traditions and stories of the group. Important to remember is the fact, noted earlier, that egalitarianism was the primary form of social organization practiced for well over 100,000 years of human evolution in hunting and gathering societies (Gurven 2006).

One could interpret the stumbling into modernity as an assertion of the need for greater equality and protection from the arbitrary whims of rulers. In England, pressure from nobles succeeded in limiting the powers of King Henry I in the *Charter of Liberties* as early as 1100 C.E. This charter later inspired the 1215 Magna Carta, which further limited the discretionary powers of royalty by guaranteeing that freemen could be punished only if they were in direct violation of the law. Though far from unique (Holt 1992), the Magna Carta has come to be seen as a forerunner in protecting various citizens from the arbitrary actions of the king by recognizing the right of (some) citizens to due process of law.

At times, revolutions instead of political pressure were used to change the nature of law and rights in the direction of inclusion and egalitarianism. The 1688 Glorious Revolution in England ended with restrictions placed on the unilateral power of royalty by the establishment of a constitutional monarchy. In the following year the English Bill of Rights was adopted, which ensured English subjects certain redress to the abuse of monarchical power and the makings of a representative democracy. The English Bill of Rights later served as inspiration for the American Bill of Rights. These limitations on what was previously thought to be the divine right of kings thus increased the relative power of the average subject, thereby reducing the amount of legal inequality separating subject and monarch.

Ishay (2008) notes that the American and French revolutions were the embodiment of the principles of the Enlightenment. Excusing themselves from the monarchical systems of old, the American colonies established a rational and secular constitution that accorded rights to ordinary citizens. "We the people," it began. The French Revolution soon followed, with such enlightenment values as *liberté, égalité, fraternité* motivating revolutionary changes. Though France struggled for some time to overcome the legacies of its past, it too eventually founded a government of the people: a democracy.

For some of the religiously inclined, it is difficult to fully comprehend how a moral system can exist without religion. Morals are dictated by God; how can morality therefore exist outside of a religion, in a secular state? It is important to note that virtually all human beings divide the world into good and bad, to moralize. Moralizing is part of the human condition, observed since Hume ([1739] 1985). While individuals moralize, collective understandings of good and bad are most often shared by groups, whether religious or not. Mothers Against Drunk Driving, for example, is a secular group that looks disparagingly at the behavior of driving while intoxicated. One need not be religious to form moral opinions. Moral systems are aspects of culture. Secular moral systems are vested not in God (necessarily), but in reason. "We take these truths to be self-evident," reads the preamble to the American Declaration of Independence. That is, these truths are considered to be obvious, verifiable, *rational*.

In forming a new constitution, the American founding fathers were directly influenced by the ideas of the Enlightenment. Moral precepts embedded in the Constitution were stated in universal and secular terms. Following the advice of Montesquieu, Americans adopted a system of legal checks and balances on various branches of government to further limit the discretion of the powerful and increase the likelihood of respect for the process. Tantamount to this new system was the accordance to citizens of certain rights of individuals, lauded earlier by the influential English philosopher and physician John Locke. The notion that individuals were endowed with certain inalienable rights at birth was a very influential idea that was embedded into the new American Constitution. Duty to God or royalty was replaced by an ethic of life, liberty, and the pursuit of happiness. This was to be the new metaphysic.

Thus, the new moral system established the state as sovereign. There would be no higher authority. The state was established as omnipotent, and the final arbiter of good and evil through the court system. Good and evil would be defined as the will of the people rather than God or rulers, though elected political representatives would have decided responsibility in discerning the people's will. Though the major world religions would continue to exist in multiple countries, the state would ultimately allow their existence, form, and means of expression. The state, and not the church, temple, or mosque, established a new moral system by describing the conditions under which people are free to practice. In time, this arrangement came to favor the divine rightness of the state as members of the same religion in different countries would call upon the same god to help their state be victorious in warfare, each believing that God was on their side.

Rights as the New Moral Code

Although added two years later as amendments to the American Constitution, a rhetoric of political equality and inalienable rights was embedded in the new Constitution in the form of the Bill of Rights. The need for such was motivated out of a desire to avoid the potential abuses of power and limitations of freedom found in the Old World. Like the English Bill of Rights that preceded it, this afterthought to the U.S. Constitution protected a limited number of civil and political rights. These included freedom of religion, free speech, free press, free assembly, and the right to petition the government for redress. The Bill of Rights forbids government infringement on the right to bear arms, and persons cannot be deprived of life, liberty, or property without due legal process. Other safety measures for federal criminal cases are described, as is an article clarifying that other rights should not be trampled in the process of protecting those listed in the Bill of Rights.

At the time, the idea of entrenching rights into a state constitution was radical, groundbreaking, and prescient. The United States was a world leader in ushering in a new age of greater equity, freedom, and protection of its citizens. Along with the constitutions of England and France, the U.S. Constitution became the gold standard and fueled the rapid rise of the nation-state in other parts of the world. In reality, of course, protection of the handful of civil rights listed in the U.S. Bill of Rights was extended to men of European descent who owned land. Women, slaves, and many racial and ethnic minorities would find little legal protection in the fledgling country. Despite the rhetoric, it takes time to realize and implement the full implications of a new moral system. Though a 20-year limit was placed on the practice of slavery, it would take decades more and a civil war to end the practice. Even today, the United States and other nations struggle to shrug off antiquated moral systems and to realize the full implication of the meaning of equitably protecting the rights of citizens.

In the new moral system, rights become embedded in the goodwill of the state. But who protects citizens from the state that chooses to be the violator? And who will defend the human rights of victims if the right is not listed in the constitution? Who will protect the rights of persons who are not citizens in a country, or who are citizens of more than one country? These are more than just esoteric questions. Aside from the Enlightenment giving birth to the notion of inalienable rights, its emphasis on reason also spawned a burgeoning quasi-scientific literature that attempted to rationalize that existing inequalities of race, class, and culture were based in nature, therefore justifying a preferential protection of rights for privileged groups. The sociologist Herbert Spencer argued that those more intelligent and highly evolved groups inevitably find themselves in the top echelons of society, a view quite popular with European and American elites. Charles Darwin would later use Spencer's catchphrase "the survival of the fittest" to help explain his new theory of evolution.

Influential individuals in the United States have at times been heavily influenced by racist, xenophobic, and intolerant perspectives. Despite a constitutional guarantee of civil liberties, the United States holds a less-than-stellar record for their protection. Many groups in the United States have had to fight for their civil liberties, taking on the very government supposed to protect them. Women were not allowed to vote in all parts of the United States until 1920, after 70 years of agitation and against the wishes of then President Woodrow Wilson. African Americans and Hispanics experienced a wide range of both de jure and de facto discriminatory practices, which have yet to be fully eliminated. Even white European minorities including the Irish, Italians, and Jews found themselves victims of extreme discrimination on the basis of religious differences, and were denied basic civil rights (Adalberto and Turner 2008).

In addition to this poor record of protecting civil rights, human rights violations in the United States abound. With increasingly severe repercussions, protecting citizens from poverty, unemployment, and access to health care is not enshrined in the 200-plus-year-old Bill of Rights. Blau et al. (2008) offer an insightful—if not damning—analysis of how the United States today lags behind virtually every other modern nation in quality-of-life indicators for its citizens, including housing, health, workers' rights, indigenous peoples' rights, cultural rights, and more. Americans tend to regard the Constitution as a universal declaration of democratic rights (Turner 2008), but to the observant, something is clearly wrong with the system.

A Universal Moral System

The events of World War II and its aftermath changed everything. It brought to the fore the severe limitations of state sovereignty in guaranteeing universal rights for citizens. It saw a completely rationalized (Ritzer 2011) yet diabolical institutionalization of genocide on a national level in Germany—a modern "civilized" state, drawing on values not of equality and democracy but of bigotry, intolerance, and racial supremacy. It instilled in people around the globe the importance of human rights. The visceral, aesthetic reactions of revulsion against the Holocaust, felt by people from around the world, resulted in universal condemnation. "Never again" became the universal moral goal. It set in place a revolution of peoples to protect themselves against governments, creating the conditions for the most universal moral revolution in human history: the human rights revolution. Legal advocates for human rights found a paucity of international law protecting human rights, making it difficult to hold Nazis accountable for their atrocities during the Nuremberg Trials after the war. Gandhi's peaceful revolution for Indian independence further exposed the brutality and inequality of British colonial rule; Great Britain was a superpower that thought itself to be culturally superior and morally benevolent. This too provided a catalyst to embrace a moral system that transcended the nation-state.

World leaders also recognized that something had to change. Firm agreement between Churchill, Roosevelt, and Stalin to form a United Nations (UN) had been secured by 1945. This move, however, was an attempt to create a balance of power in the post–World War II era. It wasn't until the formative UN conference in San Francisco later that year that an emphasis on human rights was added by U.S. consultants, in the form of amendments to the UN constitution draft (Schlesinger 2004). U.S. President Roosevelt had popularized the notion of universal rights in a famous speech in 1941, in which he described four freedoms that *all* people of the world should enjoy. The first two, freedom of religion and freedom of speech, were enshrined in the American Bill of Rights. Roosevelt, however, added freedom from want and fear, going beyond the U.S. articulation of rights. In his 1944 State of the Union address, Roosevelt also suggested an as-yet-unrealized dream: that a Second Bill of Rights be added to the U.S. Constitution.

Creating an Institutional Framework

The notion of universal rights resonated with people the world over. Morsink (1999) documents the many voices of global citizens, NGOs, religious organizations, and others who wrote in support of the creation of an international bill of rights. Countries submitting drafts for such a document to the organizing committee of the San Francisco conference, Cuba, Chile, and Panama being the first. Given this pressure, the only commission of the entire United Nations system to be mandated by the UN charter was the Human Rights Commission. The commission was designated as the body to draft the Universal Declaration of Human Rights (UDHR), under the direction of Eleanor Roosevelt. The drafting process was deliberately inclusive and open, with a successful effort to create a religiously, politically, and ethnically diverse drafting committee. That agreement on a universal moral statement of 30 articles would be achieved, let alone accepted, by the UN General Assembly on December 10, 1948, is testament to its applicability and relevance and to the readiness of the world at that time to embrace a new moral statement universal in its intent.

The impact of this new moral system was immediately felt in the United States. After risking life and limb to defend liberty and to free Europe from totalitarianism, Hispanic, Asian American, and African American soldiers returned home to experience ongoing discrimination and racism. With a renewed sense of confidence, the civil rights movement was launched, ending Jim Crow segregation in the southern United States. Hispanics successfully challenged de jure discriminatory practices in the U.S. Supreme Court and organized to end child labor among migrant workers. Women, in turn, launched the second wave of the women's movement, challenging dozens of discriminatory laws and informal sexism. Further movements lobbied for gay rights, for the protection of children's rights, and for people with disabilities. The Bill of Rights had failed to provide adequate protection for these and other groups. Now, with the burgeoning international interest in human rights, minority groups challenged the status quo.

Revolutions in moral systems can take time to be digested, accepted, and internalized, with a fuller understanding of the implications of the system realized. The larger the population, the more difficult the task. Today, the population of the globe approaches 7 billion, more than double the 3 billion alive in 1960. Institutionalization of new moral systems can also take time. Two binding covenants, the International Covenant on Civil and Political Rights (ICCPR) and the International Covenant on Economic, Social, and Cultural Rights (ICESC), were not available for ratification until 1966 and became effective as recently as 1976. But this does not explain the about-face the United States made in supporting, protecting, and expanding human rights in a movement that it began. Though a forerunner globally by enshrining the notion of rights into its Constitution, cooperating with world leaders to create the UN, and taking a leadership role in articulating the UDHR, the United States today has shown little support for furthering the human rights agenda worldwide. It promotes itself as the world's primary protector of human rights but objects to scrutiny of its own practices, has failed to ratify a majority of key human rights treaties and covenants, and greatly encumbers the treaties it does sign so as to severely restrict their application.

The Human Rights Revolution

Despite this, the explosion of interest and work in human rights around the globe is substantial. Hundreds of organizations around the globe work for the protection of human rights. More than 50 state constitutions today make specific reference to human rights. Newer state constitutions have even included statements that integrate international laws and agreements into their own legal system. Kosovo's 2008 constitution suggests that authority of the state is based on the respect for human rights (Article 1.2), and states, "Ratified international agreements and legally binding norms of international law have superiority over the laws of the Republic of Kosovo" (Article 19.2).[1] Statements such as these are indicative of an emerging world that increasingly pays homage to human rights agreements. As countries of the world continue to embrace human rights, ratify treaties, and recognize human rights within their own constitutions, the United States is conspicuous by its absence. At best, it is perceived to be a political backwater, refusing to move from an increasingly outdated view of the world system. At worst, America is perceived to be arrogant and ethnocentric, stubbornly clinging to a hope of acting unilaterally and with impunity despite the development of international norms that recognize interdependence and rely on cooperation and respect.

Regional human rights treaties are an important illustration of the trend to establish an international moral framework. It too is one in which the United States initially took a lead role. Regional treaties transcend the jurisdictional privilege of the nation-state, in line with the growing spirit of international cooperation that has existed since World War II. Though a variety of international human rights instruments exist, four important statements recognized by the UN are discussed here.

Just prior to the formation of the UN, representatives from states in the western hemisphere met in April 1948 in Bogotá, Colombia, to adopt the world's first general human rights document, the American Declaration of the Rights and Duties of Man (ADRDM). This document, signed by the United States, was an inspiration for the UDHR, which was to follow. It identifies 38 rights and 10 responsibilities of relevance to humankind. The preamble to this document is presented in Figure 5.1. Note the explicit reference to the notion of culture as a spiritual development. The United States was an enthusiastic participant in the creation and signing of the ADRDM. When the document was further revised and expanded into the American Convention on Human Rights in 1969, however, the United States refused to ratify it, along with Cuba.

After establishing the Council of Europe, European countries sought to develop a regional system of human rights. Inspired by the UDHR, the Convention for the Protection of Human Rights and Fundamental Freedoms (CPHRFF) was opened for signature in 1950 and went into effect in 1953. There is much congruence in the content of the ADRDM, UDHR, and

Figure 5.1   Preamble to the American Declaration of the Rights and Duties of Man, O.A.S. Res. XXX, adopted by the Ninth International Conference of American States (1948)

WHEREAS:	PREAMBLE
The American peoples have acknowledged the dignity of the individual, and their national constitutions recognize that juridical and political institutions, which regulate life in human society, have as their principal aim the protection of the essential rights of man and the creation of circumstances that will permit him to achieve spiritual and material progress and attain happiness;	All men are born free and equal, in dignity and in rights, and, being endowed by nature with reason and conscience, they should conduct themselves as brothers one to another.
The American States have on repeated occasions recognized that the essential rights of man are not derived from the fact that he is a national of a certain state, but are based upon attributes of his human personality;	The fulfillment of duty by each individual is a prerequisite to the rights of all. Rights and duties are interrelated in every social and political activity of man. While rights exalt individual liberty, duties express the dignity of that liberty.
The international protection of the rights of man should be the principal guide of an evolving American law;	Duties of a juridical nature presuppose others of a moral nature which support them in principle and constitute their basis.
The affirmation of essential human rights by the American States together with the guarantees given by the internal regimes of the states establish the initial system of protection considered by the American States as being suited to the present social and juridical conditions, not without a recognition on their part that they should increasingly strengthen that system in the international field as conditions become more favorable.	Inasmuch as spiritual development is the supreme end of human existence and the highest expression thereof, it is the duty of man to serve that end with all his strength and resources.
	Since culture is the highest social and historical expression of that spiritual development, it is the duty of man to preserve, practice and foster culture by every means within his power.
	And, since moral conduct constitutes the noblest flowering of culture, it is the duty of every man always to hold it in high respect.

Source: http://www1.umn.edu/humanrts/oasinstr/zoas2dec.htm.

CPHRFF. Figure 5.2 contains the preamble to the latter document, which makes specific reference to the maintenance and realization of human rights, as well as fundamental freedoms.

Figure 5.2   Preamble to the European Convention for the Protection of Human Rights and Fundamental Freedoms (1950)

The governments signatory hereto, being members of the Council of Europe,

Considering the Universal Declaration of Human Rights proclaimed by the General Assembly of the United Nations on 10 December 1948;

Considering that this Declaration aims at securing the universal and effective recognition and observance of the Rights therein declared;

Considering that the aim of the Council of Europe is the achievement of greater unity between its members and that one of the methods by which that aim is to be pursued is the maintenance and further realisation of human rights and fundamental freedoms;

Reaffirming their profound belief in those fundamental freedoms which are the foundation of justice and peace in the world and are best maintained on the one hand by an effective political democracy and on the other by a common understanding and observance of the human rights upon which they depend;

Being resolved, as the governments of European countries which are likeminded and have a common heritage of political traditions, ideals, freedom and the rule of law, to take the first steps for the collective enforcement of certain of the rights stated in the Universal Declaration,

Have agreed as follows.

Source: http://conventions.coe.int/treaty/en/treaties/html/005.htm.

After surviving the slave trade and shrugging off centuries of brutal colonial rule, African countries also sought to establish recognition and respect for human rights on their continent. To this end, the Organization of African Unity was formed in 1963 (and replaced by the African Union in 2002). By 1981 it had created the African Charter on Human and Peoples' Rights, which came into effect in 1986. Figure 5.3 contains the preamble to this document, which speaks more specifically to the past human rights issues relative to Africa, and a desire to achieve "total liberation." Also important to note is the interconnection made between civil and economic rights and economic, social, and cultural rights. The United States has been very reluctant to recognize or respect these latter issues.

The League of Arab States was formed in 1945, with the expressed purpose of facilitating collaboration, maintaining safety and independence, and considering the interests of Arab countries. In 2004 it ratified the Arab Charter on Human Rights, which came into effect as recently as 2008. Figure 5.4 contains the preamble to this document. Though unique in some

Figure 5.3   Preamble to the African Charter on Human and Peoples' Rights (1981)

PREAMBLE

The African States members of the Organisation of African Unity, parties to the present Convention entitled "African Charter on Human and Peoples' Rights",

Recalling Decision 115 (XVI) of the Assembly of Heads of State and Government at its Sixteenth Ordinary Session held in Monrovia, Liberia, from 17 to 20 July 1979 on the preparation of "a preliminary draft on an African Charter on Human and Peoples' Rights, providing inter alia for the establishment of bodies to promote and protect human and peoples' rights";

Considering the Charter of the Organisation of African Unity, which stipulates that "freedom, equality, justice and dignity are essential objectives for the achievement of the legitimate aspirations of the African peoples";

Reaffirming the pledge they solemnly made in Article 2 of the said Charter to eradicate all forms of colonialism from Africa, to coordinate and intensify their cooperation and efforts to achieve a better life for the peoples of Africa and to promote international cooperation having due regard to the Charter of the United Nations and the Universal Declaration of Human Rights;

Taking into consideration the virtues of their historical tradition and the values of African civilization which should inspire and characterize their reflection on the concept of human and peoples' rights;

Recognizing on the one hand, that fundamental human rights stem from the attitudes of human beings, which justifies their international protection and on the other hand that the reality and respect of peoples' rights should necessarily guarantee human rights;

Considering that the enjoyment of rights and freedoms also implies the performance of duties on the part of everyone;

Convinced that it is henceforth essential to pay particular attention to the right to development and that civil and political rights cannot be dissociated from economic, social and cultural rights in their conception as well as universality and that the satisfaction of economic, social and cultural rights is a guarantee for the enjoyment of civil and political rights;

Conscious of their duty to achieve the total liberation of Africa, the peoples of which are still struggling for their dignity and genuine independence, and undertaking to eliminate colonialism, neo-colonialism, apartheid, Zionism and to dismantle aggressive foreign military bases and all forms of discrimination, language, religion or political opinions;

Reaffirming their adherence to the principles of human and peoples' rights and freedoms contained in the declarations, conventions and other instruments adopted by the Organisation of African Unity, the Movement of Non-Aligned Countries and the United Nations;

Firmly convinced of their duty to promote and protect human and peoples' rights and freedoms and taking into account the importance traditionally attached to these rights and freedoms in Africa;

HAVE AGREED AS FOLLOWS.

Source: http://www1.umn.edu/humanrts/instree/z1afchar.htm.

Figure 5.4   Preamble to the Arab Charter on Human Rights, Adopted by the League of Arab States (2004)

Preamble

Given the Arab nation's belief in human dignity since God honoured it by making the Arab World the cradle of religions and the birthplace of civilizations which confirmed its right to a life of dignity based on freedom, justice and peace,

Pursuant to the eternal principles of brotherhood and equality among all human beings which were firmly established by the Islamic Shari'a and the other divinely-revealed religions,

Being proud of the humanitarian values and principles which it firmly established in the course of its long history and which played a major role in disseminating centres of learning between the East and the West, thereby making it an international focal point for seekers of knowledge, culture and wisdom,

Conscious of the fact that the entire Arab World has always worked together to preserve its faith, believing in its unity, struggling to protect its freedom, defending the right of nations to self-determination and to safeguard their resources, believing in the rule of law and that every individual's enjoyment of freedom, justice and equality of opportunity is the yardstick by which the merits of any society are gauged,

Rejecting racism and Zionism, which constitute a violation of human rights and pose a threat to world peace,

Acknowledging the close interrelationship between human rights and world peace,

Reaffirming the principles of the Charter of the United Nations and the Universal Declaration of Human Rights, as well as the provisions of the United Nations International Covenants on Civil and Political Rights and Economic, Social and Cultural Rights and the Cairo Declaration on Human Rights in Islam,

In confirmation of all the above, have agreed as follows.

Source: http://www1.umn.edu/humanrts/instree/arabhrcharter.html.

respects, the Arab charter affirms the principles of the UDHR and other human rights instruments.

Taken together, these instruments are indicative of the continuing acceptance of a new global moral system. Because of the widespread interest and input during the creation of the UDHR and the ongoing global interest in and expansion of human rights principles, it is logical to identify it as an *indigenous global movement.*

An Invitation

As a moral system, human rights have much to offer the human species. They promote a sense of equality among human beings and create a sense of unity, much in the same way as noting that we are part of a human family. Every person in the world is at least your 50th cousin. As articulated in the UDHR, human rights include freedoms from restrictions—the right to worship, freedom of speech, and freedom from slavery are examples. Sometimes called *negative rights*, they allow human beings the ability to pursue their own destiny unhindered by others. But rights also exist in which resources or support from society is accessed— the rights to education, a fair trial, health care, and the like are examples. These *positive rights* find less support in the United States, but offer the possibility of unlocking the huge human potential currently underdeveloped due to a lack of education, support, health care, and the like. It is worth pondering how much we've hindered the development of the human species by letting some of our most brilliant thinkers, artists, and others languish in squalor and die without having the opportunity to develop their skills, contribute to the betterment of humankind, and live to their fullest potential. It's worth considering how much more happiness could be produced in the world by furthering a moral system that is inclusive, respectful of all, and personally empowering.

It is also worth pondering what the world would look like if the United States once again joined the global movement to which it gave impetus. As the world's wealthiest and third most populous nation, imagine how much life—in the United States and around the globe—would improve with U.S. backing. It could happen. While this chapter has traced the general progression in human history of the expansion of moral systems that are increasingly universal, nothing is inevitable. Human beings write their own history and are in control of their own destiny. Forces are constantly in play to draw others back to a time when knowledge was more limited, ideology was more pronounced, and rights were less respected.

For example, in an appalling endorsement of ignorance and a reversal of constitutional rights, one group of determined Americans would like to see a public school curriculum that ignores the philosophical foundations for the separation of church and state and makes no mention of the contributions of Thomas Jefferson to the founding of the country. Members of this group would prefer that the U.S. government be referred to as a constitutional republic instead of a democracy, and want no requirement for students to understand that the Constitution prevents the promotion of one religion over all others. They would like to downplay the contributions of minorities such as Hispanics to American society, and make no mention of minority cultural innovations. In 2010, this group succeeded in injecting these ideas into the public school curriculum in the entire state of Texas for the next 10 years (*The Huffington Post* 2010).

The United States has been a protector of rights from its inception, thereby improving the lives of millions of people for over two centuries and providing inspiration to the rest of the world. It needs to keep in step with its own values. First, the United States needs to ratify UN human rights instruments such as the Convention on the Elimination of All Forms of Discrimination Against Women and the Convention on the Rights of the Child, which have languished without Senate approval for the past two decades. The United States needs to sign and ratify the International Convention for the Protection of All Persons From Enforced Disappearance, the Mine Ban Treaty, the Convention on Cluster Munitions, the Convention on the Rights of Persons With Disabilities, and the Optional Protocol to the Convention Against Torture. Endorsement of these rudimentary rights instruments will potentially improve the lives of millions.

Lastly, the United States needs a *constitutional revision*, to expand its very limited Bill of Rights, to ensure that economic, social, and cultural rights are protected. A country with so much can do more to develop its greatest common good: its human potential. George Bernard Shaw once said, "The reasonable man adapts himself to the world: The unreasonable one persists in trying to adapt the world to himself. Therefore, all progress depends on the unreasonable man."

Discussion Questions

1. What is a moral system? How is the concept of the moral system helpful in understanding human rights?

2. How does population growth fuel changes in moral systems? What other factors might contribute to moral revolutions?

3. How has the world benefited from the shift in values as emphasized in the Enlightenment? In what way has it been disadvantaged?

4. Would you characterize the human rights movement as an indigenous global movement as the author does? Why or why not?

5. How realistic is it to push for a revision of the U.S. Constitution? What rights would you personally like to see enshrined in the new Constitution, and why?

Note

1. http://confinder.richmond.edu/

References

Adalberto, A., Jr. and Jonathan Turner. 2008. *American Ethnicity: The Dynamics and Consequences of Discrimination.* 6th ed. Boston: McGraw-Hill.

Bolton, Gary E. and Rami Zwick. 1995. "Anonymity Versus Punishment in Ultimatum Bargaining." *Games and Economic Behavior* 10(1):95–121.

BBC. 2009. "Rich Germans Demand Higher Taxes." October 23. Retrieved August 2, 2010 (http://news.bbc.co.uk/2/hi/europe/8321967.stm).

Blau, Judith, David Brunsma, Alberto Moncada, and Catherine Zimmer, eds. 2008. *The Leading Rogue State: The U.S. and Human Rights.* Boulder, CO: Paradigm.

Bryner, Jeanna. 2007. "Monkeys Fuss Over Inequality." *LiveScience*, November 12. Retrieved August 12, 2010 (http://www.livescience.com/animals/071112-monkey-treats.html).

Cameron, Lisa A. 1999. "Raising the Stakes in the Ultimatum Game: Experimental Evidence From Indonesia." *Economic Inquiry* 37(1):47–59.

Davis, Douglas D. and C. A. Holt, eds. 1993. *Experimental Economics.* Princeton, NJ: Princeton University Press.

Dawes, C. T., J. H. Fowler, T. Johnson, R. McElreath, and O. Smirnov. 2007. "Egalitarian Motives in Humans." *Nature* 446:794–96.

Diamond, Jared. 2005. *Guns, Germs, and Steel.* New York: Norton.

Durkheim, Emile. [1933] 1984. *The Division of Labor in Society* (W. D. Halls, trans.). New York: Free Press.

Durkheim, Emile. [1912] 1962. *The Elementary Forms of the Religious Life: A Study in Religious Sociology* (J. Swain, trans.). London: Allen & Unwin.

Fehr, E. & K. Schmidt. 1999. "A Theory of Fairness, Competition, and Cooperation." *Qualitative Journal of Economics* 114:817–68.

Goodman, Lenn Evan. 2003. *Islamic Humanism.* London: Oxford University Press.

Gurven, M. 2006. "The Evolution of Contingent Cooperation." *Current Anthropology* 47:185–92.

Holt, J. C. 1992. *Magna Carta.* Cambridge, UK: Cambridge University Press.

The Huffington Post. 2010. "Texas Education Board Approves Conservative Curriculum Changes By Far-Right." March 12. Retrieved August 10, 2020 (http://www.huffingtonpost.com/2010/03/12/texas-education-board-app_n_497440.html).

Hume, D. [1739] 1985. *A Treatise of Human Nature.* London: Penguin Classics.

Ishay, Micheline. 2008. *The History of Human Rights.* Los Angeles: University of California Press.

Johnson, D. C. 2001. "Dozens of Rich Americans Join in Fight to Retain the Estate Tax." *The New York Times*, February 13. Retrieved August 2, 2010 (http://www.nytimes.com/2001/02/14/politics/14ESTA.html).

Kraemer, Joel L. 1992. *Humanism in the Renaissance of Islam*. Leiden, Netherlands: Brill.

Lenski, Gerhard and Jean Lenski. 1970. *Human Societies: A Macrolevel Introduction to Sociology*. New York: McGraw-Hill.

Lowenstein, G. F., L. Thompson, and M. H. Baserman. 1989. "Social Utility and Decision-Making in Interpersonal Contexts." *Journal of Personality and Social Psychology* 57:426–41.

Morsink, Johannes. 1999. *The Universal Declaration of Human Rights: Origins, Drafting, and Intent*. Philadelphia: University of Pennsylvania Press.

MSNBC. 2010. "Forty Billionaires Pledge to Give Away Half of Wealth." August 11. Retrieved August 15, 2010 (http://www.msnbc.msn.com/id/38556042/ns/us_news-giving).

Pagden, Anthony. 1982. *The Fall of the Natural Man: The American Indian and the Origins of Comparative Ethnology*. Cambridge, UK: Cambridge University Press.

Range, Friederike, Lisa Horna, Zso´fia Viranyib, and Ludwig Hubera. 2009. "The Absence of Reward Induces Inequity Aversion in Dogs." *Proceedings of the National Academy of Science* 106(1):340–45.

Ritzer, George. 2011. *The McDonaldization of Society*. 6th ed. Thousand Oaks, CA: Pine Forge.

Rowes, Frans, and Michel Raymond. 2003. "Belief in Moralizing Gods." *Evolution and Human Behavior* 24(2):126–35.

Schlesinger, Stephen. 2004. *Act of Creation: The Founding of the United Nations*. Cambridge, UK: Perseus.

Sen, Amartya. 1995. *Inequality Reexamined*. Cambridge, UK: Harvard University Press.

Steward, Julian. [1955] 1972. *Theory of Culture Change: The Methodology of Multilinear Evolution*. Champaign: University of Illinois Press.

Tompkinson, Paul and Judy Bethwaite. 1995. "The Ultimatum Game: Raising the Stakes." *Journal of Economic Behavior and Organization* 27(3):439–51.

Tonnies, Ferdinand. [1887] 2001. *Community and Civil Society* (J. Harris and M. Hollis, trans.). Cambridge, UK: Cambridge University Press.

Tricomi, Elisabeth, Antonio Rangel, F. Colin, J. P. Camerer, and J. O'Doherty. 2010. "Neural Evidence for Inequality-Averse Social Preferences." *Nature* 463:1089–92.

Turner, Brian. 2008. "On Individual and Social Rights." Pp. 5–15 in *The Leading Rogue State: The U.S. and Human Rights*, edited by Judith Blau, David Brunsma, Alberto Moncada, and Catherine Zimmer. Boulder, CO: Paradigm.

Underhill, Ralph. 1975. "Economic and Political Antecedents of Monotheism: A Cross-Cultural Study." *The American Journal of Sociology* 80(4):841–61.

6

Cooperating Around Environmental Rights

Rebecca Clausen

A Healthy Planet Is a Human Right

Imagine the Pennsylvania landscape in 1789, when the U.S. founders introduced the Bill of Rights. Old-growth forests of beech and hemlock covered much of the region, providing habitat for a dense and richly diverse understory. Large predators such as the wolf and cougar roamed the New England landscape, naturally regulating the deer population. Nature was intact, but not untouched by humans. Native Americans burned small areas of the forest to improve berry production, hunting, and ease of travel. In addition, European settlers had begun to clear land for agriculture and timber. Even with these modifications, however, the natural environment was wild, and its expanse must have seemed limitless. It is no wonder that the founding documents of our nation did not make provisions for environmental protection. It would have been improbable to predict in the course of a few generations the extent to which human activities could alter nature.

The environmental transformations of the twenty-first century are glaring. Figure 6.1 illustrates the change in old-growth forests as one example of environmental modifications experienced over the course of a few hundred years. These old-growth stands, also called the "lungs of the earth," now compose only 10 percent of forests in the United States. The impacts of this loss are wide ranging for species protection, ecosystem function, and climate change. The implications of ecosystem degradation directly and indirectly affect the well-being of individuals and communities by affecting quality of life, access to water and food, safe housing, and so forth. Due to these effects, people began to take action to safeguard the environment by modifying their consumption, organizing their communities, and lobbying their political representatives.

Figure 6.1   Loss of U.S. Old Growth Forests, 1600–2000

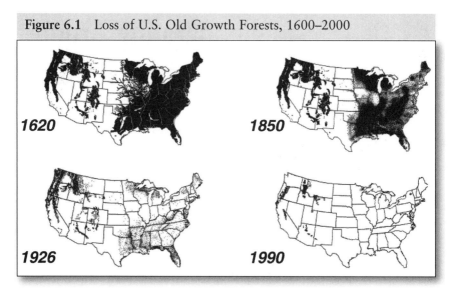

Source: http://mvh.sr.unh.edu/mvhinvestigations/old_growth_forests.htm

Data are from Paullin, Charles Oscar, *Atlas of the Historical Geography of the United States*, edited by John K. Wright, Greenwood Press, Westport, CT, 1932, 1975; Findley, Rowe, and James P. Blair, "*Will We Save Our Own?*," p. 120 in *National Geographic* 178(3), September 1990; and the Wilderness Society.

This chapter considers the possibility of a new way to look at environmental protection through a human rights-based lens. We explore the concept that a healthy environment is a fundamental human right, universal to all people. Tim Hayward (2005), a leading theorist on environmental rights, makes the claim that

a right of every individual to an environment adequate for their health and well-being should be provided in the constitution of every democratic nation. (P. 1)

Is a constitutional environmental right necessary? Or possible? What would be the consequences? To begin to address these questions, the chapter describes the history of environmental rights, their potentials and challenges, and the different conceptual approaches toward their adoption.[1] For purposes of global comparison, the chapter outlines how international governing bodies and social movements have addressed environmental rights. The chapter concludes with a description of how the discipline of sociology can contribute to national efforts of securing environmental rights for the twenty-first century.

What Are Environmental Rights?

For decades, theorists and policymakers have pondered the intersection between human rights and the environment. In his 1974 lecture, Nobel Prize winner René Cassin advocated that existing concepts of human rights protection should be extended to include the right to a healthful and decent environment (Taillant 2003). This statement was an early predecessor to sentiments expressed in more recent international and national agreements. Now more than ever, people are realizing the links between our environment and the health of humanity. The recent explosion of economic globalization has thrust environmental rights onto the agendas of academics and activists alike as communities and ecosystems feel the shared impacts of transnational investment in all parts of the globe. This recognition has led some human rights scholars to declare that violating the environment is violating our human rights (see Picolotti and Taillant 2003). Fundamentally, a constitutional environmental right would define responsibilities for a nation to care for the environment. The responsibilities can also be described as "rights of future generations" to inherit a living, life-sustaining planet (Zarsky 2002).

A Brief History and Definition

The definition of a human right to a healthy environment has been debated and modified in the international arena since the 1970s. The first authoritative statement describing environmental human rights appeared in the 1972 Stockholm Declaration (Principle 1) agreed to at the United Nations Conference on the Human Environment:

> Man has the fundamental right to freedom, equality, and adequate conditions of life, in an environment of a quality that permits a life of dignity and well-being, and he bears a solemn responsibility to protect and improve the environment for present and future generations. (UN Documents n.d.)

The sentiments expressed in the Stockholm Declaration sparked a number of international declarations supporting individual rights to a clean environment. The 1981 African Charter on Human and Peoples' Rights (Banjul Charter) stated, "All peoples have the right to a general satisfactory environment favourable to their development" (Article 24) (University of Minnesota Human Rights Library n.d.). In a more specific declaration, the 1989 United Nations Convention on the Rights of the Child provides, in Article 24, a right of the child to "the provision of adequate nutritious foods and clean drinking-water, taking into consideration the dangers and risks of environmental pollution" (Office of the United Nations High Commissioner of Human Rights 2007).

Following in line with contemporary thought of environmental rights, there are now over 50 national constitutions that grant provisions for the natural environment. Some constitutions refer to *ecological equilibrium* or *balance* while others refer to *sustainable development*. The most common wording in national constitutions is *a right to a clean and healthy environment*. This definition of an environmental right is drawn from the Brundtland Report:

> All human beings have the fundamental right to an environment adequate for their health and well-being. (United Nations World Commission on Environment and Development 1987:348)

The Brundtland Commission was convened by the United Nations in 1983 to address the growing concern about the accelerating deterioration of the human environment. It was by no means the first declaration of environmental rights; however, it has largely influenced the drafting and amending of recent constitutions and treaties. An environmental right worded in this way is a useful tool with respect to pollution, waste disposal, toxic contamination, and other environmental hazards directly related to human health.

Foundations for Environmental Rights

Public Trust Doctrine

In addition to the explicit statements that define environmental rights, there are also examples of social agreements that apply similar foundational concepts with respect to collective environmental protection. Even though the United States has not yet adopted a constitutional environmental right, the country has long respected and abided by the *public trust doctrine*. The public trust doctrine is a socially agreed-upon principle that declares certain natural resources are reserved for public use, to be maintained by the government. The doctrine holds that certain natural resources cannot be privately owned or controlled because of their inherent importance to each individual and society as a whole (McCay 1998). The public trust doctrine reaffirms the superiority of public rights over private rights for critical natural resources.

The public trust doctrine is primarily applied to waterways. For example, no one can have exclusive rights to a beach—all people must be able to have public access to stroll, swim, fish, and so forth below the high-tide line. Similarly, all people have common property rights in navigable waters and lakes for swimming, drinking, and recreating (McCay 1998). This foundational concept is not far from the declarations made by an environmental human right—that the environment is important for each and every person, and therefore it is a fundamental human right to have it protected from harm. The public trust doctrine shows that the United States has accepted some of the premises of environmental rights and that both the citizenship and the governing entities are willing to accept and enforce them.

Precautionary Principle

The *precautionary principle* is a second example of a widely accepted and enforced social contract that echoes foundational concepts of environmental human rights. The precautionary principle is a central policy instrument in the European Union, and has attained the status of a principle of customary international law (Hayward 2005). A common understanding of the precautionary principle states,

> When an activity raises threats of harm to human health or the environment, precautionary measures should be taken even if some cause and effect relationships are not fully established scientifically. In this context the proponent of an activity, rather than the public, should bear the burden of proof. (Wingspread Conference 1998)

According to the precautionary principle, ordinary citizens' right to protection from environmentally hazardous activities trumps all other individual pursuits of economic or technological research, development, and sales. The collective health of the population is given first priority over the proponents of a new technology, activity, process, or chemical that may cause harm. Christopher Miller (1995) writes that this is a "powerful and comprehensive principle which . . . would appear to endow citizens of the European

Union with something akin to the United Nations' fundamental right to an environment adequate for health and well-being" (p. 389). Most important, the precautionary principle implies that there is a social responsibility to protect the public from environmental harm, even if scientific uncertainties exist.

Taken together, both the precautionary principle and the public trust doctrine establish a social recognition that access to a healthy environment is a right shared by the entire population. Likewise, responsibility for environmental protection lies beyond individual actors and rests ultimately with overarching governing bodies. Unfortunately, neither of these principles goes far enough in securing universal environmental rights. Each has inherent uncertainties and limitations that prevent it from being a source of rights. The public trust doctrine is limited in that it mostly applies to water, while the precautionary principle mostly applies to policy decisions rather than overarching goals of a nation. To secure the highest environmental protection for even the most vulnerable populations, the United States must adopt a constitutional amendment that addresses environmental rights.

Why Do We Need Environmental Rights?

This section of the chapter outlines four reasons why a constitutionally guaranteed environmental right is necessary for U.S. society: public health, intergenerational equity, cultural integrity, and comprehensive protection. Each of these is looked at from a sociological perspective, addressing the context and interplay between communities of people and centers of power.

Public Health

Public health is concerned with the overall health of a community. Health in this context is defined as a state of complete physical, mental, and social well-being, and not merely the absence of disease or infirmity. The World Health Organization (WHO), which manages issues of health within the United Nations system, states,

> In the 21st century, health is a shared responsibility, involving equitable access to essential care and collective defense against transnational threats.[2]

If health is a shared responsibility worthy of collective defense, then an environmental right should be seen as a critical tool to supplement the goals of public health.

Environmental health is a specialty area within public health that studies how the condition of the environment affects human well-being. The WHO explains that proper environmental care is "the key to avoiding the quarter of all preventable illnesses which are directly caused by environmental factors."[3] Environmental pollution, caused by human-related activity, poses a considerable concern to public health. Westra (2008) terms any and all activities that result in harm to humans following environmental deprivation as forms of "eco-violence." She argues that eco-violence should be viewed as not only an issue of immorality but also an issue of criminality through international law. To pursue this argument, we consider two forms of eco-violence: environmental health stressors and environmental diseases.

Environmental health stressors are described as changes in the natural environment that affect the growth, development, and reproduction of humans. Air pollution is one of the most proven causes of environmental health stressors. For example, ground-level ozone is a powerful lung irritant. Short-term ozone exposure leads to shortness of breath, chest pain, wheezing, coughing, headaches, and nausea. The damage is akin to sunburn of the lungs and can lead to reduced quality of life for children and the elderly.[4] Environmental stressors are incredibly difficult to monitor and regulate on an individual basis. Therefore, the health of the community relies on the establishment of norms and rights that declare the equal protection for all from the harms of environmental stressors in general.

Environmental diseases that may have a relationship to environmental pollution include asthma, cancer, endocrine disruptions, and Parkinson's disease. While each of these diseases can be caused by factors other than environmental pollution, they can be influenced by environmental conditions to some degree. For example, endocrine disruptors are human-made chemicals that disrupt the normal functioning of human endocrine systems. The main chemicals that have been proven to disrupt endocrine functioning are PCBs (polychlorinated biphenyls), dioxin, and synthetic estrogen. The global reductions in sperm production and the increase in certain cancers (breast, testes, prostate) are attributed to endocrine disruptors.[5]

Public environmental health is often sacrificed in the name of economic growth, job creation, and return on investment. An environmental right could effectively address these public health concerns by putting more power in the hands of citizens and community groups to stop actions that threaten environmental quality and human health.

Intergenerational Equity

Intergenerational equity is a concept that views the human community as a partnership among all generations. Each generation has the right to inherit the same diversity in natural resources enjoyed by previous generations and is obligated to provide the same for future generations. While there will always be some uncertainty about the exact details of future peoples' preferences, it is reasonable to conclude that basic needs (clean drinking water, food, shelter, a habitable atmosphere) will not be radically different from current needs. As a matter of social and ecological justice, therefore, environmental rights are required not only to protect the health and well-being of the current population, but also as an obligation for future people to be able to live and thrive on the planet. In this way, intergenerational equity extends the scope of social justice into the future.

The field of ecological economics has thoroughly embraced the concept of intergenerational equity in its research. Costanza et al. (1997) have critiqued free-trade negotiations due to the absence of discussions concerning intergenerational equity and the transfer of natural and social assets to future generations. In addition, these authors claim that the management of energy resources has been based on the excessive discounting of the interests of future generations, abandoning intergenerational equity and intra-generational justice (Costanza et al 1997). Finally, intergenerational equity has deep roots in international law. Indeed, if we were to license the present generation to exploit our natural resources at the expense of the well-being of future generations, we would contradict the purposes of the United Nations charter and international human rights documents.

Cultural Integrity

Every human being has the right to culture and the development of cultural identity. Chapter 4 fully explores this concept. Here we specifically focus on the intersection between *cultural integrity* and the environment. Critical aspects of cultural identity rest on the ability to utilize and enjoy the natural world for physical, emotional, and spiritual means. Therefore, the adoption of an environmental right provides not only for the health of current and future generations but also for the cultural legacies that must be maintained.

An ecosystem exhibits "integrity" when, if subjected to a disturbance, it sustains an organizing, self-correcting capability to recover to a state that is "good" for that system (Regier 1993). Cultural integrity is the ability of both individuals and institutions to exhibit similar patterns of recovery and resiliency in the face of turbulent social context.

Westra (2008) explains that the cultural integrity model has two aspects. The first aspect emphasizes the closeness between the environment and the traditional lifestyle of indigenous people. It is this connection that defines and delimits their cultural presence as a people. Westra's argument hinges on "the specific role that land, waters and air play not only in the cultural identity, but also on the survival and basic rights of indigenous peoples everywhere" (p. 23). For example, religious customs and health practices are often directly related to the ecological integrity of a people's surrounding environment. Westra claims that perhaps the most important aspect of biodiversity in developing countries is the role of medicinal plants in the health care of indigenous peoples.

The second aspect of the cultural integrity model has traditional knowledge as its focus. MacKay (2002) notes that, in addition to recognizing indigenous rights to lands and resources, there is growing awareness to recognize indigenous legal systems and traditional knowledge. He asserts that the recognition of the rights for traditional knowledge is a precondition for the ecologically sustainable use, management, and preservation of ecosystems (MacKay 2002). A place-based lifestyle spanning many centuries garners a unique collective wisdom that many recognize as vital to holistic ecosystem management. Westra (2008) emphasized that respecting traditional knowledge is not only a question of respecting human rights but also "a question of recognizing the unique position of these peoples to foster the conservation of life-saving biodiversity" (p. 36).

The indigenous worldview is one in which the environment is embedded within the identity of humans. Environmental rights are necessary, therefore, to protect and restore the cultural integrity of diverse peoples around the world. This is critical for survival of specific indigenous cultures, as well as for what these cultures can offer to the global community in this time of environmental crisis.

Comprehensive Protection

The environmental movement made great strides in establishing a body of federal environmental laws in the 1970s, including the Clean Water Act, the Clean Air Act, and the National Environmental Policy Act. These laws improved water and air quality that had suffered tremendously during previous decades of environmental pollution. Whatever gains have since been made have been offset, however, by losses of habitat and biodiversity resulting from the cumulative effects of unplanned growth and short-term economic gains (Lavigne 2003).

Habitat and biodiversity loss continues, even though environmental laws are in place, for two reasons. First, environmental laws are reactive and follow a piecemeal approach. Our current environmental laws do not go far enough in securing environmental protection. The legislation passed in the

1970s is reactive, mitigating the amount of environmental damage and requiring its restoration once the damage is done. In part, this is due to the fact that environmental legislation focuses on technical fixes—such as discharge permits. Discharge permits set maximum harm conditions by granting permits to degrade our water, air, and land. Permits and mitigation efforts may slow the harmful effects of individual projects, but they do not address ecosystem function as a whole. Brooks, Jones, and Virginia (2002) suggest that we move from environmental mitigation law to ecosystem law.

Second, the agencies responsible for overseeing the environmental laws are not insulated from political influence, leading to *agency capture*. The Environmental Protection Agency (EPA) is the primary agency responsible for protecting nature in the United States. The EPA has the difficult task of protecting an entity (the environment) that is not truly recognized as a right. Because the EPA has no underlying right directing its operation, the executive, legislative, and judicial branches of government are able to minimize environmental protection regulations. Historically, the influence has been in the favor of industrial development interests (McKay 1994). Strict budgetary restraints and judges appointed during antienvironmental administrations undermine the mission of the EPA. Without a constitutional environmental amendment, short-term political pressure is able to influence environmental decision making and prevent long-term, comprehensive environmental protection.

Challenges of Establishing Environmental Rights

If environmental rights are critically necessary, then why hasn't the United States adopted a constitutional amendment to address these concerns? This is a complicated question that requires an understanding of both the underlying social structures of capitalism and practical considerations of law and science. Although this chapter cannot deal with each of these in its entirety, the following paragraphs provide a brief outline of primary difficulties in establishing environmental rights in the U.S. Constitution.

Capitalism is an economic system that is dependent on profit growth, oftentimes at the expense of the environment and natural resources. Two tenets of a capitalist economy are a "free market" and private property rights. Each of these notions can present points of opposition in securing a constitutional environmental right for present and future generations. A free market economy (in its ideal form) is a socially constructed system of buying and selling goods without any intervention or regulation by the government, except to enforce private property rights. Business owners and corporations that are forced to operate under a capitalist economy have little choice but to oppose any measures that may limit their profits, even if it is for the sake of a healthy environment (Costanza et al. 1997).

Private property rights present a second difficulty for securing environmental rights. The Fifth Amendment of the Bill of Rights maintains that no person will be deprived of life, liberty, or property without due process of law, nor shall private property be taken for public use without just compensation. But what if someone's private property is crucial for a country's environmental health? For example, wetlands can protect human health and well-being by filtering polluted water and providing flood protection. But if a single individual owns a wetland as private property, how can he or she be held to an environmental right to act in the best interests of all people? The wetland owner may oppose constitutional environmental rights because they conflict with his or her private property rights. These scenarios demonstrate the problems that arise when the environment is pitted against economic interests inherent in a capitalist economy.

Certain practical aspects in law and science may also cause difficulties in securing an environmental right, specifically the issues of legal enforcement and scientific uncertainties. Enforcement methods include monitoring, inspection, locating violations, and achieving compliance. The last phase of compliance enforcement requires agencies to pursue legal action or settle disputes. Ercmann (1996) explains that effective compliance enforcement for environmental rights may require reorganizing administrative organizations and crafting more precise and comprehensive legally binding instruments. In addition, lack of clarity in the meaning and definition of environmental rights could lead to enforcement difficulties.

Natural systems are imperfectly understood by science. In fact, this uncertainty is a core principle of the scientific method and propels continued research and the quest for knowledge. The exact causes of some environmental problems may be difficult or impossible to identify for a specific degree of accuracy needed to pursue legal action. For example, scientists may never achieve 100 percent certainty as to the causes and mechanisms of global climate change. Scientific uncertainty is unsettling for some in the policy arenas, especially when it comes to environmental rights. Imperfect scientific information may lead some people to oppose environmental rights on the basis of legal and political practicality.

The challenges in securing a constitutional amendment should stimulate analysis and innovation, not intellectual surrender or dismissal. Fundamental environmental rights offer many advantages and can play a key role in fostering equitable and sustainable human communities. Thankfully, activists and academics have pursued various approaches to link human rights and the environment.

Differing Approaches to Environmental Rights

Variation exists in the strategies and approaches to best achieve fundamental environmental protection for all people. This section describes four broad approaches to linking human rights and the environment. Each of these raises sociological and philosophical issues regarding instrumentalism, participatory democracy, anthropocentrism, and ecocentrism.

Underlying Precondition

One approach to linking human rights and the environment sees a healthy environment as an underlying precondition of the enjoyment of existing human rights, rather than a specific right in itself (United Nations Environment Programme 2009). Scholars who adhere to this viewpoint see environmental protection as *instrumental*—that is, an important step in the process of achieving human rights, but not an end goal in itself. This approach seeks to ensure that the natural world does not deteriorate to the point where human rights are seriously impaired; however, the main focus remains fixed on achieving previously adopted human rights goals. Picolotti and Taillant (2003:xvi) summarize the ways in which most of our basic human rights are affected by environmental degradation. These scholars state,

> The *right to health* is affected by environmental contamination of natural resources such as water, air, and sound (noise pollution).
>
> The *right to equality* is of great concern to certain sectors of society (minority and certain ethnic groups, for example) who suffer a disproportionate burden of environmental contamination.
>
> The *right to participate* is a basic premise of democratic societies . . . Undoubtedly few communities participate in the decisions that bring about severe environmental contamination in their areas and result in deterioration of health.

Each of these rights (health, equality, participation) has existing protection in international tribunals. Shelton (2003) argues that there are advantages of seeking prevention or reparation of environmental harm through procedures provided for by international human rights law mechanisms rather than national constitutional rights. One advantage is that linking environmental harm to existing international human rights law allows global and regional human rights complaint procedures to be used against those countries that violate human rights through poor environmental protection (Shelton 2003). It gives victims of environmental harm an immediate forum in which to bring complaints to an international entity. This is crucial because the most systematically affected victims of environmental harm tend to be those with limited political voices in their home countries (Dommen 2003).

A second advantage of the "underlying condition" approach is that it avoids the need to define the notion of "healthy environment." Some argue that defining the conditions of an environment suitable for human health and well-being may be a long and arduous process, thus giving more support for the idea to use existing rights law rather than creating new "right to the environment" language. Advocating for environmental rights as an underlying precondition for human rights is an instrumental calculation of the most efficient means to achieve already established goals and norms.

Procedural Rights

A second approach to linking human rights and the environment focuses on securing the procedural rights of people in relation to control over their environment. Procedural rights empower citizens to demand information relating to the environment, to actively participate in decision-making processes regarding environmental actions, and to apply for legal remedy if they have experienced harm due to environmental degradation (Hayward 2005). Procedural environmental rights can be seen as an important tool in achieving *participatory democracy* in the name of environmental protection. A goal of participatory democracy is to provide forums for people's voices to be actively engaged in decision making.

The most significant developments in implementing environmental rights have centered on procedural rights with environmental substance. The various international efforts to achieve environmental rights produced a landmark agreement on June 25, 1998, when 39 countries signed the Convention on Access to Information, Public Participation in Decision-Making, and Access to Justice in Environmental Matters, also known as the Aarhus Convention. The Aarhus Convention's primary goal was to promote democracy as well as to protect the right of everyone to live in a healthy environment. It is the aim of Aarhus procedural environmental rights to open up new areas of public debate. The third meeting of the parties that signed the Aarhus Convention explicitly addressed the themes of participatory democracy in the following statement:

> The serious environmental, social and economic challenges faced by societies worldwide cannot be addressed by public authorities alone without the

involvement and support of a wide range of stakeholders, including individual citizens and civil society organizations.

"Vision and Mission" of the Aarhus Convention Strategic Plan

The Aarhus Convention should be celebrated as a regional environmental rights agreement that sets a precedent in securing participatory democracy regarding environmental decisions. (United Nations Economic Commission for Europe n.d.)

Substantive Rights *to* the Environment

A substantive environmental right would define, apply, and protect environmental resources in the service of human welfare. Advocates of substantive environmental rights may not trust procedural rights alone to be in the best interest of nature due to the undue influence that power, status, and monetary resources may have on public participation. Democracies are entirely capable of environmental destruction, especially if the structural arrangements of capitalism lead to a populace embedded in unfettered consumption (Anderson 1996).

A substantive environmental right can be considered both a "positive right" and a "negative right." A positive right means that there are obligations on the state to establish regulation and perhaps direct resources for the provision of environmental quality. A substantive environmental right could also be considered a "negative right," where the right to a healthy environment may prevent or preclude the government from taking some action if it subjects people to environmental harm.

A substantive environmental right that guarantees universal access to an environment adequate for human health is considered an *anthropocentric* right. An anthropocentric right is inherently focused upon the human being to the exclusion of other living species. There remains a common objection by those working to protect the environment that such an anthropocentric right does not go far enough in recognizing the importance of animal rights and nature (Anderson 1996). A human right *to* the environment only considers human wants and needs, not the environment for its own sake. Those that defend a substantive environmental right admit that it is human centered, but that it is a "weak" version of anthropocentrism. That is, they recognize the interrelatedness and interdependencies of the natural world of which humans are a part. Weak anthropocentrism is less hierarchical and does not perceive the nonhuman world solely in terms of human usefulness (Redgwell 1996). Since human action occurs in a sociopolitical context, they argue the best way to alter human action is through human-centered agreements such as a constitutional environmental right.

Intrinsic Rights *of* the Environment

The most contested approach to achieving environmental rights involves establishing protections that are specifically granted to nonhuman entities. These are often called the intrinsic rights *of* the environment. Intrinsic rights value animals, plants, and ecosystem processes in their own right regardless of what they contribute to human health or well-being. Redgwell (1996) explains that there are two distinctive strands of thought that critique anthropocentric rights, identified as animal rights and deep ecology. Both perspectives are referred to as *ecocentric* philosophies, in that they adhere to a nature-centered rather than human-centered system of values.

A major component of the animal rights argument is the shared characteristics of human and other animal species. Animal rights theorists seek to explain that it is logically inconsistent to exclude animals from the consideration of equality and justice. Since animals demonstrate a capacity to suffer, Singer (1975) suggests that they should not be treated differently or granted a lower status of rights to life. These theorists exclude plants and inanimate objects from having rights based on these distinctions.

The second perspective of an ecocentric, intrinsic right of nature attempts to include all of exploited nature under the umbrella of rights protection. Christopher Stone's (1975) seminal work *Should Trees Have Standing?* argued that rights be extended to forests, oceans, rivers, and other so-called natural objects in the environment—indeed, to the natural environment as a whole. This philosophy sparked the recognition that humans should be seen on equal footing with all of nature—often called the "deep ecology" movement. Deep ecology emphasizes a shift in worldview, where the natural world's benefit to humanity is an irrelevant consideration. These thinkers reject a substantive environmental right to a healthy environment because it perpetuates the mind-set that humans dominate nature.

Environmental Rights Exist Around the World

For purposes of global comparison, this section highlights examples of international treaties, national constitutions, and declarations produced by people's movements that address fundamental environmental rights. These examples provide many models for U.S. society to draw from in pursuit of a constitutional environmental right.

International Treaties

International treaties have primarily been crafted to address single-issue environmental problems. For example, the Montreal Protocol (1990) restricts the uses of CFCs (chlorofluorocarbons) to protect the earth's ozone, the Basel Convention (1994) controls the movement of hazardous waste, and the Convention on Biological Diversity (1995) promotes international cooperation in conservation biodiversity. When it comes to actively promoting environmental rights as human rights, however, there are fewer examples. This section describes two UN documents that are making headway in this important field of international rights.

In 2002, the UN General Assembly adopted the United Nations Declaration on the Rights of Indigenous Peoples (UNDRIP). This followed more than 20 years of discussion within the UN system between nations and indigenous representatives. This universal human rights instrument passed with an overwhelming majority of 143 votes in favor and only 4 negative votes (Canada, Australia, New Zealand, and the United States). As mentioned elsewhere in this book, UNDRIP covers a broad scope of issues. One critical component addresses indigenous peoples' rights to environmental protection. This is significant because it addresses the issue of environmental rights as necessary for cultural integrity. Articles 24 and 25 relate the environmental rights of indigenous peoples to health and spiritual practices:

> Article 24
> Indigenous peoples have the right to their traditional medicines . . . , including the conservation of their vital medicinal plants, animals and minerals.

> Article 25
> Indigenous peoples have the right to maintain and strengthen their distinctive spiritual relationship with their traditionally owned or otherwise occupied and used lands, territories, waters and coastal seas and other resources and to uphold their responsibilities to future generations in this regard.[6]

Furthermore, Article 29 extends land rights to include conservation and protection of the environment. This is significant because it imparts duties and responsibilities to the nation-states to provide protection of the environment as a fundamental right of indigenous people.

> Article 29
> Indigenous peoples have the right to the conservation and protection of the environment and the productive capacity of their lands or territories and resources. States shall establish and implement assistance programmes for indigenous peoples for such conservation and protection.

Beyond the UNDRIP statement, there have been several other efforts to link environmental rights and human rights at the international level. Recently, growing recognition of the inescapable impacts of global climate change has placed the issue of environmental rights on the international agenda once more. The landmark 2009 resolution of the Human Rights Council was key to moving this process along. Resolution 10/4 "Human Rights and Climate Change" acknowledges at the international level that

> climate change-related impacts have a range of implications, both direct and indirect, for the effective enjoyment of human rights.[7]

The resolution resulted in a 2009 meeting of 40 distinguished scholars in Nairobi to discuss the link between human rights and the environment. The meeting, organized by the United Nations Environment Programme and the Office of the High Commissioner for Human Rights and titled "A New Future of Human Rights and Environment: Moving the Global Agenda Forward," provided guidance to both organizations on how to clarify the links between the two concepts on the international level. A primary goal was to consider the best strategies for pursuing an international declaration for environmental rights based on this resolution.

Even with these significant steps, the United Nations documents and treaties do not constitute an international law recognizing an adequate environment as a human right. Their significance lies in that they demonstrate a progressive pattern of movement toward achieving this goal. Countries around the world have taken it upon themselves to grant the highest legal protection for the environment through constitutional amendments and provisions.

National Constitutions

More than 50 national constitutions recognize a responsibility to protect the environment. Countries including Brazil, Costa Rica, Norway, Paraguay, Portugal, and Spain all have some form of constitutional environmental rights (Hayward 2005). Norway's constitution (Article 110b) provides a substantive environmental right:

> Every person has a right to an environment that is conducive to health and to natural surroundings whose productivity and diversity are preserved. Natural resources should be made use of on the basis of comprehensive long-term considerations whereby this right will be safeguarded for future generations as well.[8]

Norway's environmental right provides an example of language that serves to address anthropocentric concerns (conducive to human health), minimal ecocentric concerns (preservation of diversity), and the need for intergenerational equity (safeguard for future generations). Norway's constitutional language is fairly typical among nations with substantive environmental rights, and could guide U.S. efforts to draft an environmental amendment.

Ecuador provides a remarkable example of the first constitution in the world to grant ecocentric, intrinsic rights of nature. Legal scholars, policy analysts, and rights activists are closely watching Ecuador as it marks a watershed moment in the trajectory of environmental rights law. A summary of the articles makes clear the uniqueness of this language:

> Nature or Pachamama, where life is reproduced and exists, has the right to exist, persist, maintain and regenerate its vital cycles, structure, functions and its processes in evolution. (Article 1)
>
> Every person, people, community or nationality, will be able to demand the recognitions of rights for nature before the public. (Article 1)
>
> Nature has the right to an integral restoration . . . (Article 2)
>
> The State will apply precaution and restriction measures in all the activities that can lead to the extinction of species, the destruction of the ecosystems or the permanent alteration of the natural cycles. (Article 3)[9]

Ecuador voters approved the new constitution in 2008, and some feel that it may be one of the most important chapters of the country's history. Ecuador's leadership in securing ecocentric environmental rights may have a global effect, as other countries that are writing constitutions are taking notice (such as Nepal). Ecuador's extension of the intrinsic rights of nature may represent a larger shift in how humans view their place in the world. Lawyers are still cautious, however, as to how the details will be decided, and by whom. In her article "What Doctrine Should Grant Trees Standing?" Bassi (2010) raises the issue of who will enforce the rights of nature:

> While this right appears to be revolutionary for the environment and environmentalist alike, whether this right can or will be enforced is entirely dependent upon Ecuador's standing doctrine. Because nature cannot walk into a courthouse and speak for itself, it is dependent upon those who can obtain judicial review to protect its interests. (P. 462)

It remains to be seen how Ecuador will balance the intrinsic rights of nature with other economic and social needs of the country. But one thing is certain: Ecuador's constitution has breathed new life into global social movements' quest for environmental rights.

Social Movements

Social movements are leading the way in demonstrating the potential to link human rights and environmental rights. Hayward (2005) attests,

> Most mass movements at the grassroots are not just human rights, nor just environmental, but inevitably both. They have to be, if they are conscious of the role of natural resources in their lives, and of the dominant forces exploiting those resources. (P. 9)

The most recent examples of this can be found in global struggles to address climate justice. The climate justice movement seeks to address the intersection of the environmental impacts of global warming (e.g., melting sea ice) with the social justice issues of climate change (e.g., vulnerable people will be most heavily impacted). The climate justice movement has drawn heavily on the advances of environmental rights in international treaties and constitutions to make their claims. In 2009, indigenous representatives from around the world met in Alaska for the Indigenous Peoples' Global Summit on Climate Change. The leaders produced the Anchorage Declaration, which draws on the UNDRIP to motivate collective action in addressing climate change. The Anchorage Declaration states,

> We express our solidarity as Indigenous Peoples living in areas that are the most vulnerable to the impacts and root causes of climate change. We reaffirm the unbreakable and sacred connection between land, air, water, oceans, forests, sea ice, plant, animals and our human communities as the material and spiritual bases for our existence.
>
> We call on States to recognize, respect and implement the fundamental human rights of Indigenous Peoples, including the collective rights to traditional ownership, use, access, occupancy and title to traditional lands, air, forests, waters, oceans, sea ice and sacred sites as well as to ensure that the rights affirmed in Treaties are upheld and recognized in land use planning and climate change mitigation strategies.[10]

In a similar sentiment, the World People's Conference on Climate Change and the Rights of Mother Earth produced language in the Cochabamba Protocol that is heavily influenced by Ecuador's constitutional amendment.

> It is imperative that we forge a new system that restores harmony with nature and among human beings. And in order for there to be balance with nature, there must first be equity among human beings.[11]

The statement above demonstrates an explicit understanding of the connection between human rights ("equity among human beings") and the environment ("balance with nature"). Clearly, the efforts to secure environmental rights in the international and national documents are a foundation for the forward-thinking strategies coming from the global struggles for climate justice. We can only hope that the people's voices will have similar effects to guide and inspire those who are currently responsible for climate change policy decisions. In sum, it is important to recognize the variety of agreements and constitutional provisions that protect the environment (see Table 6.1).

Environmental Rights for the Twenty-First Century

Sociology's Contribution

Human rights are grounded in the practical goals and ideal dreams of the society in which we live. Surely, then, the field of sociology has much to offer in understanding the potential for where human rights can take us. In particular, the field of sociology has broadened its horizons to understand that humans are embedded in a natural world. This means that humans can affect nature and that nature has the potential to affect human organization. The subfield of environmental sociology has declared that the disciple should enter the New Ecological Paradigm where humans are not considered exempt from the natural world (Catton and Dunlap 1978). The new ground being broken in this theoretical realm can give much leverage to the pursuit of environmental rights. Interdisciplinary research studying the root causes of environmental destruction offers a new look at why the politics of social justice and environmental justice must be intertwined.

In addition to providing theoretical insight, sociology provides important data to help build the case as to why we need environmental rights. Some sociologists use quantitative models to determine the "ecological footprint" of nations in relation to their social structure (York, Rosa, and Dietz 2003). Other social science researchers conduct ethnographic fieldwork (interviews and observations) to study how people's values of the environment change over time (Norgaard 2006). These sources of data demonstrate issues of equity, identity, and context that cannot be gained by surveys alone.

Finally, sociologists are known to raise critical questions about the nature of society. For example, they may question whether constitutional environmental rights go far enough in addressing the relationships of power, politics, and economics that cause many of the environmental problems we are facing today. Or those who study the impacts of global trade may ask

Table 6.1 Samples of Existing Environmental Rights Statements

	Document	Summary Language	Environmental Rights Approach
International Treaty	Aarhus Strategic Plan	Environmental challenges cannot be addressed without involvement of a wide range of stakeholders.	Procedural, emphasis on democratic process
	UNDRIP	Indigenous peoples have the right to maintain their distinctive relationships with the land, waters, and seas.	Substantive, emphasis on cultural integrity
	UN Resolution 10/4	Climate change impacts have a range of implications for the enjoyment of human rights.	Instrumental, emphasis on public health
National Constitution	Norway Constitution	Every person has the right to an environment conducive to health and to natural diversity, safeguarded for future generations.	Substantive, anthropocentric, intergenerational equity
	Ecuador Constitution	Nature has a right to exist, persist, maintain, and regenerate its vital cycles.	Intrinsic, ecocentric
Social Movement Declaration	Anchorage Declaration	Indigenous peoples express solidarity to reaffirm unbreakable and sacred connection to nature; these rights must be recognized in climate change mitigation strategies.	Substantive, emphasis on cultural integrity
	Cochabamba Protocol	We must forge a new system that restores harmony with nature and humans. Balance in nature requires equity among humans.	Intrinsic, intergenerational equity

whether a constitutional right in the Global North will have unintentionally negative impacts in those countries of the Global South that have not yet secured constitutional protections. By continuing to interrogate human rights through the lens of global justice and social change, sociologists can help refine and revise constitutional environmental rights in the service of sustainability and human welfare.

Move to Amend

> That constitutions are not intended to be perfect is evidenced by expressly stated processes for revising or amending them. (Maddex 1995:xiv)

The quote above is meant to remind us that constitutions are living documents designed to meet the needs of a society. The U.S. Constitution provides specific instructions on how to amend when the general population recognizes the need. Thankfully, those before us have taken up this task. Today it is our turn. If environmental rights are to be shared by everyone (i.e., universal) and if we believe they should receive guarantees at the highest political level (i.e., the U.S. Constitution), then a constitutional environmental right is a logical imperative.

This is not such a far-fetched idea. In fact, it has been done before. In the heyday of the environmental movement, at least two serious proposals were made by elected officials to amend the U.S. Constitution to include environmental rights. In addition, five U.S. states (Hawaii, Illinois, Massachusetts, Montana, and Pennsylvania) have amended their constitutions to include a right to a clean environment. We must first think of the strategies for social change that would mobilize citizens to work for a constitutional environmental amendment. Just as important, we must not limit ourselves in imagining the type of political and economic change that would welcome a constitutional amendment to protect Pachamama, our Mother Earth.

Discussion Questions

1. Describe how property rights might affect the effectiveness of the public trust doctrine or the precautionary principle. How might we alter property relations in the best interest of planetary survival?

2. Is our society responsible for the health and well-being of future generations? In what ways might intergenerational equity go beyond environmental rights to include other human rights?

3. Different cultures rely on the environment in various ways, including health practices and religious customs. Can you think of other examples that link environmental rights with cultural integrity?

4. Would a constitutional environmental right be effective if the underlying political economy of capitalism remains unchanged? Would a constitutional environmental right prevent agency capture? In what ways could it promote participatory democracy on behalf of the environment?

5. Should we think about human rights and the environment within the existing framework of human rights law in which the environmental rights are instrumental in protecting of humans? Or should we talk directly about environmental rights as a means to protect the environment itself? Should we go beyond the anthropocentric in favor of the ecocentric?

Notes

1. The author wishes to acknowledge the contributions made by Christina Simeone's (2006) master's thesis, *The Necessity and Possibilities of Constitutional Environmental Rights*. Her work provided an excellent literature review and the foundation for this chapter.
2. www.who.int/about/en/
3. www.who.int/phe/en/
6. http://www.un.org/esa/socdev/unpfii/en/drip.html
7. http://www2.ohchr.org/english/issues/climatechange/index.htm
8. http://www.stortinget.no/en/In-English/About-the-Storting/The-Constitution/The-Constitution/
9. http://pdba.georgetown.edu/Constitutions/Ecuador/ecuador08.html
8. www.epa.gov/glo/
9. www.endocrinedisruption.com
10. www.indigenoussummit.com/servlet/content/declaration.html
11. www.climateandcapitalism.com/?p=2255

References

Anderson, M. 1996. "Human Rights Approaches to Environmental Protection: An Overview." Pp. 1–24 in *Human Rights Approaches to Environmental Protection*, edited by A. Boyle and M. Anderson. Oxford, UK: Clarendon Press.

Bassi, M. 2010. "La Naturaleza O Pacha mama de Ecuador: What Doctrine Should Grant Trees Standing?" *Oregon Review of International Law* 11:461–78.

Brooks, R., Ross Jones, and Ross A. Virginia. 2002. *Law and Ecology: The Rise of the Ecosystem Regime*. Aldershot, UK: Ashgate.

Catton, W. and R. Dunlap. 1978. "Environmental Sociology: A New Paradigm." *The American Sociologist* 13:41–9.

Costanza, R., J. Cumberland, H. Daly, R. Goodland, and R. Norgaard. 1997. *An Introduction to Ecological Economics*. Boca Raton, FL: St. Lucie Press.

Dommen, C. 2003. "How Human Rights Norms Can Contribute to Environmental Protection." Pp. 105–17 in *Linking Human Rights and the Environment*, edited by R. Picolotti and J. Taillant. Tucson: University of Arizona Press.

Ercmann, S. 1996. "Enforcement of Environmental Law in United States and European Law: Realities and Expectations." *Environmental Law* 26: 1213–39.

Hayward, T. 2005. *Constitutional Environmental Rights*. New York: Oxford University Press.

Lavigne, P. 2003. "Greening the U.S. Constitution." *Conservation Biology* 17(6):1485–486.

MacKay, F. 2002. "The Rights of Indigenous Peoples in International Law." Pp. 9–30 in *Human Rights & the Environment: Conflicts and Norms in a Globalizing World*, edited by L. Zarsky. London: Earthscan.

Maddex, R. 1995. *Constitutions of the World*. Washington, DC: Congressional Quarterly.

McCay, B. 1998. *Oyster Wars and the Public Trust: Property, Law, and Ecology in New Jersey History*. Tucson: University of Arizona Press.

McKay, M. 1994. "Environmental Rights and the US System of Protection: Why the US Environmental Protection Agency Is Not a Rights Based Administrative Legacy." *Environment and Planning* 26:1761–785.

Miller, C. 1995. "Environmental Rights: European Fact or English Fiction?" *Journal of Law and Society* 22(3):374–97.

Norgaard, K. 2006. "'We Don't Really Want to Know': Environmental Justice and Socially Organized Denial of Global Warming in Norway." *Organization and Environment* 19(3):347–70.

Office of the United Nations High Commissioner for Human Rights. 2007. "Convention on the Rights of the Child." Retrieved January 13, 2011.

Picolotti, R. and J. Taillant. 2003. "Introduction." Pp. xiii–xviii in *Linking Human Rights and the Environment*, edited by R. Picolotti and J. Taillant. Tucson: University of Arizona Press.

Redgwell, C. 1996. "Life, the Universe and Everything: A Critique of Anthropocentric Rights." Pp. 71–88 in *Human Rights Approaches to Environmental Protection*, edited by A. Boyle and M. Anderson. Oxford, UK: Clarendon Press.

Regier, H. 1993. "The Notion of Natural and Cultural Integrity." Pp. 3–18 in *Ecological Integrity and the Management of Ecosystems*, edited by S. Woodley, J. Kay, and G. Francis. Ottawa, Ontario, Canada: St. Lucie Press.

Shelton, D. 2003. "The Environmental Jurisprudence of International Human Rights Tribunals." Pp. 1–30 in *Linking Human Rights and the Environment*, edited by R. Picolotti and J. Taillant. Tucson: University of Arizona Press.

Simeone, Christina. 2006. *The Necessity and Possibilities of Constitutional Environmental Rights*. Master's thesis presented to University of Pennsylvania Department of

Earth and Environmental Studies. Retrieved July 26, 2010 (http://repository .upenn.edu/cgi/viewcontent.cgi?article=1006&context=mes_capstones).

Singer, Peter. 1975. *Animal Liberation: A New Ethics for Our Treatment of Animals.* New York: Review/Random House.

Stone, Christopher. 1975. *Should Trees Have Standing? Toward Legal Rights for Natural Objects.* New York: Avon Books.

Taillant, J. 2003. "Environmental Advocacy and the Inter-American Human Rights System." Pp. 118–61 in *Linking Human Rights and the Environment*, edited by R. Picolotti and J. Taillant. Tucson: University of Arizona Press.

UN Documents. N.d. "Declaration of the United Nations Conference on the Human Environment" [From *Report of the United Nations Conference on the Human Environment*, Stockholm, June 1972]. Retrieved January 7, 2011 (http://www .un-documents.net/unchedec.htm).

United Nations Economic Commission for Europe. N.d. "Introducing the Aarhus Convention." Retrieved January 13, 2011 (http://www.unece.org/env/pp/).

United Nations Environment Programme. 2009. "High Level Expert Meeting on the New Future of Human Rights: Moving the Global Agenda Forward." Retrieved January 13, 2011 (http://www.unep.org/environmentalgovernance/Events/ HumanRightsandEnvironment/tabid/2046/language/en-US/Default.aspx).

United Nations World Commission on Environment and Development. 1987. "Brundtland" Report. General Assembly A/42/427. Retrieved January 13, 2011 (http://www.un.org/documents/ga/res/42/ares42-187.htm).

Westra, L. 2008. *Environmental Justice and the Rights of Indigenous People: International and Domestic Legal Perspectives.* London: Earthscan.

Wingspread Conference. 1998. "Wingspread Statement on the Precautionary Principle." Retrieved January 13, 2011 (http://www.gdrc.org/u-gov/precaution-3.html).

York, R., E. Rosa, and T. Dietz. 2003. "Footprints on the Earth: The Environmental Consequences of Modernity." *American Sociological Review* 68(2):279–300.

Zarsky, L. 2002. "Global Reach: Human Rights and Environment in the Framework of Corporate Accountability." Pp. 31–54 in *Human Rights and the Environment: Conflicts and Norms in a Globalizing World*, edited by L. Zarsky. London: Earthscan.

7

Comparing Constitutions

Judith Blau

The U.S. Constitution has inspired people around the world, and Americans are justifiably proud that it helped to launch a new era that we now refer to as *modernity*. This constitution boldly chartered a new course by setting a high standard for the rule of law, making a decisive break with monarchical tyranny, establishing the principles of governance, and affirming individual *freedoms*. Americans tend to think that the U.S. Constitution was unique and remains so to this day. For one thing, we often overlook the great similarities between the United States' 1787 Constitution and France's 1789 Declaration of the Rights of Man and of the Citizen. The declaration begins with this phrase:

> The representatives of the French people, organized as a National Assembly, believing that the ignorance, neglect, or contempt of the rights of man are the sole cause of public calamities and of the corruption of governments, have determined to set forth in a solemn declaration the natural, unalienable, and sacred rights of man, in order that this declaration, being constantly before all the members of the Social body, shall remind them continually of their rights and duties.[1]

It is true that the French declaration ended up in smithereens by 1792 (along with the 1791 French Constitution), but it is fulsomely referenced in France's current constitution as providing the fundamental principle of equality.[2] Like the U.S. Constitution, the French declaration has profoundly influenced the constitutions of other countries. The ideas embodied in these documents launched the world into the era of *modernity*—an era in which individualism, rationality, impersonality, capitalism, and law have been ascendant. To be sure, there were undemocratic regimes that defied the new modern order, and rich nations often put aside their democratic values to pursue unjust wars and to enrich already wealthy businesses and corporations. Yet the trend until now has been the steady advance of democracy, transparency, and accountability. This is the case for very poor countries as well as rich ones (Blaustein 1993; Venter 2008).

Liberalism

To recapitulate, the U.S. Constitution, the Declaration of the Rights of Man and of the Citizen, and the 1791 French Constitution all share a liberal premise, namely, one that asserts that individuals have certain rights and freedoms in the political sphere and, inferentially, in the economic sphere as well (Blau and Moncada 2006). For example, all have the same rights, in principle, to assemble freely, to petition government officials, to practice the religion of their choice, to have a fair trial, and, inferentially, to become as rich as possible.

These foundational documents derived their justification from the principle of a "natural law"—that is, that all humankind has these universal rights (Lauren 2003:14). Yet the U.S. and French constitutions and the Declaration of the Rights of Man also derived their justification from the liberal doctrine of individual sovereign rights. This conception is widely shared around the world, and there can only be applause for that. Yet this doctrine also has pernicious consequences. First, it ignores the many ways that people have cultural and social identities. Second, liberalism ignores people's existential rights to food, shelter, a job, health care, education, and other substantive conditions of equality. Third, liberalism promotes the idea of individual autonomy without acknowledging that people live and work in groups—families, clans, communities, tribes, cities. In these groups, people often endeavor to communicate, cooperate, and reciprocate, and liberal principles do not encourage such endeavors.

What fundamentally challenged liberalism in the twentieth century was the coincidence of three historical moments, each greatly significant. One was the challenge of creating new international norms in the aftermath of the Holocaust, another the struggles of new nations as they threw off the yoke of colonial oppression, and another, throughout the world, the intensification of labor movements. All of these, together and separately, clarified the shortcomings of the liberal doctrine and helped to highlight the need to recognize universal and substantively grounded human rights. Once introduced into the imaginations of people around the world, human rights became the global clarion call, and henceforth, advocates made demands on governments, corporations, and enterprises that all their rights be recognized. These included not only liberal rights—civil and political rights—but also economic, social, cultural, and environmental rights, as well as the rights of vulnerable people, such as minorities, handicapped persons, and migrants. The United States is the anomaly.

A Close-Up Look at the
U.S. Constitution and Its Origins

The Declaration of Independence[3]

On June 7, 1776, Richard Henry Lee rose to his feet at the convening of the Second Continental Congress to declare a motion for independence. It passed, and the members of a small committee, headed by Thomas Jefferson, sequestered themselves to prepare the document. Two days later, the committee presented the declaration to Congress and proclaimed the right of revolution. The philosophical grounding of this right to revolt is important, but just as important is what Jefferson deemed to be rights. Paragraph 2 of the Declaration of Independence begins,

> We hold these truths to be self-evident, that all men are created equal, that they are endowed by their Creator with certain unalienable Rights, that among these are Life, Liberty and the Pursuit of Happiness.—That to secure these rights, Governments are instituted among Men, deriving their just powers from the consent of the governed,—That whenever any Form of Government becomes destructive of these ends, it is the Right of the People to alter or to abolish it, and to institute new Government, laying its foundation on such principles and organizing its powers in such form, as to them shall seem most likely to effect their Safety and Happiness.[4]

Jefferson misquotes John Locke, who wrote, "Life, Liberty and Pursuit of Property." All the Framers of the Constitution believed that property was a right, as I will later describe, but we might charitably speculate that the reason why Jefferson substituted "Happiness" for "Property" was because property in the colonies included slaves, and although having human chattel may have been acceptable, it probably was not comfortable to celebrate.

That equality and rights are "self-evident truths" also requires explanation. For Jefferson, this did not imply some democratic ideal of self-governance.

Instead, it is an elitist term that goes back to the Stoics' conception that a tribunal of wise men could weigh the options and arrive at good ethical judgments (Jefferson [1825] 1955). It was "self-evident" in this hypothetical and philosophical sense.[5] Additionally, the arguments of the declaration draw from a long line of writers, including Saint Thomas Aquinas, the Enlightenment philosophers—especially the French *philosophes*, Voltaire and Jean-Jacques Rousseau—but mainly the English philosopher, John Locke. The declaration could have been written line for line by Locke, with the exception of the substitution of "Happiness" for "Property."

Nor is Jefferson completely original about connecting rights to political action. The English barons had demanded concessions in the form of the Magna Carta from King John in 1215, and in the same century, King Magnus of Norway was pressed to issue the *Magnus Lagaboters Landslov*, which promised equality before the law (Lauren 2003:18). Additionally, in the sixteenth century, there had been upheavals that accompanied the advance of liberties and freedoms. Royalty in France, Holland, Spain, and England had been forced to make major concessions, relinquishing their own powers and extending rights to property holders and sometimes to others as well. Following decades of civil war in England, the Levellers, in the mid-seventeenth century, demanded guarantees of the people's "native rights," including legal rights, and the right to life, property, and the exercise of free speech and of religion. This culminated in the passage of the Habeas Corpus Act of 1679 and the Bill of Rights in 1689, which together greatly advanced people's freedoms and democracy, and the bill's provisions included trial by jury, prohibitions against cruel and unusual punishment, security of law and person, representative government, and free elections.

The Declaration of Independence provides a set of *philosophical reasons* why the colonists should rise up and rebel, and Jefferson provided a list of "the causes which impel them to the separation." Yet Jefferson did not need the Stoics and a "tribunal of wise men" for justification. He simply could have looked out the window and onto the streets. The insurrection had started more than a year before, on April 18, 1975. However, instead of praise and support for their idealism and struggles, the colonial Congress responded to the people's insurrection by sending King George an apology in its Olive Branch Petition. And, months before Jefferson penned the declaration, about February 1776, Thomas Paine's pamphlet *Common Sense* hit the streets of colonial towns. Written in England and shipped to the colonies, it presented many of the ideas that inform the vision behind the declaration. Historians Morison, Commager, and Leuchtenburg (1983:80) describe its great importance: "Within a month this amazing pamphlet had been read by or to almost every white American. It rallied the undecided and the wavering."

The Idea of Rights

Thus, while the declaration was not all that novel, and derived much from John Locke, it also rubber-stamped a revolution that had already begun. Jefferson's document was immensely helpful in spurring efforts to establish rules and procedures for governance well before the war was over. Individual colonies formed their own governments beginning in 1776, with a resolution by Congress, and each of their constitutions included a Bill of Rights, and each placed democratic control of government in the hands of the sovereign people (i.e., those who held property). Thus, Jefferson's declaration was like a cueing card for everything that came next—independence, writing a constitution, and setting up the machinery of governance. The last land battle of the War of Independence was mid-November 1782, and the Peace of Paris was signed later that month.

As authors have stressed throughout this volume, *ideas* about rights are extremely powerful on their own, since they find expression in constitutions and charters, but to matter at all, these ideas have to appeal to people's *common sense* (as Thomas Paine recognized) and relate to their understandings and experiences. While Thomas Jefferson's idea about "rights" is different from what we now term "human rights," it has been Jefferson's (as well as Madison's, Hamilton's, and the other Framers') conception that has dominated American political culture for over two and a third centuries. One important difference between early American rights and human rights is practical coverage. Only white males held rights in the new republic, and for purposes of political participation, only white males who owned property. The colonial rebellion that culminated in national independence was for political freedom; today there is much more at stake because people share the world in ways that were unimaginable in the late eighteenth century. We can say now that the freedoms spelled out in the declaration were inadequate even for their times, most egregiously so regarding slavery but also the abominable disregard for the rights of indigenous peoples, and the disentrancement of males without property and of women.

It makes sense to consider that individual political rights were prioritized in the context of the War of Independence and in the period of early nation building. But economic rights became an easy analogue to political rights as the new nation began to industrialize. Bit by bit, Americans adopted the idea that they had individual economic rights as well as political rights, but the form these rights took was not the rights to economic security, but the rights to ownership. Capitalism was beginning to bloom precisely at the time America gained its independence, and individual economic rights became increasingly salient, without much public debate. The white, male American citizen had as much right to accumulate resources as he had to go to church. Especially in rural New England, new industries sprouted everywhere— sawmills, gain mills, paper mills, factories for iron production—and with these new industries came, inevitably, class divisions. Critics at the time, and most especially Karl Marx, further contended that capitalist production leads not only to the impoverishment of workers but to their dehumanization and devaluation as well, owing to the ways that production estranges the workers from "their own nature and essence," and from what they produce, and from their relationships with other human beings (Marx 1859:81). But few, if any, were reading Karl Marx in nineteenth-century America.

In the twentieth century, socialist societies responded in a forthright way to the viciousness of capitalism, while sometimes imperiling the political freedoms of their citizens, while Europeans adopted cushions in the form of welfare capitalism (Esping-Anderson 1990). Celebrated too in Europe was an extension of political freedoms, namely the idea of social rights, which as elaborated by T. H. Marshall (1950) included some sort of economic welfare and security. Why welfare capitalism was less successful in the United States compared with other industrialized countries is complex, but a short answer is that welfare capitalism penetrates through all social classes in European countries especially, and to some extent Britain. (That is to say when all benefit from welfare programs and contribute their share, they are a *collective good*.) But in America, welfare was for the poor and divided Americans instead of unifying Americans around a sense of reciprocal responsibility. (In 1996, welfare in America was abolished with the passage of the Personal Responsibility and Work Opportunity Reconciliation Act.)

In summary, the United States has the oldest constitution in the world, but that is nothing to be proud of. Its provisions for the well-being of the citizenry are negligible, and even though laws exist pertaining to, for example, labor rights, it can be said that laws, without constitutional backing, are extremely easy to change. What I also want to stress is that contemporary understanding of human rights or *derechos humanos* or *droits de l'homme* are very different from Jefferson's "rights" and the long intellectual tradition from which he drew. This is not to imply that the elements of Jefferson's vision—equality, liberty, and the inalienability of rights—are an alternative to human rights. Instead, I wish to suggest that the American liberal tradition helped to launch an important component of what we now understand as human rights.

However—and most important—civil and political rights are not understood in the American liberal tradition as being *integral and inherent* to all other human rights, including economic, social, and cultural rights. Moreover, in this same American liberal tradition, people are the *objects of rights* bestowed by the state, whereas from the human rights perspective, human beings are the *agents of their own rights*. Human rights are deeply embedded in society, and accompany rights as well as responsibilities. This provides a background for a closer look at *The Federalist Papers* and the Bill of Rights.

The Federalist Papers

It was Jefferson's hand that penned the Declaration of Independence, but not the Constitution. The Constitution is largely based on *The Federalist Papers,* written by Alexander Hamilton, James Madison, and John Jay as serialized papers published between October 1787 and August 1788. What has become known as "Beard's thesis" is based on Charles Beard's (1913) close reading and interpretation of these papers and his conclusion that property interests played a large role in the thinking of the Framers. What the U.S. Constitution and early national laws accomplished, according to Beard, was to pave the way for the advance of capitalism. (Georges Lefebvre [1964:349–60] makes this case for the French Constitution.)

Very specifically, Beard (1913) concludes that the Framers, especially Alexander Hamilton, felt that political power ought to expressly flow from a strong economic system. Public policy according to Hamilton and the other Federalists ought to promote economic growth, while curbing the excessive self-interest of fledgling industrialists and planters. It was Hamilton who proposed measures that would promote economic self-sufficiency and prosperity, through tariffs on imported goods and an excise tax on certain goods produced domestically. John Adams likewise agreed in his contributions to *The Federalist Papers* that a main task of government (led by men of superior wisdom and capabilities) would be to protect the propertied and financial interests of the nation.

Thus, from the very beginning of the nation's history, economic interests played a major role in the nation's legal and political climate, even if these interests were not spelled out explicitly. Instead the overt emphasis, at least for public consumption, was on equality and its justification by an unseen natural law and secular justifications having to do with the social contract between ordinary citizens and the state.

Alan Pendleton Grimes draws from *The Federalist Papers* in his analysis of the drafting of the U.S. Constitution and arrives at the same conclusions that Beard had. Additionally, he argues that constitutional interpretations during the Reconstruction period drew heavily on Manchester Liberalism, an ideology of the supremacy of the values of capitalism and economic values. Grimes (1955:291) states that the view in the decades following the Civil War was that "the greatest good of the greatest number was, therefore, interpreted to mean the greatest acquisition for the greatest number of people." Furthermore, Grimes writes, "Equal opportunity gave way to each man an equal chance to prove the extent of his inequality. In a pecuniary value scheme, it was evident that not all men were worth the same."

In sum, the political culture in which the Constitution has been applied has always supported economic rights of property holders, although the Constitution says very little about property rights per se, and the legal culture in which the Constitution has been interpreted has always supported corporations, although the Constitution says nothing about corporations. Yet we do not want to convey the idea that the Constitution is merely a vehicle for property rights and the rights of corporations, but we wish to further show how capitalist ideals were confounded with political ones in the eighteenth century.

Bill of Rights and Other Constitutional Amendments

Whereas Lockean Jefferson highlighted people's inalienable rights, it was the vision of the Hobbesian Federalists that prevailed in the Constitution. The Constitution puts constraints on people's democratic rights. It does so by diluting voters' influence through the electoral system, but also because power is divided between states and the federal government and the people are marginalized by the tensions between the competing jurisdictions. True, the system of checks and balances has been relatively successful in deterring would-be tyrants, but the same system provides disincentives for citizen involvement in governance. However, we are concerned not with the nature and structure of governance, but rather with constitutional provisions for individual rights, which are laid out in the ten 1791 amendments (the Bill of Rights), and in a few subsequent amendments. Although well known to Americans, it is useful nevertheless to again examine the constitutional amendments that are related to rights and freedoms. They are reproduced in Figure 7.1.

Figure 7.1   Amendments to the U.S. Constitution

Article [I] 1791

Congress shall make no law respecting an establishment of religion, or prohibiting the free exercise thereof; or abridging the freedom of speech, or of the press; or the right of the people peaceably to assemble, and to petition the Government for a redress of grievances.

Article [II] 1791

A well regulated Militia, being necessary to the security of a free State, the right of the people to keep and bear Arms, shall not be infringed.

Article [III] 1791

No Soldier shall, in time of peace be quartered in any house, without the consent of the Owner, nor in time of war, but in a manner to be prescribed by law.

Article [IV] 1791

The right of the people to be secure in their persons, houses, papers, and effects, against unreasonable searches and seizures, shall not be violated, and no Warrants shall issue, but upon probable cause, supported by Oath or affirmation, and particularly describing the place to be searched, and the persons or things to be seized.

Article [V] 1791

No person shall be held to answer for a capital, or otherwise infamous crime, unless on a presentment or indictment of a Grand Jury, except in cases arising in the land or naval forces, or in the Militia, when in actual service in time of War or public danger; nor shall any person be subject for the same offence to be twice put in jeopardy of life or limb; nor shall be compelled in any criminal case to be a witness against himself, nor be deprived of life, liberty, or property, without due process of law; nor shall private property be taken for public use, without just compensation.

Article [VI] 1791

In all criminal prosecutions, the accused shall enjoy the right to a speedy and public trial, by an impartial jury of the State and district wherein the crime shall have been committed, which district shall have been previously ascertained by law, and to be informed of the nature and cause of the accusation; to be confronted with the witnesses against him; to have compulsory process for obtaining witnesses in his favor, and to have the Assistance of Counsel for his defense.

(Continued)

(Continued)

Article [VII] 1791

In Suits at common law, where the value in controversy shall exceed twenty dollars, the right of trial by jury shall be preserved, and no fact tried by a jury, shall be otherwise re-examined in any Court of the United States, than according to the rules of the common law.

Article [VIII] 1791

Excessive bail shall not be required, nor excessive fines imposed, nor cruel and unusual punishments inflicted.

Article [IX] 1791

The enumeration in the Constitution, of certain rights, shall not be construed to deny or disparage others retained by the people.

Article [X] 1791

The powers not delegated to the United States by the Constitution, nor prohibited by it to the States, are reserved to the States respectively, or to the people.

Article [XI] [Judicial Jurisdiction, 1795]

Article [XII] [Electoral College, 1804]

Article [XIII] 1865

Neither slavery nor involuntary servitude, except as a punishment for crime whereof the party shall have been duly convicted, shall exist within the United States, or any place subject to their jurisdiction.

Article [XIV] 1868

Section 1. All persons born or naturalized in the United States, and subject to the jurisdiction thereof, are citizens of the United States and of the State wherein they reside. No State shall make or enforce any law which shall abridge the privileges or immunities of citizens of the United States; nor shall any State deprive any person of life, liberty, or property, without due process of law; nor deny to any person within its jurisdiction the equal protection of the laws.

Section 2. [Population apportionment for number of Representatives]

Section 3. [Any engaged in insurrection or rebellion may not hold major political office.]

Section 4. [Public debt]

Article [XV] 1870

The right of citizens of the United States to vote shall not be denied or abridged by the United States or by any State on account of race, color, or previous condition of servitude.

Article [XVI] [Income Tax, 1913]

Article [XVII] [Vacancies in Senate, 1913]

Article [XVIII] [Prohibition of Liquor, 1919]

Article [XIX] 1920

The right of citizens of the United States to vote shall not be denied or abridged by the United States or by any State on account of sex.

Article [XX] [Terms of President, Vice President, and members of Congress, 1933]

Article [XXI] [Repeal of eighteenth article of amendment (Prohibition) 1934]

Amendment [XXII] [Term limits for president, 1951]

Amendment [XXIII] [District of Columbia, 1961]

Amendment [XXIV] 1964

The right of citizens of the United States to vote in any primary or other election for President or Vice President, for electors for President or Vice President, or for Senator or Representative in Congress, shall not be denied or abridged by the United States or any state by reason of failure to pay any poll tax or other tax.

Amendment [XXV] [Provisions for filling vacancies of elected officials, 1967]

Amendment [XXVI] [Voting age set to 18 and older, 1971]

Amendment [XXVII] [Salaries of congressional representatives, 1992]

Note: Ratification history and notes excluded; omitted amendments in brackets.

Source: www.whitehouse.gov/constitution/constitution.html.

The important First Amendment states people's rights as they relate to religious freedom, and freedom of speech, of the press, the right to assemble, and to petition government. The wording is important—"Congress shall make no law"—which is to say, in colloquial but apt terms, "Just watch your back, because the State may sneak up and take those freedoms away." In the language of Isaiah Berlin (1969), these are negative freedoms, liberties held defensively against the state, but given by the state.

The controversial amendment on the right to bear arms (sometimes interpreted as the rights of the individual states to keep a militia) is stated in Article II, and Article III offers qualified privacy protection to citizens when soldiers want access to their homes. The important provisions ensuring legal rights—for protection against unreasonable search and seizures, illegal imprisonment, double jeopardy, self-incrimination, and excessive bail; due process; and trial by jury—are all spelled out in Articles IV through VIII, with IX stating the coherence of rights. Articles X and XI specify that the national government is supreme only within its own sphere and that individual states have their own sovereign power. Article XII clarifies that electors vote, not persons.

Enactment of Article XIII liberated about 3 million slaves, but they were not free in any modern sense. As Frederick Douglass stated at the time, "The black was free from the individual master, but a slave of society . . . He was turned loose, naked, hungry, and destitute to the open sky" (quoted in Morison et al. 1983:326) No constitutional amendment was ever proposed that would give African Americans or the members of any minority group full equality, nor does the Civil Rights Act, a piece of legislation that addresses discrimination (again, in the negative sense of rights), and not full rights. Besides, like any piece of legislation, it can be as easily repealed as it was passed into law.

Southern states did everything in their power to circumvent the 1865 Thirteenth Amendment, leading to the enactment of the Fourteenth Amendment in 1868. It overrides the power of individual states to abridge the rights of citizens, to uphold due process and equal protection of the laws. As we elaborate below, it subsequently became the basis of the legal doctrine of corporate personage rights. Ratification of the Fifteenth Amendment in 1870 was presumed to guarantee black suffrage, but was sabotaged by states that rushed to impose poll taxes and other restrictions to limit the black franchise, and it was not until nearly a century later, in 1964, with the ratification of the Twenty-Fourth Amendment, that the Constitution expressly prohibited states from imposing poll taxes. Women achieved the vote with the ratification of the Nineteenth Amendment in 1920.

Amendments XVI, XVII, XVIII, XX, XXI, XXII, XXIII, and XXV are not of particular interest here. Amendment XXVI lowers the voting age to 18, and XXVII prohibits Congress members from giving themselves a raise, at least during the current session of Congress.

I argue that the freedoms laid out in the Constitution are political and civil rights, but not human rights, at least in the contemporary sense. To be clear, political rights are the individual rights of liberal democracy, including the right to vote, the right to hold office, and the right to participate in governance. Civil rights are more complex, but essentially involve the protection of the person's existence (Nowak 2000), and include freedom of thought and opinion, freedom of religion, the right to recognition before the law, the right to a fair trial, freedom of movement, and the right to a nationality.

Moreover, civil and political rights can undermine human rights because they exclusively focus on the individual and thereby sever humans from their societies, social networks, and communities. They do nothing to promote solidarities, but instead promote competition and the defense of personal rights as opposed to the rights of others, thereby impairing people's complex interdependencies within communities, societies, states, and now the globe.

Corporate and Property Rights

The rights of corporations are not formally spelled out in the Bill of Rights, but are nevertheless protected through precedent. It is an interesting story because the precedent traces back to a simple clerical error that, once publicized, became the foundation on which corporations derive their power and autonomy in America.

In the 1886 case, *Santa Clara County v. Southern Pacific Railroad*, Chief Justice Waite asserted in an oral argument that "the court does not wish to hear argument on the question whether the provision in the Fourteenth Amendment to the Constitution, which forbids a State to deny any person within its jurisdiction the equal protection of the laws, applies to those of corporations. We are all of the opinion that it does" (Hammerstrom 2002). What is the precedent for this? In an earlier case that year, Southern Pacific Railroad 118 U.S. 294, a court stenographer had made an error in transcription, giving Southern Pacific the rights of a person—immunity from a state's authority—and when this was discovered by a newspaper reporter, it was flashed to many newspapers via the telegraph. Whatever their reasons, the justices did not revoke the error and embraced it as their own.[6]

Corporate personhood rights are extensive: (1) They and shareholders are immune from persecution, and corporations can spend an unlimited amount on political lobbying;[7] (2) corporations are offered some First Amendment rights;[8] (3) under the Fourteenth Amendment corporations may establish a business virtually anywhere they want and have considerable power over citizens' groups to endanger natural habitats; (4) under the Fifth Amendment, corporations may hire real persons who will protect their rights against self-incrimination;[9] (5) under the Fourth Amendment's search and seizure provisions, corporations are protected against surprise visits by government officials, such as Occupational Safety and Health Administration inspectors;[10] and (6) under due process provisions, corporations are protected in courts.[11] Moreover, (7) they have the right to airtime to lobby against legislation that they perceive as harmful to them (Meyers 2000), and (8) under the Sixth Amendment, they have the right to trial in criminal cases.[12] Because the U.S. courts rejected in the famous 1886 case the idea that corporations and businesses were a matter of "special privilege" and determined that they were instead a matter of "general utility with certain person-age rights," corporations and businesses have been shielded from considerable regulation and control by state authorities ever since.

Corporate rights, according to Carl Mayer (1990; also see Edwards 2002), dramatically expanded in the 1990s, as the Supreme Court further elaborated corporations' personhood rights, while their responsibilities to workers, communities, consumers, and the environment have shrunk. Additionally, as Anthony Ogus (1990) explains, the U.S. Constitution is moot on contract rights, and that is why there are virtually no constitutional cases dealing with contracts of, for example, sale, credit, housing, and, most significantly, employment. This makes the United States virtually unique in matters of contract law—as other countries recognize especially labor contracts—and gives business entities and corporations unusual power (Ogus 1990).

We highlight these issues here because the media, as well as elected office-holders, have been less than forthright with the American public about the extent to which corporations' rights have been expanded while those of American citizens have not.

"Life, liberty, and the pursuit of happiness," especially in the context of the American Revolution, would have been understood by colonists as freedom from the British and, likewise, as personal freedom. Thomas Paine, who was avidly read by the colonists, describes freedom as individuals having autonomy and independence. To illustrate his point, he wrote that the servants accept servitude in looking after the interests of their master, but when servants "encounter the world, in their own persons, they repossess the full share of freedom." Thus, freedom is something that all freemen inherently possess even if in their society their station in life conceals it. Yet he went on to explain that freedom is possessive: "I consider freedom as personal property . . . wherever I use the words *freedom* or *rights*, I desire to be understood to mean a perfect equality of them" (Foner 1976:143). Clearly, Paine did not mean that only holders of property had freedom, but what he did want to convey, according to Eric Foner, is that holding freedom is like holding property insofar as it secures one's autonomy.

An interesting aspect of Paine's thinking that he shared with Locke was his conception of property rights. Within natural rights theory generally, property was a natural right of free people before they founded governments. According to Locke, in the state of nature, property was a natural right because after eating the Apple and falling into Sin, "men employed their labor," and acquired rights to property (the trees, land, and so forth), and when they founded a government, it became the government's responsibility to help individual men protect their natural right to it (Locke [1689] 1980:30, 61). The difference between Locke and Paine, on one hand, and Jefferson, on the other, is really like splitting hairs, since Jefferson believed that property was a means to happiness and ought to have all the protections of civil law.[13]

When "freedom" hit the ground, so to speak, in the newly independent nation, it was put to immediate, practical use in laws protecting the freedoms of commerce, trade, and property holders. The greatest beneficiary by far of freedom was capitalism. Writes Zygmunt Bauman (1988:45), "The capitalist economy is not only the territory where freedom may be practiced in the least constrained fashion, un-interfered with by any other social pressures or considerations; it is also the nursery where the modern idea of freedom was sown and cultivated, to be later grafted on other branches of increasingly ramified social life." Thus, the term *freedom* in the United States so confounds capitalists' freedoms with individuals' freedoms that when Americans embrace the latter it only serves to reinforce the former.

Hypercapitalism and Economic Inequality

Former Labor Secretary Robert Reich (2010) describes changes in the concentration of wealth in the following historical terms. In 1928, the richest 1 percent of Americans received 23.9 percent of the nation's total income. After that, the concentration of wealth declined due to the New Deal reforms, and then after World War II, the GI Bill, civil rights legislation, and the Great Society programs. By the late 1970s, the top 1 percent took in only around 8 percent of America's total income. Yet after that, inequality began to widen again. By 2007, the richest 1 percent were right back where they were in 1928. They received 23.5 percent of the nation's total income.

The implications of such economic inequalities are profound. The human consequences are quickly grasped. People cannot save for retirement. Families lose their homes in excessively high numbers—around 360,000 a month in 2009, and this did not decline appreciably in 2010. In the southern states, nearly 20 percent of all children are food insecure. Cities simply no longer have the capacity to provide shelter to all who are homeless. Nearly 36 million Americans, including 12.9 million children, live below the poverty level.

We tend to think that food insecurity, loss of one's home, and poverty are unjust at the level of individuals and, in a vague sense, that excessive wealth is not fair. However, it is possible to reframe economists' writings on economic inequality and indications of poverty and so forth in terms of human rights, and, more specifically, in terms of human rights as a collective good. I elaborate in the conclusion, but suffice it to say here that American liberalism justifies the accumulation of wealth and therefore economic inequalities.

Constitutions

As the authors of chapters in this volume have variously argued, a main purpose of state constitutions has been to elaborate citizens' human rights. Since around 1950 with the decolonization of India, Pakistan, and African countries, new states forged ahead to write constitutions that would better protect their people than colonists had ever done. Constitutional reforms along these lines gained further momentum with the breakup of the Soviet Union and political transformations in Latin America. These *new nations* adopted constitutions that were far-reaching, and, more specifically, departed in fundamental ways from older constitutions of Western countries. To some extent, constitutions of Western countries have been revised to reflect contemporary realities, and we might say that they have "caught up" with constitutions of Third World countries. For example, Spain's 1997 constitution is in some sense comparable to South Africa's 1996 constitution. Both highlight welfare and labor rights as well as cultural rights. Both protect same-sex marriage. Both have sweeping nondiscriminatory provisions. Both emphasize cooperative government throughout all levels. And both constitutions draw from international human rights treaties.

Of course, it is the case that the people of new nations in Africa and elsewhere struggle with staggering levels of poverty, with exploitation by multinationals, sometimes with tyrants, and often with environmental disasters that are induced by climate change, but most began the twenty-first century with constitutions that embrace fundamental human rights. Comparatively, the U.S. Constitution remains frozen in the eighteenth century (Sabato 2007). Authors of chapters in this book give examples of constitutional provisions, and thus, there is no need to elaborate in much detail. However, it is useful to simply understand how rapidly new nations adopted constitutions in the latter decades of the twentieth century. These new nations incorporated into their constitutions the political freedoms that had been developed earlier in the West, but also incorporated the economic, social, and cultural rights that are spelled out in the Universal Declaration of Human Rights and the two covenants. Additionally, as African countries became involved in the pan-African process involving the drafting and ratification of the 1981 Banjul Charter on Human and Peoples' Rights[14] and subsequent treaties[15] (including the protocol on the rights of women[16] and the Youth Charter[17]), these individual African countries revised their constitutions to encompass provisions from these various treaties.

There is not space here to outline all of these constitutional provisions, but Figure 7.2 illustrates some of the rights outlined in some of the constitutions of African countries. The doctrine implied by the expression *living constitution* is fully applicable. This is not to deny that most African countries have extremely high rates of poverty. Nor is it to deny that some African governments are tyrannical and corrupt. For example, Chad and Cameroon, which have exemplary constitutions, rank among the lowest countries on an index of the perception of corruption (Transparency International 2009). Human Rights Watch (2009) urges the government of Nigeria to better uphold human rights standards, and the U.S. Department of State (2010) reports that the police in South Africa used excessive force during the World Cup events. The point that can be made, however, is that once a constitution affirms human rights, civil society groups (i.e., INGOs and NGOs) become mobilized to help achieve these human rights by putting pressure on the government, and watchdog groups, such as Human Rights Watch, Amnesty International, Global Watch, and Social Watch, develop metrics for whether a government lives up to its own constitution.

Most countries have provisions for either constitutional or judicial review boards that are the ultimate guarantors of how well a constitution does its job. Maddex (2008) distinguishes between the two in this way: Judicial review bodies are charged with ruling on the constitutionality of laws whereas constitutional review bodies are extrajudicial bodies that determine the constitutionality of laws. The former are nearly ubiquitous. In the United States, the Supreme Court exercises the power of judicial review. Constitutional review boards are relatively rare, but they are noteworthy because of their

Figure 7.2   Selected African Countries: Illustrative Constitutional
Provisions[18]

Algeria	Language rights.
Angola	Fundamental freedoms and rights of individuals.
Cameroon	Adherence to the Universal Declaration of Human Rights, the Charter of the United Nations, and the African Charter on Human and Peoples' Rights.
Chad	Equality of the sexes; right to belong to a union and to strike; to have access to public culture and education.
Egypt	Discrimination of any sort is prohibited; right to social and health insurance.
Ethiopia	Rights and freedoms that are interpreted in conformity with the Universal Declaration of Human Rights and the International Covenants on Civil and Political Rights and on Economic, Social, and Cultural Rights.
Gambia	Rights of women; rights of children; rights of individuals with disabilities; entitlement to enjoy and promote "any culture, language, tradition or religion."
Ghana	Article 27 provides equal rights for women and special care during pregnancy.
Kenya	Protection of conscience and expression.
Liberia	People have certain natural, inherent, and inalienable rights to which all are entitled regardless of ethnic background, race, sex, creed, place of origin, or political opinion.
Morocco	Equal rights to education and employment; right to property ownership.
Mozambique	Men and women are equal before the law in political, economic, social, and cultural affairs, and full rights are extended to individuals with disabilities
Nigeria	Guaranteed access to the high court for violations of the constitution's provisions on fundamental rights.

Rwanda	Discrimination based on race, ethnicity, clan, tribe, color, sex, region, social origin, religion, opinion, economic status, differences of culture, language, social situation, physical or mental deficiency, or any other form of discrimination is prohibited.
South Africa	Nonderogable (unconditional) rights that cannot be put aside by law or during an emergency include "human dignity" and life.
Tanzania	Citizens are obligated to work because they create the material wealth in society, which is the "source of the well-being of the people and the measure of human dignity."
Tunisia	The inviolability of the home, confidentiality of correspondence, protection of personal data, and the right to move freely within the country or to leave it are guaranteed.
Uganda	Fundamental rights are *inherent* rather than being granted by law. (That is, they cannot be abrogated.)
Zambia	Rights include life, liberty, security of the person and the protection of the law; freedom of conscience, expression, assembly, movement, and association; protection of young people against exploitation; and protection for the privacy of the home and other property and from deprivation of property without compensation.

relative independence from the courts and government and most especially because they are appellate bodies for citizens who wish to challenge the courts or the government on constitutional grounds. Figure 7.3 is a list of countries that have constitutional review boards.

Conclusion

Human rights, as laid out in treaties—such as the Convention on the Rights of the Child, the Convention on the Elimination of All Forms of Discrimination Against Women, and the Convention on the Rights of Persons With Disabilities—are most often interpreted, at least in the United States, in terms of individual rights. But even a glance at the text of any human rights treaty shows that it is also framed in terms of collective rights.

Figure 7.3   Countries With Constitutional Review Boards[19]

Argentina – Armenia – Austria – Bangladesh – Colombia – Croatia – Denmark – East Timor – Estonia – Finland – Ghana – Guyana – Haiti – Hungary – Lithuania – Macedonia – The Netherlands – Norway – Panama – The Philippines – Poland – Portugal – Russia – Rwanda – Serbia – Slovakia – Slovenia – South Africa – Sri Lanka – Sweden – Tanzania – Uganda – Zimbabwe

Let's take as an example the treaty that draws most from the Western tradition of liberal, individual rights, namely, the International Covenant on Civil and Political Rights. Included in the short preamble is this statement:

> Recognizing that, in accordance with the Universal Declaration of Human Rights, the ideal of free human beings enjoying civil and political freedom and freedom from fear and want can only be achieved *if conditions are created whereby everyone may enjoy his civil and political rights*.[20]

A mirror statement appears in the preamble of the International Covenant on Economic, Social, and Cultural Rights. A premise, in fact, of all human rights treaties and declarations is that rights are embedded in collectivities, namely communities and societies, and the members of all communities and societies have the responsibility to create the conditions whereby fundamental human rights are protected. Governments are the allies of the people in this ambitious project, but the action is on the ground. Ordinary citizens do the heavy lifting, holding enterprises and governments responsible. Importantly, citizens create spaces in their communities to protect the most vulnerable—minorities, migrants and refugees, children, the handicapped, and the aged. Increasingly important in this age of globalism, transnationalism, migration, and multicultural diversities is the human capacity for empathy across lines of difference and the recognition of human equality.

Without question, the advance of human rights depends on a broad understanding of what a *decent society* is and how that understanding can be widely shared. The knowledge bases and methodologies of the social sciences as well as of many other fields, including those that are interdisciplinary, will be extremely useful to people, enterprises, organizations, and governments in their pursuit of a decent society. It can be stressed here that a scientific revolution is now underway that posits that the realization of human rights is the objective (*telos*) of any scientific endeavor. Besides, although academic institutions have not retooled in all respects to accommodate this revolution-in-the-making, it is very likely that the great divide between science and the humanities can be bridged. None can predict now how in any detail the intellectual, practical, and institutional dimensions of this revolution-in-the-making will unfold, but there is little question that it will. The human costs of economic inequality, the degradation of the earth's ecosystem, and the destruction of cultures and languages are now too great for scientists to continue to pursue knowledge-for-the-sake-of-knowledge (or corporate profits). Yet there is no question that challenging times are ahead for all of the sciences, and as the pace of globalism continues, in all likelihood it will quicken with increasing interdependencies.

Discussion Questions

1. Having *freedoms* has a twofold meaning. It can mean that people can be self-determining since they are freed from traditional authority, but it can also entail powerlessness and isolation. How can societies, communities, and people themselves preserve the positive aspects of freedoms while dampening down the latter?

2. *Modernity* is a contested term. Many argue that late capitalism or postmodernity or globalism or globalization has replaced modernity. This is complicated, but it's good to grapple with these issues since we are living in the midst of complex change.

3. America's War of Independence and *rebellion* was justified in philosophical terms and in commonsense terms by Thomas Paine. Which is more compelling, or did the colonists benefit from both?

4. What are some examples of *collective goods* (sometimes called common goods or public goods)? When are they provided by governments, and when are they created by people in communities?

5. What are ways of distinguishing between a *nation* and a *state*? (It is useful to note that indigenous peoples often refer to themselves as a nation.)

6. There is a debate in America about the merits of a *living constitution*. You might look at the Wikipedia article and generate your own class debate.

7. *Telos* is a philosophical concept that refers to purpose, and for social scientists it refers to the pursuit of shared goals, including, or especially, a *decent society*. The *telos* that motivated the Framers of the U.S. Constitution is different from the one that lies behind contemporary constitutions. Discuss.

Notes

1. Declaration of the Rights of Man and of the Citizen: http://www.hrcr.org/docs/frenchdec.html

2. French Constitution, 1958, and as subsequently amended: http://www
.servat.unibe.ch/icl/fr00000_.html

3. This section is adapted from Blau and Moncada (2006).

4. http://www.archives.gov/exhibits/charters/declaration_transcript.html

5. The core premise of the American Declaration of Independence—"that all men are created equal with unalienable rights"—and of its near contemporary, the French Declaration on the Rights of Man and of the Citizen—"men are born free and equal in rights"—goes back a long, long way. It is possible to trace the central idea back to the Egyptians, Greeks, and Romans, as well as to Chinese, Islamic, and Hindu philosophers. For example, remarkable ancient Egyptian texts refer to the equality between "the son of any of importance and any of humble origins." The formalization of the principle of equality started as early as the first century A.D. with Marcus Tullius Cicero and then later continued in the seventeenth century in the works of Hugo Grotius, a Dutch jurist. This detailed account can be found in Lauren (2003:11–14); also see Bronner (2004:56–59) and Grimes (1955:88–92).

6. The 1886 case of *Santa Clara County v. Southern Pacific Railroad* became the key precedent for subsequent decisions. With that, corporations became legal persons in the United States, and gained the ability to challenge regulatory actions. In 1893, corporations won a major victory in the case of *Noble v. Union River Logging*, which gave them Fifth Amendment due process rights against the federal as well as state governments.

7. *Citizens United v. Federal Election Commission* (2010)

8. *National Bank of Boston v. Bellotti* (1978); *Pacific Gas & Electric Co v. Public Utilities Commission* (1980)

9. *Hale v. Henkel* (1906)

10. *Hale v. Henkel* (1906)

11. *Noble v. Union River Logging R. Co.* (1903)

12. *Armour Packing Co. v. United States* (1908)

13. It cannot be forgotten that Jefferson owned slaves, and had children with Sally Hemings.

14. http://www.dfa.gov.za/foreign/Multilateral/africa/treaties/banjul.htm

15. http://www.africa-union.org/root/au/Documents/Treaties/treaties.htm

16. http://www.africa-union.org/root/au/Documents/Treaties/Text/ Protocol%20on%20the%20Rights%20of%20Women.pdf

17. http://www.africa-union.org/root/au/Documents/Treaties/Text/African_ Youth_Charter.pdf

18. These constitutions also include the civil and political rights enshrined in the U.S. Constitution. Sources: University of Richmond "Constitution Finder" (http:// confinder.richmond.edu/); Maddex (2008)

19. A constitutional review board may investigate and act on citizens' complaints that their constitutional rights have been infringed by government bodies (Maddex 2008).

20. http://www2.ohchr.org/english/law/ccpr.htm

References

Bauman, Zygmunt. 1988. *Freedom*. Minneapolis: University of Minnesota Press.

Beard, Charles A. 1913. *An Economic Interpretation of the Constitution of the United States*. New York: Macmillan.

Berlin, Isaiah. 1969. *Four Essays on Liberty*. Oxford, UK: Oxford University Press.

Blau, Judith and Alberto Moncada. 2006. *Justice in the United States: Human Rights and the U.S. Constitution*. Lanham, MD: Rowman & Littlefield.

Blaustein, Albert P. 1993. *Constitutions of the World*. Littleton, CO: Fred B. Rothman.

Bronner, Stephen Eric. 2004. *Reclaiming the Enlightenment*. New York: Columbia University Press.

Edwards, Jan. 2002. "Challenging Corporate Personhood." *Multinational Monitor* 23(10, 11). Retrieved January 7, 2011 (http://multinationalmonitor.org/mm2002/02oct-nov/oct-nov02interviewedwards.html).

Esping-Anderson, Gosta. 1990. *The Three Worlds of Welfare Capitalism*. Cambridge, UK: Polity Press.

Foner, Eric. 1976. *Tom Paine and Revolutionary America*. London: Oxford University Press.

Grimes, Alan Pendleton. 1955. *American Political Thought*. New York: Holt.

Hammerstrom, Doug. 2002. "The Hijacking of the Fourteenth Amendment." Retrieved January 7, 2011 (http://reclaimdemocracy.org/personhood/fourteenth_amendment_hammerstrom.pdf).

Human Rights Watch. 2009. "Ten Steps the Yar'Adua Administration Can Immediately Take to Improve Nigeria's Poor Human Rights Record." Retrieved January 7, 2011 (http://www.hrw.org/en/news/2009/06/05/ten-steps-yar-adua-administration-can-immediately-take-improve-nigeria-s-poor-human-).

Jefferson, Thomas. [1825] 1955. "Letter to Richard Henry Lee." P. 89 in *American Political Thought,* edited by Alan Pendleton Grimes. New York: Henry Holt.

Lauren, Paul Gordon. 2003. *The Evolution of International Human Rights: Visions Seen*. Philadelphia: University of Pennsylvania Press.

Lefebvre, Georges. 1964. *The French Revolution, Vol. II*. London: Routledge & Kegan Paul.

Locke, John. [1689] 1980. *Second Treatise of Government*. Indianapolis, IN: Hackett.

Maddex, Robert L. 2008. *Constitutions of the World*. Washington, DC: Congressional Quarterly Press.

Marshall, T. H. 1950. *Citizenship and Social Class, and Other Essays*. Cambridge, UK: Cambridge University Press.

Marx, Karl. 1859. *Economic and Philosophic Manuscripts of 1844*. Moscow, Russia: Progress.

Meyer, Carl J. 1990. "Personalizing the Impersonal: Corporations and the Bill of Rights." Retrieved January 7, 2011 (http://reclaimdemocracy.org/personhood/mayer_personalizing.html).

Morison, Samuel Eliot, Henry Steele Commager, and William E. Leuchtenburg. 1983. *A Concise History of the American Republic*. New York: Oxford University Press.

Meyers, William. 2000. "The Santa Clara Blues." Redwood Coast Alliance for Democracy. Retrieved January 7, 2011 (http://www.iiipublishing.com/alliance.htm).

Nowak, Manfred. 2000. "Civil and Political Rights." Pp. 69–108 in *Human Rights: Concept and Standards*, edited by Janusz Symonides. Burlington, VT: UNESCO and Ashgate.

Ogus, Anthony. 1990. "Property Rights and the Freedom of Economic Activity." Pp. 125–50 in *Constitutionalism and Rights: The Influence of the United States Constitution Abroad*, edited by Louis Henkin and Albert J. Rosenthal. New York: Columbia University Press.

Reich, Robert B. 2010. *Aftershock: The Next Economy and America's Future*. New York: Random House.

Sabato, Larry J. 2007. *A More Perfect Constitution: Twenty-five Proposals to Revitalize Our Constitution and Make America a Fairer Country*. New York: Walker.

Transparency International. 2009. "Corruption Perception Index." Retrieved January 7, 2011 (http://www.transparency.org/policy_research/surveys_indices/cpi/2009/cpi_2009_table).

U.S. Department of State. 2010. "Human Rights Report: South Africa." Retrieved January 7, 2011 (http://www.state.gov/g/drl/rls/hrrpt/2009/af/135977.htm).

Venter, Francois. 2008. "Globalization of Constitutional Law Through Comparative Constitution-Making." *Verfassung und Recht in Übersee* 41(1):16–31.

PART II

Citizenship, Identity, and Human Rights

8

Arizona's SB 1070

Setting Conditions for Violations of Human Rights Here and Beyond

Rogelio Sáenz, Cecilia Menjívar,
and San Juanita Edilia García

The United States has experienced major shifts in the racial and ethnic composition of its population over the last half century. In particular, due to a variety of demographic patterns alongside globalization forces stimulating the international movement of capital, goods, and people, the presence of the Latino population has increased dramatically over the last several decades. Indeed, Latinos represent the engine of the U.S. population— without Latinos, the country would be much older and would be growing at a slower rate. While the Latino population has moved into places where historically it has been absent (dubbed new-destination areas), it continues to be concentrated along the Mexico-U.S. border. As Latino immigration has expanded in the country, a common reaction has been the implementation of measures to halt it and to criminalize the immigrants' presence, and to round up and deport Latino undocumented (and, in some cases, documented) immigrants already in the country. It is in this region where we have seen the militarization of the border through increasing governmental and vigilante surveillance and the erection of walls and fences to keep immigrants out.

Arizona is the latest, and perhaps most visible, state to initiate draconian policies to apprehend and deport undocumented immigrants and to deter others from coming into the state. In 2007, Arizona passed the Legal Arizona Workers Act, a measure to identify and punish businesses that "knowingly" and "intentionally" hire unauthorized workers. The U.S. Ninth Circuit Court of Appeals upheld this policy in March 2009. More recently, Arizona passed Senate Bill 1070 (SB 1070) in April 2010. This policy requires law enforcement agents of the state of Arizona and its political subdivisions (counties, cities, and towns) to enforce and completely comply with federal immigration policies. In essence, Arizona law enforcement agents are required to carry out the functions of Immigration and Customs Enforcement (ICE) agents associated with checking the immigration status of individuals. The policy outlines the numerous offenses pertaining to SB 1070 (see below), including requiring law enforcement agents to check the legal status of an individual during a routine stop or during any "legal contact" as well as the hiring and transporting of undocumented immigrants. While many in Arizona and in other parts of the country have voiced support for the policy, many others have expressed major concerns related to the potential violation of basic human rights embedded in this law. In July 2010, Judge Susan Bolton blocked key parts of SB 1070 involving the requirement to check the immigration status of persons suspected of being undocumented. Although the more controversial portions of the law have been temporarily blocked, the effects of signing the law have reverberated through neighborhoods and meeting halls, as other states consider passing similar legislation and immigrants and their families throughout the country wait and hope that this will not be the case.

This chapter provides an overview of the policy and how it creates conditions for multiple violations of human rights, not only of immigrants but of U.S. citizens as well. The chapter has three sections. First, we discuss the demographic context in which policies such as SB 1070 in Arizona have been constructed. Second, we provide an overview of SB 1070, discuss its implications for the violation of human rights, and illustrate fears and actions that it has already generated in Arizona. Third, we suggest that the "long arm" of SB 1070 reaches beyond the confines of Arizona by illustrating how persons in other parts of the country are already facing fears and distress due to the rising anti-immigrant sentiment taking hold in the country.

Latinos and Whites and the Shifting Demography of Arizona

The United States since its inception has been a white country. Indeed, for over 150 years beginning in 1790 and ending in 1952, by barring nonwhites from citizenship, U.S. immigration policy essentially stipulated that only whites were eligible for U.S. citizenship. While many European immigrants who arrived in the United States during this period were initially viewed as nonwhite socially, there was no question that they were white legally and thus eligible for U.S. citizenship. Nonwhite racial and ethnic groups who were ineligible for U.S. citizenship but who were incorporated into the country through aggressive and forced immigration were eventually granted U.S. citizenship through the "back door." This was the case for African Americans (Fourteenth Amendment to the Constitution in 1868), Mexican Americans (Treaty of Guadalupe Hidalgo in 1848), Puerto Ricans (Jones Act of 1917), and Native Americans (Indian Citizenship Act of 1924). Other groups who were not considered white fought in the courts for whiteness and for eligibility to become U.S. citizens (see López 2006).

In this environment, to be white has meant to be included, incorporated, and welcomed, and to essentially be part of mainstream American society across its institutions. Even when groups were excluded and received with hostility, such as the case of the Irish, once they were deemed white, they became incorporated and "assimilated" into the mainstream. Thus, to be white is to be part of the "club" where one feels comfortable in one's environment; it signifies to be "normal." Indeed, whites often do not see themselves as having a race; rather it is nonwhites (read: those who are outside the mainstream) who have a race and are preoccupied with issues of race. Whites are comfortable in the space where they are the dominant group in terms of numbers, power, and leadership, for this is what is "normal." Indeed, while blacks and other persons of color regularly report that they would prefer to live in integrated settings alongside a significant portion of whites, whites prefer to live mostly with other whites. Many places including our societal institutions are "white space" where whites feel comfortable and welcome (see Moore 2008). White space then is a precious commodity for whites because it supports and sustains their power and, importantly, reproduces racial inequality.

When whites feel that this environment is altered, they feel invaded, and forces are set in motion to maintain white space and white benefits. For example, whites felt threatened by the passage of civil rights legislation in the mid- to late 1960s. Quickly we saw policies and actions taken to circumvent school desegregation, affirmative action, fair housing, and so forth. In a short period of time, gains that persons of color made through civil rights legislation were overturned. Indeed, today public schools are as segregated as they were prior to civil rights legislation, the term *affirmative action* has become taboo, and the standard inclusion of the "Affirmative Action/Equal Opportunity Employer" statement in job ads rings hollow.

It is in this context that we have seen the rise of policies and actions directed against Latinos in Arizona and throughout the country. For instance, in 2005 there were 300 bills introduced and 38 immigration-related laws throughout the country; by 2007 the numbers had increased to 1,562 bills and 240 laws (Hegen 2008). These actions have come in the form of policies involving English as the official language, attacks on bilingual education, Propositions 187 and 209, anti–affirmative action legislation, and municipal policies such as making it illegal for landlords to rent to undocumented immigrants or for day laborers, presumably undocumented immigrants, to seek work at street corners. The hallmark of these pieces of legislation is their aim to debilitate the "magnet" for immigration by relying on enforcement and the criminalization of an ever wider range of immigrant behaviors and practices. In doing so, they bar undocumented immigrants (and their families) from a wide range of public spaces where their presence is visible, those reminders that the demographic landscape of the country is changing. We now turn to the shifting demography of the state of Arizona.

The Shifting Demography of Arizona

The population of Arizona has grown significantly over the last several decades. Indeed, the state's population more than doubled from 2.7 million in 1980 to 6.5 million in 2008. During this period, Arizona rose from the 29th to the 14th most populous state in the country. The state's population expansion has increasingly been tied to growth in its Latino population. Over the period from 1980 to 2008, Latinos made up two fifths of the nearly 3.8 million people that were added to the Arizona population during this time. The Latino population more than quadrupled from nearly 441,000 in 1980 to almost 2 million in 2008 (see Figure 8.1).

Furthermore, the magnitude of the Latino population in the growth of the Arizona population has expanded progressively over time. For example, of the approximately 947,000 people added to the Arizona population between 1980 and 1990, whites constituted nearly two thirds of the change, and Latinos accounted for about one fourth (see Figure 8.2). More recently, however, of the nearly 1.4 million persons added to the state population between 2000 and 2008, Latinos accounted for nearly half of the growth compared to less than two fifths among whites.

These differences in the growth rates of Latinos and whites have led to major changes in the share of each of these groups in the Arizona population over time. The percentage of Arizonians who are Latino rose from 16 percent in 1980 to 30 percent in 2008 (see Figure 8.3). In contrast, the share of the state inhabitants who are white fell from 75 percent in 1980 to 58 percent in 2008.

Figure 8.1   Latino Population in Arizona, 1980–2008

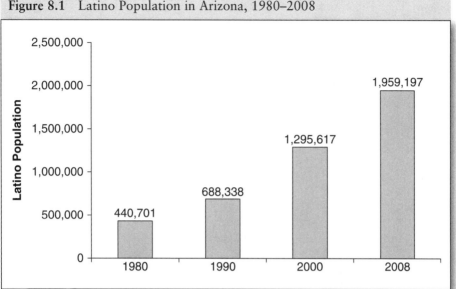

Source: Hobbs and Stoops (2002); U.S. Census Bureau (2010).

Figure 8.2   Percentage of Arizona Population Change Due to Latino and White Population Growth for Selected Periods

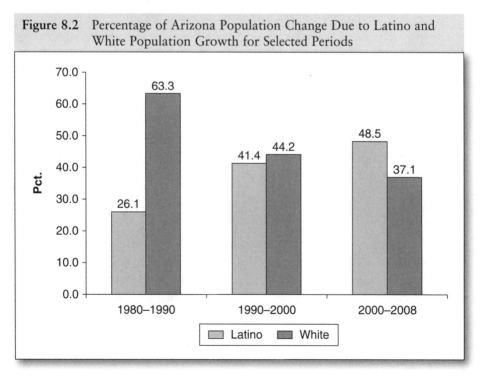

Source: Hobbs and Stoops (2002); U.S. Census Bureau (2010).

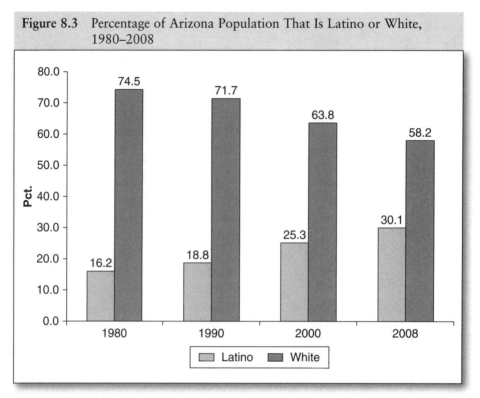

Figure 8.3 Percentage of Arizona Population That Is Latino or White, 1980–2008

Source: Hobbs and Stoops (2002); U.S. Census Bureau (2010).

The shifting demography of Arizona has been produced by variations in the age structure of Latinos and whites as well as by the increasing levels of internal and international immigration in the state.

Youthful Latinos and Aging Whites

The age structure of a population is one of the most important demographic factors associated with the magnitude and direction of population change. Populations that are young tend to produce rapid population growth as a large share of persons in the population are in or will be entering the period associated with family formation and childbearing. By way of contrast, populations that are older generally grow at slow rates or may even decline in numbers as deaths and births tend to approximate each other, or deaths outnumber births.

The Latino and white populations of Arizona differ significantly on the basis of the age structure. The median age of Latinos is 17 years younger than that of whites, with the median age of Latinos being 26 and that of whites being 43. Indeed, there is a major demographic divide between Latinos and whites across Arizona's age spectrum. Whites account for over half of the state's population beginning at age 35 and comprise at least 80 percent across elderly age categories (see Figure 8.4). In contrast, Latinos outnumber whites in the two youngest age cohorts (0–4 and 5–9). This bodes a greater presence of Latinos in the coming decades.

The varying pace of future growth between Latinos and whites in Arizona is evident in one other way—the ratio of births to deaths for Latinos and whites. In 2006, while there were 1.2 births to every 1 death among whites, there were 8.9 births to every 1 death among Latinos, reflecting the much greater youthfulness of Latinos (Centers for Disease Control and Prevention 2010; Martin et al. 2009; see also Haub 2006). As such, Latinos are growing

Figure 8.4   Percentage of Latinos and Whites in Arizona Across Age Categories, 2008

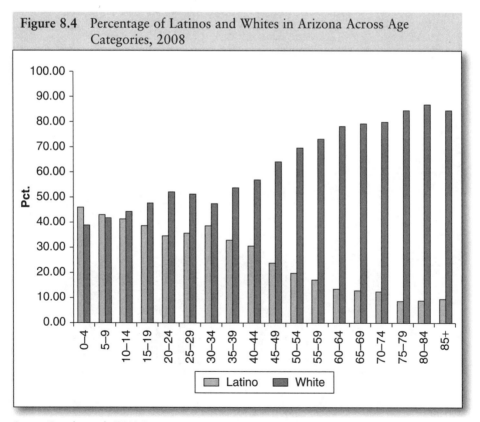

Source: Ruggles et al. (2010a).

much more rapidly in number than whites due to natural increase (births minus deaths).

Rising Latino Immigration

The Latino population is also growing disproportionately due to rising levels of immigration. Nonetheless, it is important to point out that a significant majority of Latinos in Arizona were born in the United States, with two of every three born in this country. Still, the percentage of Latinos who are foreign born increased from 18 percent in 1980 to 33 percent in 2008 (see Figure 8.5). Note that the share of the foreign-born among Latinos peaked in 2000 during this period.

A variety of factors have contributed to Arizona's rising immigration. For example, the passage of the North American Free Trade Agreement (NAFTA) in 1994 stimulated immigration to the United States as many farmers in rural areas of Mexico could not compete effectively with U.S. agriculture. In addition, starting in the early to mid-1990s, the Immigration and Naturalization Service (INS) formed blockages in California and Texas

Figure 8.5   Percentage of Latinos in Arizona Who Are Foreign Born, 1980–2008

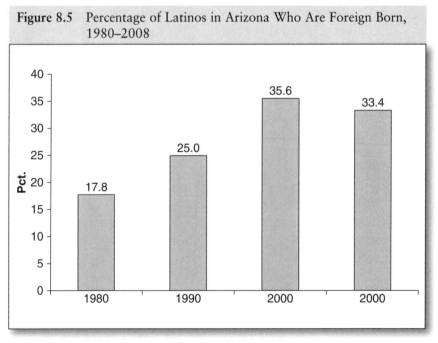

Source: Ruggles et al. (2010a, 2010b, 2010c, 2010d).

to avert the entry of immigrants in these areas, with the result being that the main entry point shifted to Arizona (see Eschbach et al. 1999). This movement of the main entry point to Arizona can be seen in the fact that more than half of foreign-born Latinos living in Arizona in 2008 entered the United States after 1994. Moreover, the weakening California economy has also pushed many Latino immigrants to other states, many to Arizona. While California's share of all foreign-born Latinos in the four border states (Arizona, California, New Mexico, and Texas) declined from 71 percent in 1980 to 60 percent in 2008, that of Arizona rose from 3 percent in 1980 to 7 percent in 2008. It is still apparent that the large majority of foreign-born Latinos in the four border states are concentrated in California and Texas.

In sum, these demographic patterns have upset the comfortable white space of Arizona for many whites. As the Latino population has expanded in Arizona, we have seen the creation of practices and policies, such as SB 1070, and the patrolling of its border by vigilante and reputed neo-Nazi groups (Amster 2010). The goals of these actions have been to halt immigration to Arizona and to round up and deport those already in the state. We now turn to our discussion of SB 1070 in Arizona, its implications for the violation of human rights, and the fears and actions that it has already generated in the state and beyond.

SB 1070 and Violations of Human Rights

After a string of laws passed in recent years that have sought to penalize the activities and behaviors of undocumented immigrants in the state, Arizona Senate Bill 1070 was signed by Governor Jan Brewer on April 23, 2010, as an attempt to get the state to cooperate with federal immigration agencies in enforcing federal law. The objective was to make "attrition through enforcement" the local policy, meaning that conditions for immigrants in the state were going to be so inhospitable that they were going to deter and discourage immigrants from coming in and create enough of a disincentive for those already in the state to leave voluntarily. Those already in the state would "self-deport." And though not the first (or last) attempt to criminalize the presence and activities of undocumented immigrants (in Arizona or in other states), SB 1070 is unique in its reach and in its inclusion of a variety of behaviors and actions associated with Latino immigrants.

The law, temporarily blocked just before it was supposed to go into effect on July 29, 2010, requires police officers to verify a person's immigration status in the course of "lawful contact" when "practicable" if there is "reasonable suspicion" that the person is an undocumented immigrant. The law included the provision that officers may not solely consider race, color, or national origin in complying with this law. House Bill 2162 amended the law; it eliminated the word *solely* (from "solely consider race") and changed "lawful contact" to "lawful stop, detention, or arrest." The law also makes it illegal for undocumented workers to seek work in public places and for employers to stop at a street to pick up and hire undocumented workers (the last two are directed at day laborers). The law specifies that in addition to committing a federal violation, a person is guilty of trespassing if the person is present on any public or private land and cannot produce an alien registration card. According to the law, it is unlawful to transport an "alien" in Arizona, and the means of transportation is subjected to vehicle immobilization or impounding. Furthermore, it would allow law enforcement agents to arrest a person without warrant if there is probable cause to believe the person has committed a public offense that makes the individual removable from the United States (Arizona State Senate 2010).

SB 1070 and the state-level laws that preceded it have a direct impact on human rights, whether directly violating them or indirectly creating conditions that lead to violations. Thus, one must remember that SB 1070 does not stand alone, as previous laws that were passed since 2004 in Arizona are still in place, as are those at the federal level, particularly the Illegal Immigration Reform and Immigrant Responsibility Act (IIRIRA) of 1996 that has facilitated the deportation of thousands. Indeed, Maricopa County (the most populous county in the state) has been one of the most vigorous users of the 287(g) agreement, a federal program that seeks to identify for deportation undocumented immigrants who have committed crimes, but that has been used mostly to conduct raids in businesses where Latino immigrants work or to carry out traffic stops in the neighborhoods in which they live. SB 1070 was passed within this backdrop, not to supersede any of these laws or independent of them but to exacerbate the effects of what was already there. It is this multipronged legal context that is ripe for the infringement of rights.

Some of the most noted local-level laws in Arizona include Proposition 200 ("Protect Arizona Now" or "Arizona Taxpayer and Citizen Protection Act"), a voter-approved initiative passed in 2004 to require proof of eligibility to receive social services such as retirement, welfare, health, disability, public or assisted housing, postsecondary education, food assistance, unemployment, or similar benefits that are provided with appropriated funds of state or local governments, and to require state and local workers to report immigration violations to federal authorities in writing. In 2006, Arizona voters approved Proposition 100, which denies bail to undocumented immigrants accused of felonious crimes; Proposition

102, which bars undocumented immigrants from collecting punitive damages in civil lawsuits; Proposition 103, which makes English the official language of the state; and Proposition 300, which denies in-state college tuition to immigrants who cannot produce proof of permanent legal residence or citizenship, and bars undocumented immigrants from accessing subsidized child care and adult education programs (Arizona Legislative Council 2006). And then in January 2008, the Legal Arizona Workers Act went into effect; it seeks to punish businesses that hire undocumented workers with severe penalties, including the suspension of a business license or its revocation for a second offense.

According to the Universal Declaration of Human Rights, a basic right of individuals is to be able to secure employment and to not be deprived of means of subsistence; it also includes the right to wages sufficient to support a minimum standard of living, equal pay for equal work, and the opportunity for advancement. Furthermore, the United Nations International Convention on the Protection of the Rights of All Migrant Workers and Members of Their Families, adopted in 1990 but not ratified by the United States (or any of the wealthy nations that receive immigrants today), stipulates that migrant workers and members of their families should have the right at any time to enter and remain in their country of origin and that migrant workers or members of their family should not be subjected to arbitrary or unlawful interference with their privacy, family, home, correspondence, or other communications, or to unlawful attacks on their honor and reputation. It affirms that migrant workers and members of their family shall have the right to the protection of the law against such interference or attacks, and that they are not to be subjected individually or collectively to arbitrary arrest or detention (Menjívar and Rumbaut 2008). This convention also stipulates that migrant workers and their children should have access to a range of social services, such as educational institutions, vocational guidance, placement services, and training on the basis of equality of treatment for their children.

There are several provisions of SB 1070 that directly infringe on individuals' universal rights, but in the interest of space we will only address those that directly affect workers. The Arizona laws that target on one hand the business owners who hire undocumented immigrant workers (Legal Arizona Workers Act 2007) and on the other the workers themselves who seek employment (SB 1070) directly infringe on this right. SB 1070 goes further, as it penalizes different activities associated with day labor work, a specific kind of employment that is common among Latino immigrants. Thus, it does not penalize all workers in the same way but seeks to be particularly punitive of day laborers, a group mostly composed of immigrant and/or Latino workers. The multipronged legal system in place today has created conditions that impinge directly and indirectly on the rights of immigrants as workers, and it has done so from multiple angles in a way that slowly asphyxiates the efforts of those who are seeking dignified employment in the state.

In addition to addressing the "supply side" (by seeking to deter immigrants from coming to or staying in Arizona) as well as the "demand" (by penalizing employers who hire immigrants, an action that was already punishable under federal law, the Immigration Reform and Control Act of 1986), it creates conditions for immigrants to become more vulnerable and to live more clandestine lives. Fear of detection, for instance, is a powerful force that can keep immigrants from reporting abuses and crime, from seeking services and help when needed, and even from sending their children to school. Importantly, even though the law cannot overtly target Latinos, by going after the jobs that they are likely to take and focusing on neighborhoods where they live, the law essentially aims to drive out Latino immigrants. And it does so by creating a climate of fear and insecurity for them. As Olivas (2007) argues, in a critique of these "pigtail ordinances in modern guise, . . . the blowback in affected communities, and the resultant prejudice sure to follow from [them] . . . are sure signs of an ethnic and national origin 'tax' that will only be levied upon certain groups, certain to be Mexicans in particular, or equally likely, Mexican Americans."

Immigrant workers in Phoenix live with this sense of insecurity on a daily basis. A Guatemalan woman in Phoenix told Cecilia Menjívar that when they go clean model homes at night, she and her husband never ride together in the same car for fear that they might be stopped and sent to a detention center, and separated from their children. In her words,

> Look, Cecilia, this situation is scary; it gives us fear. Every day, I don't lie to you, it's constant. So no, we don't drive together. What if we are stopped and we get deported? We'll be taken to jail, right? And the kids, what? Who'll take care of them? Who's going to stay with them? We worry; we live anguished. So he goes in one car, with our neighbor, and I go in another one, with my cousin. The same when we go to the market. He goes in one car and I go in another. So no, we try to never, no, we're never in the same car. Never. Who knows what can happen. We need to be careful. We must take precaution.

In addition, workers become more vulnerable to abuses. Even though they recognize abusive practices, such as not getting paid overtime, not being paid what was agreed for a job, or receiving regular threats of being fired, they know they have few places to go. They are cognizant that reporting an abusive employer will bring them to the attention of the authorities, and thus, they do not take the risk. A Salvadoran woman recounted the time when her husband was told to stop by and pick up what he was owed by his boss. "'On Thursday, I'll pay you on Thursday.' But Thursday, there was nothing. And another Thursday went by and nothing." When asked if she was afraid her husband would not be paid at all, the woman said, "That's the thing. You never know because there are people who work and don't get paid. The boss closes the business or says that he has no money. And what can one do? Go to the police to file a complaint? Go to the sheriff [laughs]?" Obviously, unscrupulous employers are well aware that in today's climate, very few of these workers, if any, will turn them in to the authorities.

Thus, the context that a law like SB 1070 creates violates immigrant workers' rights by closing options for work, by making the context so inhospitable that workers will leave, but also by pushing the workers into more vulnerable situations ripe for abuse. However, SB 1070 has attracted the attention of politicians in other states, and even in other countries, who quickly started to contemplate whether similar policies could be implemented in their jurisdiction. Indeed, a few days after the governor of Arizona signed SB 1070 into law, legislators in approximately 22 other states, including Alabama, Colorado, Delaware, Florida, Idaho, Indiana, Maryland, Michigan, Minnesota, Mississippi, Missouri, Nevada, North Carolina, Ohio, Oklahoma, Oregon, Pennsylvania, Rhode Island, South Carolina, Texas, Utah, and Virginia, declared their intent to introduce similar legislation (Waslin 2010). In the process, just the consideration of implementing such laws sends a message to Latino immigrant communities across the country. Thus, the fear and insecurity that immigrants experience in Arizona are not contained within the state borders; SB 1070 is creating similar experiences in states where similar laws are being considered.

The Reach of SB 1070 Beyond Arizona

The anti-immigrant movement and sentiment that abounds perpetuates racism and the devaluation of immigrants and even those who *appear* to be immigrants (Romero 2006). In the current anti-immigrant climate, being an undocumented immigrant, or just an immigrant, has major implications for immigrants and their families. The meaning, stigma, and experiences of undocumented immigrants especially today may also affect not only the immigrant community but the Latino community overall, including U.S.-born Latinos/Latinas (Romero 2006). Given the rise of anti-immigrant sentiment coupled with the increase in enforcement as evident by the augmentation of raids, deportations, and anti-immigrant legislation, we argue that this further excludes and marginalizes undocumented immigrants by putting daily strains and structural barriers in their lives. Moreover, we argue that these constant pressures ultimately have a significant impact on their mental health, specifically contributing to feelings of distress.

In this section, we present the voices of undocumented Mexican immigrant women to illustrate how policies such as SB 1070 send a widespread message that causes distress in immigrant communities throughout the United States. The voices of these women portray sentiments of fearing the police and immigration officials, or of being separated from their families due to deportations. They fear being apprehended or questioned by police or immigration officials. This constant fear, similar to experiences of the couple in Phoenix mentioned above, contributes to feelings of living in the shadows, imprisoned, secluded, limited, and hidden.

These findings from Houston, Texas, have implications for the mental health of immigrants particularly with respect to how anti-immigrant hostility contributes to feelings of fear and subjugation. More specifically, our observed patterns reveal the social significance of undocumented status and how the unequal social structure of the United States prevents the integration of these women. We now provide data from interviews conducted with undocumented Mexican immigrant women in Houston to show that the effects of policies like SB 1070 are not contained solely in the states where they are passed but become a powerful message sent to immigrants across the United States.

Take, for instance, Zenaida, a 23-year-old immigrant from Guanajuato. Her words capture the fear she constantly lives with due to her undocumented status. Living in an anti-immigrant climate in a society where racism is ingrained and shapes other dynamics creates fear and distress that affect the lives and minds of individuals. An increase in hate crimes toward immigrants, the militarization of the border, draconian legislative policies, and so forth demonstrate how the current climate further pushes to the margins an already marginalized community. Zenaida shares the following:

> I feel sadness and fear at the same time. I'm always with that fear that something may happen, like if the police stop me, or that immigration will be there and I won't be able to make it home or if I'm not with my kids . . . I'm scared . . . I'll always be with that fear, sadness, and frustration . . . You become frustrated because you can't do anything . . . like you can't fix your papers to be here legally.

"Fear Consumes Us"

Living with constant fear is a daily reality for undocumented immigrants, as well as for their documented and U.S.-born relatives. Study participants in Houston spoke about a fear of being apprehended by immigration or police officials—they expressed feeling closed in, limited, or imprisoned. They described the raids, the mass deportations, the roadblocks in immigrant communities, and the militarization of the border enforced by the U.S. government. For example, Liliana, a 28-year-old woman who migrated to the United States as a tourist, overstayed her visa, and was then considered an undocumented immigrant but later obtained legal residency via marrying a third-generation Mexican American, provides an example of living with fear. When asked to describe retrospectively how she felt when she was undocumented, she stated the following:

> You don't go to many places, like to other states, because you think you'll get stopped. In other words, you stay in the same circle, doing the same thing. It's sadder. You feel like you're in prison but bigger because you drive to go buy groceries, you take the kids to school, and you bring them back but you continue to feel like you don't belong here.

Liliana describes what it was like living as an undocumented immigrant. She describes feelings of isolation and seclusion and not being able to live worry-free. She relates her experiences of living in the United States as an undocumented immigrant to living in a prison, describing how she must remain within the same circle, such as going to buy groceries and taking her children to and from school. She also describes feeling as if she is not wanted in the United States. Later in her interview, she vocalized the existence and presence of anti-immigrant views particularly against Mexican immigrants.

Liliana's description, along with other respondents' similar sentiments, is reminiscent of a song titled *"La Jaula de Oro"* by *Los Tigres del Norte* (The Tigers of the North). *Los Tigres del Norte,* a norteño genre group, represent the voice of the working-class communities in Mexico and of Latino immigrants in the United States (Ragland 2009). *"La Jaula de Oro"* is about an undocumented Mexican immigrant man who has been in the United States for 10 years. In this song, the United States is portrayed as a great but confining nation, a "golden cage." This metaphor relates to feeling confined in a golden cage that remains a prison particularly for the undocumented population or for those who hold uncertain legal statuses and find themselves in legal limbo. This song personifies the ways in which respondents described what it meant to live in the United States as an undocumented immigrant.

Going further in describing what it means to live in constant fear among immigrants is Deyanira from Nuevo León, who states, "You're fearful. You feel scared like if the police stop you, like lately even the police officers can ask for people's Social Security [number]." Although policies like SB 1070 are not in effect in Houston, they nevertheless send a chilling message to the city. Since July 20, 2008, the Harris County Sheriff's Office has agreed to enforce the 287(g) program in Houston (U.S. Immigration and Customs Enforcement 2010, n.d.). Section 287(g) allows local law enforcement officials to question the immigration status of the community working in conjunction with ICE agencies. The implications of legislative policies such as these are discomforting for the Latino community, and especially for the undocumented population.

Anti-immigrant legislation demonstrates intolerance and racism. Furthermore, legislation such as SB 1070 and similar laws will only increase and legitimize racial profiling. It is evident that individuals who appear to be of Latin descent are likely to be stopped and questioned about their citizenship or residency status. As is reminiscent in Deyanira's quote, the fear of being apprehended by local law enforcement is fierce, a concern that is likely to heighten tension and distrust between the undocumented immigrant community and law enforcement.

The fear of being stopped and questioned by police or immigration officials is a reality for many immigrants. Participants regularly reported being scared of police and immigration officials who had conducted raids, roadblocks, and deportations in the Houston area. Zenaida, one of the immigrants mentioned above, stated that living as an undocumented immigrant is living "with fear, fear that they'll get you in a roadblock, for instance that they'll be outside the apartment complex asking for your papers, for your Social Security [number]. One feels like you are always hiding, like you always live with fear of going anywhere." She actually lived through that experience when she was driving to her apartment. She described the logistics and location of the roadblock:

> There were about four cop cars on the corner . . . I was coming through here and the police was right here [as she drew the logistics of the situation] and then the cars came this way and the cops signaled them to go over where they were at. Another car and I were signaled to keep going . . . Yes, I have been so close to those roadblocks, and yes, I am extremely scared because I don't have a license. I only have my [Mexican] consulate ID card . . . I was so scared and frightened because I had my three children with me. I felt so scared and said I

will never drive through that route. I will never go through there anymore because there are too many cops.

This fear of being stopped by police officers expressed numerous times by respondents indicates how legislation like the 287(g) agreement heightens tension between the local law enforcement officials and the undocumented population. This has major implications for a number of contacts with authorities, including reporting crimes. Crime reporting is already a problem in minority communities as individuals do not always trust authorities (Menjívar and Bejarano 2004). This legislation exacerbates this situation and may prevent undocumented immigrants from calling the police for the fear of being deported. For example, Zenaida had been a victim of domestic violence, and she shared that she never reported her husband even though he had hit her numerous times before. She believes her neighbor called law enforcement officials because she never sought help from them due to the fear of being deported. Her husband had been deported to Mexico three weeks prior to the date she was interviewed. Zenaida was struggling to decide what would be the best outcome for her and her children given her status as an undocumented immigrant, as a single mother, and as having only limited family support in the United States. Given these circumstances, she was contemplating returning to Mexico. This is only one example that shows how restrictive policies can heighten fear of authorities and the police among the undocumented population.

Consistent with the sentiment of being fearful of having her undocumented status discovered, Daniela, a 31-year-old immigrant, states the following:

> You feel secure [with papers] but since I don't have papers you have to put up with things because the last thing you want is to be noticed. You don't want this country to find out that you are here. You don't want anyone to find out. It's like they say: We live in the shadows. We live in the shadows so that no one, not police officers, not immigration, not the government, not anyone, should know that we do not have papers.

Again the theme of feeling isolated and constrained reappears. Daniela makes the comparison to living in the shadows or in confinement. She describes living life as far from public view as possible. She also makes a connection of having to endure certain things for the fear of being found out. This type of seclusion could lead to a worse situation, particularly when these immigrants have been the victims of crime. Eugenia, a 39-year-old undocumented immigrant from the state of Coahuila, also described being undocumented as living in the shadows. In her words,

> Living in the shadows is living with fear . . . living in, like they say, in the shadows and darkness . . . It means you cannot live freely . . . You can't even go out freely to the stores, to run errands, because you are always fearful that they will deport you.

Again, we see how prevalent the fear of being deported is and what it means to live in the United States as an undocumented person. This constant fear has been intensified especially in the post-9/11 enforcement era. What it means to be an undocumented immigrant now, in a negative, anti-immigrant context of reception, has major implications for all immigrants, undocumented or not. For instance, there are serious implications from living in a constant state of fear for individuals' mental and overall health. Additionally, these implications play a major role in the integration process of immigrants and their children. Feelings of having to hide and of fear on a routine basis can have detrimental health consequences. Living with constant fear and internalizing social injustices without being able to speak up or challenge them is similar to the concept of "racial battle fatigue," which has been found to have severe health impacts (Smith, Allen, and Danley 2007).

Smith and colleagues (2007) introduce the concept of "racial battle fatigue" to address "the physiological and psychological strain exacted on racially marginalized groups and the amount of energy lost dedicated to coping with racial microaggressions and racism" (p. 555). Moreover, the feelings immigrants experience today, described in the above quotes, impact the ways in which immigrants integrate into U.S. society. These quotes show the fear that undocumented immigrants face daily, a fear of being deported and of the consequences should they be deported.

Conclusion

Over the last couple of decades, communities and states have created policies to deter immigrants from migrating into these areas and to encourage those already in place to leave due to the fear of being apprehended and deported. The state of Arizona is the latest to establish such policy with the signing of SB 1070 in April 2010. This chapter has provided an overview of the context in which SB 1070 and related policies have been constructed. We argue that the disproportionate growth of the Latino population has led to whites feeling that their comfort associated with white space where they are in control and where inequality is reproduced is being assaulted. As a way to reconstruct white space and to protect privileges that come with whiteness, policies such as SB 1070 have been put in place. The rabid anti-immigrant sentiments in the country along with the expansion of the Latino population in areas away from the Mexico-U.S. border will likely lead to the enactment of similar policies elsewhere.

We also provide an overview of SB 1070. As we show, this law did not emerge in isolation in Arizona but has been part of a larger effort beginning a few years earlier to make Arizona an uncomfortable and unwelcoming place for immigrants and, more generally, Latinos. We show the fear that SB 1070 has already generated in the local Latino community and emphasize the potential it has for violating the basic human rights of Latinos in Arizona. Moreover, we argue that SB 1070 and similar policies have a long reach as their effects are felt beyond the confines of the states in which they are formed. In particular, we provide an illustration of the fear and apprehension that Mexican immigrant women in a setting outside of Arizona—Houston, Texas—report as they lead their daily lives in an environment that increasingly targets them for apprehension and deportation.

Thus, we have shown how anti-immigrant and draconian policies such as the recent SB 1070 serve to dehumanize unauthorized immigrants and their families. The constant fear felt by undocumented immigrants and even U.S.-born Latinos is a social reality that violates human and constitutional rights. Fear is a form of oppression that limits, belittles, and confines Latino immigrants. Policies such as SB 1070 send a national and even international message, one that relates and paints the United States as a nativist, racist, and anti-immigrant country, particularly targeting Latino immigrants. In this sense, the current immigration regime and its implementation can be conceptualized as "legal violence" (Menjívar 2009).

This chapter shows how immigrants are racialized and demonstrates the social costs associated with undocumented immigrants living in a nativist and racist society and how this ultimately affects their psychological well-being. This chapter contributes to a timely reality that Arizonians and, even more broadly, Latino immigrants are facing given their marginalized position in the social structure. This group endures discrimination at every turn, but heightened nativism among anti-immigrant groups, alongside enforcement policies, makes undocumented immigrants much more vulnerable for deportation. In this hostile context, the Mexican-origin population is particularly at risk for negative mental health outcomes. Yet, scant attention has been given to the relationship between this social environment and ethnic minority mental health outcomes (Vega and Rumbaut 1991; Viruell-Fuentes 2007). Particular attention needs to be placed on a vulnerable group that continues to be marginalized and oppressed (Viruell-Fuentes 2007).

Specifically, in addressing the social ills that contribute to a system of inequality where currently undocumented Mexican immigrants are targeted, we encourage scholars to focus on the unequal and racist society that immigrants enter and on how undocumented immigrants are not provided with the necessary resources to successfully integrate into society. Therefore, by failing to consider the larger social factors that impact people's lives differently depending on their social locations—their structurally unequal position in society based on their undocumented status, along with their race/ethnicity, class, gender, sexual orientation, and so forth—our discourse holds people of color responsible for their positions in society and reinforces prevailing ideas of individualism and meritocracy (Romero 2008). It is imperative to focus on the structural factors and ideological processes that have limited and continue to limit the opportunities for groups of color in the United States.

Discussion Questions

The International Convention on the Protection of the Rights of All Migrant Workers and Members of Their Families was adopted by the United Nations General Assembly in December 1990.

By 2010 it had 31 signatories and 43 parties, but these participating states did not include wealthy states, such as the United States, that attract migrants. Below are extracts from that long and complex international treaty.

1. Please discuss the global economics and politics that probably motivated UN state actors to craft this treaty. Why is it long? Why is it complex?

2. This treaty not only has legal ramifications for state parties, but it also provides a very humanistic perspective on the well-being of vulnerable people. How can we think of laws as being humanistic? Or motivated by humanistic concerns?

3. Article 36 attempts to distinguish state responsibilities to undocumented and documented workers. Discuss how clear or ambiguous this is.

International Convention on the Protection of the Rights of All Migrant Workers and Members of Their Families

Adopted by General Assembly Resolution 45/158 of 18 December 1990
(http://www2.ohchr.org/english/law/cmw.htm)

Article 5

For the purposes of the present Convention, migrant workers and members of their families:

(a) Are considered as documented or in a regular situation if they are authorized to enter, to stay and to engage in a remunerated activity in the State of employment pursuant to the law of that State and to international agreements to which that State is a party;

(b) Are considered as non-documented or in an irregular situation if they do not comply with the conditions provided for in subparagraph (a) of the present article.

Article 7

States Parties undertake, in accordance with the international instruments concerning human rights, to respect and to ensure to all migrant workers and members of their families within their territory or subject to their jurisdiction the rights provided for in the present Convention without distinction of any kind such as to sex, race, colour, language, religion or conviction, political or other opinion, national, ethnic or social origin, nationality, age, economic position, property, marital status, birth or other status.

Article 14

No migrant worker or member of his or her family shall be subjected to arbitrary or unlawful interference with his or her privacy, family, correspondence or other communications, or to unlawful attacks on his or her honour and reputation. Each migrant worker and member of his or her family shall have the right to the protection of the law against such interference or attacks.

Article 22

1. Migrant workers and members of their families shall not be subject to measures of collective expulsion. Each case of expulsion shall be examined and decided individually.

Article 25

1. Migrant workers shall enjoy treatment not less favourable than that which applies to nationals of the State of employment in respect of remuneration ...

(Continued)

(Continued)

Article 36

Migrant workers and members of their families who are documented or in a regular situation in the State of employment shall enjoy the rights set forth in the present part of the Convention in addition to those set forth in part III.

Article 43

1. Migrant workers shall enjoy equality of treatment with nationals of the State of employment in relation to:

   (a) Access to educational institutions and services subject to the admission requirements and other regulations of the institutions and services concerned;

   (b) Access to vocational guidance and placement services;

   (c) Access to vocational training and retraining facilities and institutions;

   (d) Access to housing, including social housing schemes, and protection against exploitation in respect of rents;

   (e) Access to social and health services, provided that the requirements for participation in the respective schemes are met;

   (f) Access to co-operatives and self-managed enterprises, which shall not imply a change of their migration status and shall be subject to the rules and regulations of the bodies concerned;

   (g) Access to and participation in cultural life.

References

Amster, Randall. 2010. "Climate of Fear: SB 1070 and Extremist Violence on the Arizona Border." *Commondreams*, July 27. Retrieved January 15 (http://www.commondreams.org/view/2010/07/27-12).

Arizona Legislative Council. 2006. "2006 Ballot Proposition Analyses." Retrieved January 10, 2011 (http://www.azleg.state.az.us/2006_Ballot_Proposition_Analyses/).

Arizona State Senate. 2010. "Fact Sheet for S.B. 1070." January 15. Retrieved September 5, 2010 (http://www.azleg.gov/legtext/49leg/2r/summary/s.1070pshs.doc.htm

Centers for Disease Control and Prevention. 2010. "Compressed Mortality File Underlying Cause of Death: Mortality for 1999–2006 with ICD 10 Codes." Atlanta, GA: Author. Retrieved January 20, 2011 (http://wonder.cdc.gov/wonder/help/cmf.html).

Eschbach, Karl, Jacqueline M. Hagan, Nestor Rodriguez, Ruben Hernández-León, and Stanley Bailey. 1999. "Death at the Border." *International Migration Review* 33:430–40.

Haub, Carl. 2006. "Hispanics Account for Almost One-Half of U.S. Population Growth." Washington, DC: Population Reference Bureau. Retrieved July 21, 2010 (http://www.prb.org/Articles/2006/HispanicsAccountforalmostOneHalfofUSPopulationGrowth.aspx).

Hegen, Dirk. 2008. "2007 Enacted State Legislation Related to Immigrants and Immigration." Washington, DC: National Conference of State Legislatures.

Hobbs, Frank and Nicole Stoops. 2002. "Demographic Trends in the 20th Century, Census 2000 Special Reports, Series CENSR-4." Washington, DC: U.S. Census Bureau.

López, Ian Haney. 2006. *White By Law: The Legal Construction of Race*. Revised and updated 10th anniversary ed. New York: New York University Press.

Martin, Joyce A., Brady E. Hamilton, Paul D. Sutton, Stephanie J. Ventura, Fay Menacker, Sharon Kirmeyer, and T. J. Matthews. 2009. "Births: Final Data for 2006." *National Vital Statistics Reports* 57(7). Hyattsville, MD: National Center for Health Statistics.

Menjívar, Cecilia. 2009. "Latino Immigrant Workers and Legal Violence in Phoenix, Arizona." Paper presented at the "Migration during an Era of Restriction Conference," University of Texas, Austin, November 4–6.

Menjívar, Cecilia and Cynthia Bejarano. 2004. "Latino Immigrants' Perceptions of Crime and of Police Authorities: A Case Study from the Phoenix Metropolitan Area." *Ethnic and Racial Studies* 27(1):120–48.

Menjívar, Cecilia and Rubén G. Rumbaut. 2008. "Rights of Migrants." Pp. 60–74 in *The Leading Rogue State: The United States and Human Rights*, edited by Judith Blau, David L. Brunsma, Alberto Moncada, and Catherine Zimmer. Boulder, CO: Paradigm.

Moore, Wendy Leo. 2008. *Reproducing Racism: White Space, Elite Law Schools, and Racial Inequality*. Lanham, MD: Rowman & Littlefield.

Olivas, Michael A. 2007. "Lawmakers Gone Wild? College Residence and the Response to Professor Kobach." Public Law and Legal Theory Series, 2007-A-51, University of Houston, Texas. Retrieved January 10, 2010 (http://ssrn.com/abstract=1028310).

Ragland, Cathy. 2009. *Música Norteña: Mexican Migrants Creating a Nation Between Nations*. Philadelphia: Temple University Press.

Romero, Mary. 2006. "Racial Profiling and Immigration Law Enforcement: Rounding Up of Usual Suspects in the Latino Community." *Critical Sociology* 32(2):447–73.

Romero, Mary. 2008. "Crossing the Immigration and Race Border: A Critical Race Theory Approach to Immigration Studies." *Contemporary Justice Review* 11(1):23–37.

Ruggles, Stephen, J., Trent Alexander, Katie Genadek, Ronald Goeken, Matthew B. Schroeder, and Matthew Sobek. 2010a. "Integrated Public Use Microdata Series: Version 5.0" [Machine-readable database: 2008 American Community Survey Sample]. Minneapolis: University of Minnesota. Retrieved July 21, 2010 (http://usa.ipums.org/usa/index.shtml).

Ruggles, Stephen, J., Trent Alexander, Katie Genadek, Ronald Goeken, Matthew B. Schroeder, and Matthew Sobek. 2010b. "Integrated Public Use Microdata Series: Version 5.0" [Machine-readable database: 1980 5% Public Use Microdata Sample]. Minneapolis: University of Minnesota. Retrieved July 21, 2010 (http://usa.ipums.org/usa/index.shtml).

Ruggles, Stephen, J., Trent Alexander, Katie Genadek, Ronald Goeken, Matthew B. Schroeder, and Matthew Sobek. 2010c. "Integrated Public Use Microdata Series: Version 5.0" [Machine-readable database: 1990 5% Public Use Microdata Sample]. Minneapolis: University of Minnesota. Retrieved July 21, 2010 (http://usa.ipums.org/usa/index.shtml).

Ruggles, Stephen, J., Trent Alexander, Katie Genadek, Ronald Goeken, Matthew B. Schroeder, and Matthew Sobek. 2010d. "Integrated Public Use Microdata Series: Version 5.0" [Machine-readable database: 2000 5% Public Use Microdata Sample]. Minneapolis: University of Minnesota. Retrieved July 21, 2010 (http://usa.ipums.org/usa/index.shtml).

Smith, William, Walter R. Allen, and Lynette L. Danley. 2007. "Assume the Position . . . You Fit the Description: Psychosocial Experiences and Racial Battle Fatigue Among African American Male College Students." *American Behavioral Scientist* 51(4):551–78.

U.S. Census Bureau. 2010. "2008 American Community Survey 1-Year Estimates, Detailed Tables." Retrieved July 21, 2010 (http://factfinder.census.gov/servlet/DTGeoSearchByListServlet?ds_name=ACS_2008_1YR_G00_&_lang=en&_ts=303827884148).

U.S. Immigration and Customs Enforcement. 2010. "Delegation of Immigration Authority Section 287(g) Immigration and Nationality Act." Washington, DC: Department of Homeland Security. Retrieved January 20, 2011 (http://www.ice.gov/news/library/factsheets/287g.htm).

U.S. Immigration and Customs Enforcement. N.d. "Memorandum of Agreement." Retrieved January 20, 2011 (http://www.ice.gov/doclib/foia/memorandumsof AgreementUnderstanding/r_287gharriscountyso111609.pdf).

Vega, William A., and Rubén G. Rumbaut. 1991. "Ethnic Minorities and Mental Health." *Annual Review Sociology* 17:351–83.

Viruell-Fuentes, Edna A. 2007. "Beyond Acculturation: Immigration, Discrimination, and Health Research among Mexicans in the United States." *Social Science & Medicine* 65:1524–35.

Waslin, Michele. 2010. "SB 1070-Inspired Activity Continues in the States." Washington, DC: Immigration Policy Center. Retrieved September 26, 2010 (http://immigration impact.com/2010/08/19/sb1070-inspired-activity-continues-in-the-states/).

9

Beyond Two Identities

Turkish Immigrants in Germany

Tugrul Keskin

Human migration has been an important phenomenon throughout history with critical impacts on populations and events. Societies and ethnic groupings and tribes are not static, but migrate from one place to another for economic, cultural, and political reasons. Therefore, immigrants have never been far from the center of domestic and international political discussion. The immigration issue shapes and informs the heart of the modern state structure and its definition of citizenship. Over time, the interaction between the state and immigrant communities challenges and modifies the essence of national identity. A more flexible national policy takes into account the inevitable challenge from globalization and human mobility, and will enable the society to adapt and respond. This chapter examines the identity of immigrants in relation to citizenship, through the lens of the case of Turkish immigrants in Germany.

There are three levels of political and social actors to consider in the citizenship and immigration issue. One is immigrant identity, the second is national identity, and the third is supranational identity of the European Union or other forms of supranational identity. A starting point for an analysis of national identity should account for the mutually constitutive relationship that exists between the state and its immigrants; the state shapes and is also shaped by immigrant identities. It is a relationship that takes time to form and solidify, and at the end of the process, a third identity emerges—both for the state and for the immigrant community. Each is somehow responsible for shaping the other in immutable ways. In the more successful cases, a nation-state responds with a fluid and open approach, and in other cases, the response is more rigid and exclusive. The rigid response is in practice most likely to disregard the cultural and political rights of immigrant communities, and it is in response to some of the more rigid practices and their negative consequences, as well as more social practices that are not directly addressed by the legal system, that the International Convention on the Protection of the Rights of All Migrant Workers and Members of Their Families was conceived, and is aimed to remedy.[1]

The International Convention on the Protection of the Rights of All Migrant Workers and Members of Their Families was established by the General Assembly of the United Nations in 1990 to ensure the protection of the rights of immigrants across borders. The convention protects immigrants from cultural, religious, and other forms of discrimination in the workplace, and guarantees them equal status with state nationals in such diverse areas as their conditions of work and terms of employment; access to education, vocational guidance, and placement services; access to housing, social, and health services; and access to and participation in cultural life. This convention was adopted in 1990 with the explicit recognition that "the rights of migrant workers and members of their families have not been sufficiently recognized everywhere and therefore require appropriate international protection" (Article 14). The convention also references the awareness "of the impact of the flows of migrant workers on States and people concerned, and desiring to establish norms which may contribute to the harmonization of the attitudes of States through the acceptance of basic principles concerning the treatment of migrant workers and members of their families" (Article 11). This is presumably with the understanding that the continuous flow of populations across national borders is an international issue that should be addressed at the supranational level.

Immigration movements became a focus of national and political identity in the twentieth century because of the creation of the nation-state in Europe. The nation-state emerged as a by-product of capitalism and industrialization, as a model of national identity based on territoriality because of the creation of the domestic market and the need for labor. The nation-state is therefore directly linked to territorialization of society, politics, and economy in this era. This process in turn fueled national domestic immigration, and led to the emergence of industrial cities in Europe. However, in the second part of the twentieth century, the discovery of the international market and the development of global capitalism produced another type of immigration: cross-border and cross-regional immigration. One of the most important examples of this is the Turkish immigration to Germany.

In later periods of twentieth-century European history, the nation-state model was characterized by de-territorialization, and the increased power of supranational institutions such as the European Union and supranational associations such as multinational corporations and institutions on international diplomatic territory including the World Bank, the International Monetary Fund, and the United Nations. This new set of challenges has prompted national reforms and changes to laws and regulations that provide an ever-expanding concept of citizenship. The model of national identity has slowly shifted to what I describe as a de-territorialized model, based more on economic than on traditional territory-based characteristics. These shifts have taken place as a direct consequence of globalization and the weakening power of the nation-state. When powerful global actors challenge the rigid nation-state, its borders (territoriality) become less stable, and as a result, the social cohesiveness of national identity is redefined by new powerful economic structures—even though according to some scholars, such as Ernest Gellner and Eric Hobsbawm, the nation-state is a by-product of capitalism, and social and political actors are dominant in the marketplace. Since the state is the key element in the economy in the early stages of capitalism, national identity is based on social and political territoriality. However, in global capitalism, the state loses its control over economic actors, and these actors modify the role of the state and redefine social and political characteristics. Hence, these dynamics are in some cases challenging the structure of national identities and in other cases eliminating them. In contrast to the state rhetoric and its desire to have one cohesive national identity, it is instead confronted with ethnic diversity and multiculturalism, which challenges the idea of nationality based only on territory.

National identity that was once based on nationality alone is now replaced with an identity characterized more easily by citizenship. This type of identity is more diverse and multicultural in character and enables a broader concept that takes into account and gives rights to populations that migrate and therefore may have citizenship in a nation but not belong to that nation in terms of their national identity. After all, the greatest consequence of globalization is that different ethnic and minority groups live, are educated, and work together, but this does not make them "American" or "Turkish" or "German."

Global capitalist culture interacts with and eliminates more traditional types of social structures and cultural forms of organization. For example, Turkish "guest workers" as they are called in Germany, Mexican immigrants in the United States, or Tamil political asylum seekers in Canada are each influenced by the same cultural icons. They each like to watch the sitcom *Friends* on television; they are all affected by increasing gas prices or by expensive health care and in so doing move further away from traditional forms of association. In this context, territoriality-based national identity is being threatened by global capitalist culture and its consequences. Therefore, identity has become a problematic issue for the nation-state, particularly in Europe, as it becomes more fluid in a region struggling with a vast amount of immigration and having a difficult time keeping pace with changes, including a changing concept of national identity.

A useful case study to demonstrate these dynamics is the Turkish immigrant identity in Germany within the larger context of the European Union. It is important to understand the social, political, and cultural structures of the Turkish immigrant population in Germany and its relationship to the decreasing power of the nation-state due to globalization, migration, and the European Union. This research looks at the relationship between nationality, ethnic identity, and citizenship among Turkish immigrants, within the larger context of the relationship between Germany and the European Union.

Turkish guest workers have been in Germany for decades. At first, they were considered to be short-term visitors or foreign workers, a much-needed labor pool for post–World War II reconstruction in Germany. The plan was that guest workers were to return to their home country after some time, but this plan, as it was understood at the time by the German government and immigrant communities alike, did not actually take place. Immigrants were unable to earn enough money to comfortably return home, and so the waves of migration continued without any parallel repatriation of immigrant groups back to Turkey. The Turkish immigrant community grew exponentially, as the breadwinners in Turkish households played a central role in bringing more members of their immediate family to Germany, and replicated the model of the large interdependent Turkish family within their new environment. The next generation of Turks, specifically those born in Germany, were the sons and daughters of immigrants and torn between two national identities. Not completely Turkish, having been born in Germany, and yet not allowed to be German citizens, the situation of Turkish immigrants may be described as follows: "Even where new, immigrant communities equipped with their own historic cultures have been admitted by the state, it has taken several generations before their descendants have been admitted (in so far as they have been) into the circle of the nation and its historic culture through the national agencies of mass socialization" (Smith 1991:11).

The German government did not expect Turkish immigrants to form a permanent community in Germany. In this case, citizenship regulations are extremely inflexible, although there have been small modifications in recent years. These regulations have also followed a more complex and rigid trajectory than in most European nation-states. From the years 1913 to 1999, German citizenship was based not on territory, but on blood connection. A German citizen was anyone of direct German blood descent, regardless of where in the world an individual lived. This policy completely disregarded any citizenship rights of those who had migrated to Germany until the year 2000, when the prior citizenship law was repealed. This was the ultimate exclusionist approach to nationality and citizenship, because no one who descended from a country other than Germany could become a citizen, regardless of contribution to society, taxpaying, or any other form of participation. For example, after the collapse of the Soviet Union, Germans who were forced to migrate to Kazakhstan by Stalin after World War II and were not born in Germany and had never lived in Germany were granted German citizenship in 1991, whereas Turkish guest workers living there more than 20 years did not have citizenship. This is a clearly exclusionist approach to citizenship and did not demonstrate any intention to integrate immigrants.

The new German citizenship regulations that took effect as late as the year 2000 have a more territoriality-based model of citizenship. Immigrants can become German citizens today even if they are born to non-German parents, if one parent has had a permanent residence permit for at least three years and has been residing in Germany for at least eight years. This new model takes into account time spent in Germany and not German descent. Today, 10 years after the more moderate citizenship laws took effect, Germany is dealing with an even more complex set of issues. Germany has since had to review the realities that have been imposed by the continuing waves of immigrants. The current concept of German national identity is more closely characterized by citizenship. German citizenship now takes into account populations that migrated many years ago, but this development has been a long time coming, and German society is having a difficult time in its late absorption of diverse populations. This can be seen in many facets of society, including the residential segregation of immigrant populations. Article 43 of the International Convention on the Protection of the Rights of All Migrant Workers and Members of Their Families addresses this issue as follows: "Migrant workers shall enjoy equality of treatment with nationals of the State of employment in relation to access to housing, including social housing schemes, and protection against exploitation in respect of rents." Article 25 of the convention also addresses the issue of rights to equal treatment in the workplace: "Migrant workers shall enjoy treatment not less favourable than that which applies to nationals of the State of employment in respect of remuneration and: (a) Other conditions of work, that is to say, overtime, hours of work, weekly rest, holidays with pay, safety, health . . . (b) Other terms of employment, that is to say, minimum age of employment, restriction on work and any other matters which, according to national law and practice, are considered a term of employment."

Due to economic, cultural, and political circumstances, the influx of Turkish "guest workers" has become a central issue in German politics and has generated a challenging problem for German identity in the public sphere. Today, Turks are not guest workers anymore. Even though they establish and own businesses, participate fully in the German education and political system, and no longer have the status of "immigrant," they are still extremely segregated socially. This presents a dilemma for German identity in the public sphere because there are now many segregated German identities instead of the earlier state objective of one cohesive whole.

While the more traditional politicians and power-holders cling to the old concept of nationality, challenges to this concept are coming from within and also from without—from external factors. Within the country, there are now several generations of immigrant populations that have set up their homes and raised families in Germany. The second and third generations of immigrant children are German citizens, are educated in German schools, speak the German language, attend German universities, work in German companies, and pay taxes to the nation-state. Increasingly, they celebrate both German and Turkish cultural events and holidays and participate in society as German citizens do. But this has only been in place for a mere 10 years, and full integration is very slow.

Important external factors also come into play concerning the European Union and the additional complexity this adds to the concept of national identity. The German nation-state has been weakened in some sense due to membership in the European Union. As just one example, Germany changed its immigration and citizenship laws in part due to EU pressures regarding citizenship policies. Certain aspects of German national identity have been relinquished, and some token economic and political decisions are now made above the nation-state at the European level.

The European Union may in fact be a key element that will shape and reconstruct the citizenship identity in Europe as it wrestles with navigating the challenge of continuing waves of immigrants throughout Europe. Although the European Union has successfully expanded its membership to include states that would benefit in economic, security, and political terms, there have also been significant challenges in this process. These challenges arise from states that may not have the same cultural or legislative traditions, and may therefore have more difficulty fulfilling their membership requirements. The Eastern European and Mediterranean states are two such regions that have presented significant dilemmas for the union in its establishment of a common set of values. The case for their being included among the states that are obviously "European" has been harder to make. Essentially, the "European identity" has become something of an enigma as the union has continued to enlarge, and this set of dynamics has trickled down to the microcosm of the nation-state. Interestingly, Germany has been the most vocal opponent of including Turkey in the European Union, even though its largest immigrant population is Turkish.

Today in Europe, there is an emerging supranational identity that has been called Eurocentrism. Fuchs, Gerhards, and Roller (1996) argue that "the constitutive points of reference are for the construction of being part of a supranational state, and secondly the awareness of partaking in a shared European culture" (Martiniello 1996:176). Moreover, the authors assert that the differentiation between immigrant identity and national identity creates an "us versus them" discourse; however, as various waves of migration from different cultures continue, this identity is constantly changing. The boundary of who is part of the nation and who is not is therefore being challenged from within the state, and also externally at the European level. Fuchs et al. (1996:167) state that "while a shift of the external boundary between 'us' and 'them' could be expected as a result of western European integration, the migration waves should provoke a change in the definition of 'others' within the nation state." In essence, the authors suggest that the process of increased immigration may generate the construction of a new and much broader Eurocentric identity. The boundary between "us" as national citizens and "them" as noncitizens is continually blurred and renegotiated.

Globalization and Immigration

Examined in a broader perspective, the issue of national identity in the globalized world extends beyond the case of Germany. The renowned ethnopolitical scholar Anthony D. Smith (1991) asserts that territoriality is important to building national culture and identity in the globalized world order. Furthermore, he argues, "the US is a prime example of the territorial national type of political community and of the power of territorial nationalism" (p. 150). According to this view, the United States is an example of a new form of national identity that is based on territoriality, rather than ethnic and cultural origin. On the other hand, and in stark contrast to this idea, Samuel Huntington (2004) claims that ethnic origin and cultural unity should be considered vital elements of the American identity, and refers to the cohesion of the white Anglo-Saxon Protestant identity. Huntington's view is similar to the approach taken by nation-state models of identity, in the sense that ethnic origin and cultural identity play a more central role than territory and citizenship.

Huntington (2004) examines national identity in the American nation-state. His definition of American identity is highly divisive because he does not accept multiculturalism as an inclusive approach, in which a nation opens its doors freely to other cultures. Rather, he asserts that multiculturalism is likely to be exclusionist in practice, because ethnic and cultural groups are forced to adapt and assimilate and in effect must leave behind their ethnic and cultural identity in order to do so. Huntington's approach presupposes the cultural unity rather than the diversity of American society. Accordingly, he blames the Mexican community for not being able to assimilate into Anglo-Protestant culture. The United States is understood to possess an independent cultural and political identity only in the event that different ethnic groups are able to adapt and assimilate to Anglo-Saxon culture. In effect, Huntington believes that American society is defined by a dominant cultural identity and that all others should try and emulate this one best practice. This is the melting pot analogy, and the idea that all groups shed their unique ethnic identities in favor of an American identity.

According to Huntington (2004), the cohesiveness of the American identity is at risk of domination by other cultural identities, particularly in the case of Spanish immigrants: "The inflow of immigrants would again become highly diverse, creating increased incentives for all immigrants to learn English and absorb US culture. And most important of all, the possibility of a de facto split between a predominantly Spanish-speaking United States and an English-speaking United States would disappear, and with it, a major potential threat to the country's cultural and political integrity."

It is useful to delve into why the existence of a large Spanish-speaking population would be perceived as a threat to the cultural and political integrity of the United States. After all, a large percentage of Spanish-speaking citizens cannot in itself be a problem. In most cases, when the first generation of immigrants does not speak English immediately, the chances are very good that the children of immigrants will. Huntington's (2004) perspective regarding American identity is only one viewpoint; other scholars view American cultural and national identity more inclusively to account for a variety of ethnicities and cultural identities as a normal fact of life in a multicultural society.

Mexican immigrants in the United States, Turkish immigrants in Germany, and immigrants in the wider European context have had similar experiences with multiculturalism in their respective societies, because there are common elements and dynamics at work on the national and supranational level. Scholars such as Raymond Aron asserted 20 years ago that "there are no such animals as European citizens. There are only French, Germans, or Italian citizens" (Meehan 1993:2). Today, Aron's view is under discussion among the immigrant community as well as political leaders and parties in Europe. According to his view, the nation-state is undergoing a transformation. It is not *disappearing* from the political arena, but is being re-formed within the structure of the European Union. Importantly, the relationship between immigrant communities and their host countries is one issue that will determine the future identity of the European Union and the role of the nation-state within the union.

As an additional source of comparison on these themes of national and pan-national identity, Yasemin Soysal (1994) argues that Europe recruited the foreign labor force specifically as a temporary solution for its labor needs. Despite the objectives of this early initiative, foreign workers have now become permanent fixtures on the respective national landscapes, and consist of large communities in all European countries. Immigrants participate in the educational system, welfare programs, and labor markets of their host countries. They have also become an important part of political circles; they join political parties and trade unions, among other political interest groups. Soysal uses the term *guest workers* to describe immigrants; however, this term is a poor one for immigrants who are likely to be taxpayers of their respective countries. Soysal describes the role of the citizenship model in contemporary Europe. According to her view, there is a new citizenship model that has been shaped by more recent, post–World War II immigrant realities in Europe. She describes this new model as one of "postnational citizenship." This is unlike and more inclusive than other models, which attempt to account for and describe the consequences of massive immigration at the beginning of this century to the United States, Canada, and Australia. Soysal (1994) defines the postnational model as one that provides "every person the right and duty of participation in the authority structures and public life of a polity, regardless of their historical or cultural ties to that community" (p. 3). This new model appears to rely much more on the idea of individual rights than the nation-state model of old Europe. What matters is not the cultural or historical ties to any particular national or ethnic community, but rather that the individual belongs to and participates in a particular political sphere or polity. This in itself provides the citizen with rights.

Migration Theories and the Construction of Immigrant Identity

Migration theories are discussed within many disciplines including sociology, economics, geography, demography, and political science. The movement of large populations has had a significant impact on each of these fields of study. Migration as a movement has had demographic implications on the societies that have experienced the greatest impacts. Mass migration is able to change and influence the social, political, and economic structure of a nation, country, and society. Jackson (1986) claims that "migration must involve a distinct social transition involving a change of status or a changed relationship to the social as well as the physical environment" (p. 4). Therefore, there is always a social reaction to immigration, which will involve the renegotiation of identity. He furthermore argues that migration can be either temporary or permanent. This issue of longevity—how long a group intends to remain in its host country—is a key element in this process and how it is responded to.

When Turkish guest workers arrived in Germany at the beginning of the 1960s, they were considered temporary immigrants. Today, after a few decades have passed, they have become permanent immigrants. Another example of this kind of longevity in patterns of migration might be the Pakistanis and Hindus in England. They have followed a very similar pattern to the Turkish immigrants in Germany; several generations have been born and raised in England. The adaptation and integration of these ethnic groups to their "host" countries has become a very complicated issue, and this process has had both positive and negative consequences for the immigrant community and the U.K. government. These groups have been an important source of low-cost labor for certain sectors of society in the United Kingdom, and have filled jobs that British nationals have been less willing to pursue; however, these groups have also had more trouble assimilating to British society. The groups themselves have done well economically within certain limits of economic operation and have been successful at exploiting and operating in low-income niches and predominantly operate in the running of newsstands and newsagents. However, movement beyond these lower economic sectors has been more difficult. It is still likely that these groups have fared better economically than they would fare in their country of origin.

There are many reasons for a group to migrate from its country of origin to a host country. The causal factors for migration should be taken into consideration by a host country, and should in part determine its reaction to each case. Causes may include migration for voluntary, forced, internal, or international reasons or perhaps cases of return migration. Voluntary migration describes a situation in which a person decides to undertake his or her own move, and economic factors most frequently play the largest role in the decision-making process in this type of migration. Forced migration describes a situation in which people are forced to migrate either internally or internationally because of persecution or to escape mass killing of minority groups. This is an example of politically motivated migration. The best examples of forced migration are the Muslim groups in Bosnia and the population exchange between Turks and Greeks in Cyprus.

The internal migration model applies most frequently to groups that migrate or have been forced to migrate for either political or economic reasons. Migration from the rural to the urban side of the country is a good example of an internal migration process that corresponds to economic factors. Examples of international migration such as Turkish workers in Germany or Mexican immigrants in the United States also are most often economically motivated.

A comprehensive understanding of the complexity surrounding the issue of migration would involve economic factors and their relationship to theories of migration. Alan A. Jackson divides economic factors into two different categories based on where a group migrates to, and where it migrates from. These two categories are described as "push and pull factors." The push factors involve a lack of access to land, lack of employment, low wages, wasted land, drought and famine, and population increase. The most important element of the pull factors is the attractiveness of the destination city or country. Jackson (1986) asserts that "the basic push-pull model for migration behavior drawn from classical economic theory is closely related to the theory of the labor market" (p. 17). The more advanced labor markets in Western Europe and the United States have drawn immigrants from more underprivileged regions. These factors are intricately connected to the labor market. Easterners are able to move within their own country to the more developed urban areas or cities, and one step beyond this pattern of immigration would involve migration to developed cities in another country.

Host nations are concerned about the issue of immigration for many reasons. The immigration process has resulted in some of the most important demographic changes in recent years, and this trend has had many impacts on the social and political structure of societies. International migration in particular may have both negative and positive impacts on the social and demographic structure of a country, and will be likely to escalate and exacerbate many of the preexisting social and economic tensions and conflicts in that society. As just one example of the vast implications of immigration flows to a nation, Jackson (1986) argues that "in demographic terms the age and sex structure may be substantially altered and this may distort the age and sex balance if there is a specific sustained flow. Apart from demographic considerations the implications for the social, cultural and economic life of the community at each end of the spectrum must be considered" (p. 40). A nation that is dealing with changes in age or sex balance as a result of increased patterns of migration must be prepared to address these issues in its handling of policy and community challenges. These are considerations that domestic politicians must take into account in the domestic policy of a nation and that European politicians must also take into account at the European level.

Historical Overview of Turkish Immigrants in Germany

Germany was beginning to recover from World War II at the end of the 1950s. As a result, the German economy needed a strong labor force from which to draw resources. Part of this reconstruction effort required menial labor that the upper ranks and certain groups of German society were unwilling to participate in. This meant that the types of labor required would need to be drawn from a foreign labor force that was willing to accept low wages for menial tasks. This took place only after the available and willing German workforce had been exhausted.

Today, 2.5 million Turks live in Germany, a nation that consists of roughly 82 million people. The Turks began to settle in Germany in 1961, following agreements that were made between the two nations. In the first few years following World War II, millions of mainly German refugees arrived in West Germany from East Germany and Eastern Europe. They provided the labor that was needed to rebuild the postwar German economy. However, by the late 1950s and early 1960s, this supply proved to be insufficient, so the government began to look abroad to poorer countries of Southern Europe.

In 1961, there were approximately 500,000 job vacancies, and this same year, Germany and Turkey signed the "Guest-worker Agreement," so state-contracted flows of Turkish labor started and 6,800 Turkish workers arrived in Germany in order to make money and then return home in better economic conditions (Sen 2003). Poorer countries of Europe such as Italy, Spain, Portugal, Greece, Yugoslavia, and Turkey sent workers to Germany during the 1960s and 1970s. The citizens of these countries accepted the employment that was available to them in Germany very easily, as they had no jobs or their jobs at home did not pay enough. This population consisted mainly of single men without families who wanted to use the opportunity to work abroad to learn new skills and, more important, to earn higher wages. "The immigrants dreamed of earning good money, starting a small business and then going back to a more secure life back at home. Germany was insistent in its invitation and the workers were greeted enthusiastically during these years of fast economic growth, when labor was short in supply" (Ardagh 1995:274). It was not only Germany that benefited from the situation. The governments of the labor-supplying countries also benefited from the migration because it helped to minimize high levels of unemployment in their countries; the expatriates would send deutsche marks into the country to their families or would bring them when they returned home, and this would provide a boost to the economy of their country of origin. The host country was also able to train workers for free, and it was expected that some of these trained workers would return home eventually.

In 1970, the German economy was doing well again, and thus even more immigrants were needed. However, by that time, the Greek, Italian, and Spanish economies were improving, and Greece and Spain became members of the European Community in 1981 and 1986, respectively. Parallel to this, labor supplies from these countries were also drying up, and many Italians, Spanish, and Greeks were returning home. Therefore, the Bonn government turned to the best alternative source of labor, which was Turkey. Because of domestic problems in the Turkish economy with wages, work conditions, and high unemployment rates, Turkish workers stayed far longer in Germany than they had planned to stay.

At the end of 1973, with the oil crisis and the first signs of recession, the German government imposed a ban on further recruitment from outside of the European Community. However, this ban had a paradoxical effect. Whereas it did succeed in reducing the number of active foreign workers from 2.6 million in 1973 to 1.9 million in 1983, the overall foreign population continued to rise in the same period from 4 million to 4.6 million, then to 4.8 million in 1990 (Ardagh 1995), and to nearly 7.5 million today. Knowing they would lose their work permits once they left Germany for more than three months, many of the immigrants decided to settle, bringing their wives and children with them. Ironically, despite the ban, the overall Turkish population rose from 1.028 million in 1974 to 1.581 million in 1982, 1.6 million in 1990, and 2.5 million in 2002. This increase was the direct result of continuous inflows of family members as well as high birth rates. Accordingly, "Today, family dependants account for 60% of the total foreign worker population, while in the 1960s 90% of the workers were single men" (Ardagh 1995:276). The law that was adopted in 1983 encouraged foreign workers to return home with their families permanently, and had a similar paradoxical effect on the number of foreigners. The German government tried to reduce the number of immigrants, but again its efforts were not effective. What took place instead was an increase in the number of immigrants in Germany due largely to external factors.

Many Turkish people in Germany decided to stay as a result of improving conditions in Germany for them. The benefits of remaining in Germany, despite initial problems of first- or second-generation adaptation, outweighed the benefits that would be gained by returning to Turkey. Therefore, immigration continued, and immigrant groups remained in Germany: "Since the Second World War, more than 30 million people have moved to Germany, including millions of ethnic German refugees, asylum seekers, 'guest workers,' and their families" (International Organization for Migration n.d.). Today, Turks constitute the largest group of foreigners, making up 30 percent of all foreigners living in Germany.

Today, 7.3 million immigrants live in Germany, which amounts to approximately 8.9 percent of the total German population. In its *State of World Population 2006* report, the United Nations Population Fund lists Germany as hosting the third-highest percentage of international migrants worldwide. Recent studies have shown that many of the early immigrants from the mass migration that began in the early 1960s remain in Germany: "At the end of 2002 around two thirds of these immigrants had been living in Germany for eight years or longer. One third had been resident in the Federal Republic for more than 20 years. More than two thirds of the children and young people descended from immigrants living in Germany were born here, too."[2]

Despite the large number of Turkish immigrants who decided to remain in Germany, they were always seen as temporary guests. As a consequence, the term *gastarbeiter*—meaning "guest workers"—was routinely applied to them. This understanding of immigrant workers led consecutive German governments to avoid adopting policies of work and immigration that would allow further absorption of such groups into German society.

Exclusion of Immigrants From German Society

One of the most important social implications of immigration is a process of long-term exclusion of immigrant communities from central parts of society in "host" nations. Scholars conclude that exclusion of ethnic minorities from political participation has led to racism in its different forms being experienced in different ways in all of the European countries (see, for example, Martiniello 1996). This exclusion itself has perpetuated the cycle of alienation of minority immigrant groups from society and has led to a situation in which migrant groups exist on the fringes of society, and do not have the political power necessary to address their own concerns and needs.

The alienation of migrant groups from core parts of society has led to patterns of racism and xenophobia. Xenophobia and racism come mainly from economically disadvantaged groups that view the foreign workforce as a threat to their own levels of employment. Social and political factors such as exclusion and alienation intensify these latent problems: "Racism, violence and exclusion are many factors that influence the definition and structuring of minority groups. In 1984 the murder of two young Turks by skinheads impelled Keskin to create the Union of Turkish Migrants of Hamburg" (Kastoryano 2002:132). Political groupings such as this are able to represent the interest of Turkish immigrants, and are critical to the welfare of German Turks. They also lend political legitimacy that the German government does not provide to minority groups such as the Turks.

The Turkish immigrant population in Germany is looked at as a group that is there due to economic necessity, and these immigrants are a known element whose work is seen as critical to the running of certain sectors of German economic life. However, as a group they are not well liked and are poorly assimilated into German social and political structures.

Between Two Cultures: Almanci

The situation of Turkish guest workers in Germany has always been a problematic issue for both Germany and Turkey. Besides their difficulty with adaptation and integration into German society, these individuals have faced cultural difficulties in Turkey as well, when they return or visit. Because most of the guest workers from the end of the 1950s and beginning of the 1960s were from the rural side of Turkey, culturally they were more traditional and religious in comparison to other segments of Turkish society. The term *Almanci*, or *Germanist*, is widely used in Turkey to describe Turkish guest workers in Germany. These populations therefore face criticism and alienation in their country of origin and are not fully able to belong to either society.

Islam as a Reactionary
Identity Among Turkish Immigrants

The role of religion cannot be ignored in the context of the relationship of different ethnic identities within the nation-state. It is one more layer of complexity that is added to the experience of immigrant communities both by the immigrants themselves and by the host nation. In the case of immigrants with a different religion that arrive in a host nation, this has the potential to cause cultural and religious clashes between communities. A common reaction by immigrant groups is to identify themselves by looking at groups that are most different from them and then to use reactionary mechanisms to justify their own cultural and religious identity. This is a process in which the outward differences that immigrant communities face every day exacerbate the insecurity of living in a new land and living far from family and traditions. The reaction of these groups tends to be to seek comfort as close as possible to home, by observing cultural traditions perhaps more closely than they would have in their country of origin, and by seeking validation of their understanding and experience. This can be described as a "pulling in" where immigrant groups collaborate closely in all facets of life and cling more tightly to traditional facets of their cultural, ethnic, or religious life than they may otherwise be inclined to do in their country of origin.

Religion is another facet of identity that is used as a reactionary mechanism, and can involve symbolism and extremism. Of this tendency, author Yasemin Soysal (1997) claims that

> a significant outcome of the postwar labor migration has been Europe's rediscovery of Islam. In response to vitalization of religious associational life among immigrants, there has been arisen a visible interest in Islam as an object of political cultural curiosity and scientific inquiry. On the axis of Birmingham, Marseilles, and Berlin, the experience of Pakistani, Maghrebine, and Turkish migration reveals the counters of Muslim community formation within European democracies to researchers, politicians and the public. At issue is the compatibility of Islam—its organizational culture and practice—with European categories of democratic participation and citizenship. Formation of Islamic community is identified as either a divisive, anti-democratic threat or a contribution to the political and cultural plurality of Europe. (P. 509)

Because Turkish immigrants are not able to participate fully in the social and political lives of their host communities, their reaction has been to draw further inward to the associational life within their communities. One of the mechanisms they have used to do this has been to focus on their religious identity, and to form associations with others based on religion. "Whether or not European states recognize Islam as an official religion, Islamic groups are allowed to organize under public law as regular associations. One consequence has been the proliferation of religious organizations that practice and advocate Islam in its most radical forms" (Soysal 1997:509). In response to their separation from German society, their tendency has been to radicalize their identity based on religion and religious affiliation. This provides a community to an otherwise alienated group.

Unwanted Immigrants in the European Union

After the Soviet Bloc collapsed, one result was the formation of new and accelerated political and economic forms of unity among the European nation-states. Importantly, the stated goal of the European Union is to produce a transnational system and identity based on a common set of values and social and human rights that its citizens can be responsible to and responsible for.

From a cultural perspective, however, some scholars have argued that the European Union may be conceptually more of a Christian "cultural club." If this is the case, then we must assume that the European identity to those who believe this is the case is based on religion. Cultural arguments for the European identity that favor an emphasis on common descent and shared history have been numerous and well documented. These references have ranged from a focus on the Christian foundations of the European Union, to those that focus on shared political histories. On the other hand, more leftist politicians argue that European identity is geographical and historically not culturally based.

Throughout the last 30 years, the immigrant population in Europe, especially from Muslim-populated countries, has grown dramatically. Turkish immigrants in Germany and France; Moroccan, Tunisian, and Algerian immigrants in Spain, Italy, and France; Indian and Pakistani immigrants in England; and Albanians and Bosnians in Germany are just a few examples, and these groups and the associated dynamics have changed the social and cultural structures in Europe. The impact of immigrants on European social, economic, and political structures cannot be ignored. The citizens of what has been referred to as Old Europe had different, more insular, and more traditional values than new European citizens (Keskin and Watkins 2008:217). The new trend of Europe is more globalized and diverse, more tied to the economic interests of Europe, and less tied to culture and heritage.

Conclusion

The issue of national and immigrant identity in Europe has reached a turning point. Within the European Union, there are many thousands of immigrant and minority groups to integrate socially and politically, and nation-states have come to realize that the concept of national identity must shift to account for and reflect greater diversity. This is the model for a new, more open and inclusive Europe, guided by a new third identity, that is both national and guided by a supranational and regional identity solidified through common rights and responsibilities.

Germany has a unique case of identity problems with respect to its immigrant population. This relationship provides valuable lessons and may contribute in an important way to the larger project of creating new citizenship models within the European Union and its component nation-states that are more flexible and inclusive.

A few decades ago, the Turkish guest workers went to Europe as a labor force for the capitalist market. Today, they still act as a valuable source of labor. But they also contribute greatly as citizens of European countries. Whereas they did not have much influence on the political landscape of Germany 30 years ago, today they are better educated and work side by side with Germans—in some cases entering German politics and even the parliament.

Discussion Questions

1. How do diverse forms of identity—including but not limited to immigrant identity, national identity, European identity, and other forms of supranational identity—interact with one another? Is one form of identity more salient than another, and if not, why not?

2. What does it mean to describe the existence of a "mutually constitutive relationship" between the state identity and its immigrant communities? How is the state shaped by its immigrants?

3. What types of rights are protected by the International Convention on the Protection of the Rights of All Migrant Workers and Members of Their Families, and which rights may be harder to identify and protect/enforce in practice?

4. How does the German model of citizenship compare and contrast to the American model historically? Which may be more effective in protecting the rights of immigrant communities, and why?

5. Why is there a need for a supranational convention on the human rights of migrant communities? Why may it not be sufficient to address the issue of migrant rights purely on a case-by-case basis, according to national policies?

Notes

1. http://www2.ohchr.org/english/law/cmw.htm
2. http://www.unfpa.org/swp/2006/english/introduction.html

References

Ardagh, John. 1995. *Germany and Germans*. London: Penguin Books.

Fuchs, Dieter, Jürgen Gerhards, and Edeltraud Roller. 1996. "Nationalism versus Eurocentrism? The Construction of Collective Identities in Western Europe." Pp. 165–78 in *Migration, Citizenship and Ethno-National Identities in the European Union*, edited by Marco Martinello. London: Ashgate.

Huntington, Samuel. 2004. "The Hispanic Challenge." *Foreign Policy*, March–April. Retrieved January 12, 2011 (http://www.foreignpolicy.com/articles/2004/03/01/the_hispanic_challenge).

International Organization for Migration. N.d. "Germany." Retrieved January 16, 2011 (http://www.iom.int/jahia/Jahia/germany).

Jackson, Alan A. 1986. *Migration: Aspect of Modern Sociology*. New York: Longman.

Kastoryano, Riva. 2002. *Negotiating Identities: States and Immigrants in France and Germany*. Princeton, NJ: Princeton University Press.

Keskin, Tugrul and Sharon Watkins. 2008. "Redefining the State and Society in the March Toward Europe." Pp. 215–38 in *Turkey-European Union Relations: Dilemmas, Opportunities and Constraints*, edited by Meltem Muftuler-Bac and Yannis A. Stivachtis. Boulder, CO: Rowman & Littlefield.

Martiniello, Marco, ed. 1996. *Migration, Citizenship and Ethno-National Identities in the European Union*. London: Ashgate.

Meehan, Elizabeth. 1993. *Citizenship and the European Community*. London: Sage.

Sen, Faruk, 2003. "The Historical Situation of Turkish Migrants in Germany." *Immigrants and Minorities* 22:208–27.

Smith, Anthony D. 1991. *National Identity*. Las Vegas: University of Nevada Press.

Soysal, Yasemin Nuhoglu. 1994. *Limits of Citizenship: Migrants and Postnational Membership in Europe*. Chicago: University of Chicago Press.

Soysal, Yasemin Nuhoglu. 1997. "Changing Parameters of Citizenship and Claims-Making: Organized Islam in European Public Spheres." *Theory and Society* 26:509.

PART III

Vulnerability and Human Rights

10

The Rights of Age

On Human Vulnerability*

Bryan S. Turner

Introduction: Vulnerability and the Body

There has been much discussion in recent decades about the possibility of "life extension," namely the idea that the application of new medical technologies can dramatically extend life and in addition help people overcome the disabilities typically associated with old age (Callahan 2009). The prospect of a radical, if not revolutionary, change in the human life span raises intriguing questions about the rights of such geriatric survivors and their entitlements in relation to the generations that come after them. The issue of the relationship between human rights and generational rights is, however, strangely absent from much of the utopian literature on technology and aging that is in the so-called immortalist project for indefinite prolongevity (de Grey 2008). Perhaps more surprisingly, the problems of aging populations and the consequences for human rights and obligations have also been largely absent from the human rights literature, which has

---

*This chapter first appeared in a different form in *Vulnerability and Human Rights*, by Bryan S. Turner, 2006, University Park: Penn State University Press; and *Can We Live Forever? A Sociological and Moral Inquiry*, by Bryan S. Turner, 2009, London: Anthem.

been focused more on dramatic violations of rights associated with genocide, war, and natural disasters than on the humdrum infirmities of the elderly. Nevertheless, as I shall argue here, the victims to whom human rights are typically addressed share one important thing in common with the elderly and the frail, namely their human vulnerability (Turner 2006).

An aging population is a fundamental fact of all developed societies. Consider the United States. According to data from the National Center for Health Statistics in August 2009 (Centers for Disease Control and Prevention 2010), in 1900 the average life expectancy for Americans at birth was 47.3 years, but by 2007 that figure had risen for all groups (white females, nearly 81 years; black females, nearly 77 years; white males, 76; and black males, 71). However, the United States was ranked 27th out of 37 countries in the health survey, demonstrating the lack of adequate health coverage, inadequate welfare provisions, and significant income inequality. The life extension project of modern medicine promises even more significant increases in life expectancy, but does it promise longevity equally?

My critical assessment of the immortalist project of indefinite prolongevity is based on four fundamental assumptions about human existence: the vulnerability of all human beings as embodied agents, the interdependency of humans (especially during both the early and late stages of the life cycle), the overarching reciprocity or interconnectedness of social life, and finally the precariousness of social institutions. There is a dialectical relationship between these four components that becomes obvious when one thinks about the process of technological modernization. Within this complex balance among vulnerability, dependency, reciprocity, and precariousness, modern technologies, especially medical technologies, have powerful and far-reaching implications. Medical innovations have obviously beneficial consequences for health, but they are largely disruptive of the relationship among these four social components. If our shared embodiment is the real source of our common sociability, then changes to embodiment must have implications for both vulnerability and interconnectedness. The new microbiological revolution in medical sciences holds out the promise of "the mirage of health" (Dubos 1959), including the prospect of "living forever"; it is driven by a powerful commercial logic and has (largely unrecognized) military and security applications and implications that are problematic for human rights and democracy. New medical procedures such as therapeutic cloning, new reproductive technologies, regenerative medicine, stem cell research applications, procedures to cryonically freeze patients, fetal surgery, and organ transplants create the possibility of a medical utopia, but they also as a matter of fact reinforce social divisions and inequalities, especially between rich and poor societies. Medical advances make no direct or automatic contribution to social equality, and often create new social hierarchies and divisions.

Human beings are ontologically vulnerable and socially insecure, and their natural environment is often inhospitable. In order to protect themselves from such uncertainties in the everyday world, they must ongoingly build social institutions (especially political, familial, and cultural institutions) that come to constitute what we call "society." We need trust in order to build companionship and friendship to provide us with the means of mutual support. We depend upon the creative force of ritual and the emotional ties of common festivals to renew social life and to build effective institutions, and we need the comforts of social institutions as means of fortifying our individual existence. Because we are biologically vulnerable, we need to build political institutions to provide for our collective security. These institutions are, however, themselves precarious and cannot work without effective leadership, political wisdom, and good fortune to provide an enduring and reliable social environment. Rituals typically go wrong, social norms offer no firm blueprint for action, and the guardians of our social values—priests, academics, lawyers, and others—turn out to be open to corruption, mendacity, and self-interest. However, these afflictions and uncertainties of everyday life also generate intersocietal patterns of dependency and connectedness, and in psychological terms, this shared world of risk and uncertainty creates conditions that can, but do not always, result in sympathy, empathy, and trust, without which society would not be possible. All social life is characterized by this contradictory and delicate balance between scarcity, solidarity, and security (Turner and Rojek 2001). The development of such institutions as the rule of law, citizenship, and human rights is an essential ingredient of a social and political framework to provide some degree of security as a defense against our inescapable vulnerability. Human beings do not stand, however, in a fixed or stable relationship to these institutions; because all human beings are themselves passing through time and toward the end of their individual trajectory, they are invariably frail and characteristically disabled. Any study of human rights needs to take into account the passage of individuals and generations through time and hence their ever-changing relationship to society and its (fixed) resources. Modern medical utopian thought promises to change this relationship between time and society.

Following Pierre Bourdieu (2000) in his *Pascalian Meditations*, we acquire practical reason through the everyday use of our bodies and come to assume a habitus that expresses our tastes or preferences for various goods, including symbolic goods. In the process of creating this habitus, we also develop a reflexive self that is always expressed through embodiment. Our selfhood is reflected in the peculiarities of our own embodiment; our eccentricity is articulated through these practices and our habitus. Two processes—embodiment and "enselfment"—express the idea that mind and body are never separated. Who we are is a social process that is always constructed in terms of a particular experience of embodiment. Suffering (the loss of dignity) and pain (a loss of comfort) are always intertwined, and so vulnerability is both a physical and a spiritual condition. Finally, our experience of the everyday world involves a particular place and time—a location within which experiences of the body and our dependency on other humans unfold. The emphasis on the temporal nature of our social being is taken from Martin Heidegger's (1962) account of *Being and Time* in which the concept *Dasein* or literally "there-being" specifies the temporality of being in space. Heidegger's philosophy of being-in-time perfectly conceptualized the inevitable contingency of human existence. Given the ineluctable contingency of the everyday world, embodiment is crucial for our sense of identity, security, and continuity. Human beings need comfort in order to experience security, certainty, and confidence. As a result, serious human rights violations typically involve some attack on the body through torture and deprivation, an assault on the dignity of the self through psychological threat, and some disruption to place through confinement or exclusion (imprisonment, rendition, deportation, seizure of land, and exile). Human rights abuses disrupt, disconnect, and destroy the conditions that make secure or stable embodiment possible.

Human rights are often discussed in relation to traumatic and dramatic events—the Holocaust, the Balkan crisis, the Armenian massacres, or the conflicts in Darfur. The ordinary grinding and routine problems of aging, frailty, and geriatric disabilities are somewhat neglected. As a feature of human frailty, our ontological vulnerability includes the idea that human beings of necessity have an organic propensity to disease and sickness, that death and dying are inescapable, and that aging bodies are subject to impairment and disability. The human life cycle is characterized by its finite possibilities, and hence, it is inescapably tragic. As a result of these conditions, human beings are through their life cycle involved in various relationships of dependency. Arnold Gehlen (1988) employed Nietzsche's aphorism that we are "unfinished animals" to develop an anthropological view of the frailty of human beings. Given this incompleteness, human beings need to build institutions to compensate, as it were, for their lack of instincts. Human beings are characterized by their "instinctual deprivation," and as a result they do not have a stable structure within which to operate.

These arguments about vulnerability and precariousness can be given an economic dimension by grasping the relationship between vulnerability and economic studies of environment. In his *Entropy Law and the Economic Process*, Nicholas Georgescu-Roegen (1971) argued that waste is an unavoidable aspect of the development process of modernization, and that human beings inevitably deplete natural resources and create environmental pollution. Economic progress merely speeds up the inevitable exhaustion of the earth's natural resources. Georgescu-Roegen's theory suggested that economics had neglected to study the problem of natural scarcity, thinking that technology and entrepreneurship could solve the Malthusian problem of population growth in relation to fixed assets. His economics of waste applied the biological ideas of Alfred Lotka (1998) to the accumulation of capital. Human beings rely on what Lotka called "exosomatic instruments" to develop the environment, unlike animals that depend on "endosomatic instruments." In some respects this is an old anthropological argument. Birds evolve wings to fly; human beings create airplanes. However, wings involve low-entropy solutions and do not deplete natural resources while technological solutions, such as jet-propelled airplanes, are high-entropic recipes that use up finite energy. Because humans are somatically vulnerable, they develop high-entropy strategies that have the unfortunate and unin-tended consequence of creating a precarious environment. More important, the entropy law says that social conflict is inevitable; because resources are scarce, humans degrade their environment, and they must compete within limited space. These Malthusian conditions of social conflict in modern times have been further exacerbated by the industrialization of violence and by the destabilizing impact of new wars. We can as a result see the growth of social citizenship as an attempt to reduce conflict through typically mod-est income redistribution in the framework of the nation-state and human rights as conflict-reducing instruments between and within states. A robust framework of rights may not solve the problems raised by Alfred Lotka, but such a framework may depress the level of social violence that is the his-torical companion of scarcity.

Some Objections to the Vulnerability Argument

There has in modern social science been a widespread acceptance of the idea of cultural relativism, and these arguments have important implications for human rights by bringing into question their relevance across cultures. In short, the universalism of human rights has been challenged by anthropo-logical relativism. The argument about vulnerability and precariousness is intended to be a fruitful basis for the defense of the universalism of human rights. As a defense of human rights, it is partly grounded in the notion of the ubiquity of human misery and suffering. Arthur Schopenhauer ([1850] 2004) opened his essay *On the Suffering of the World* with the observation that every "individual misfortune, to be sure, seems an exceptional occurrence; but misfortune in general is the rule." While the study of misery and misfortune has been the stuff of philosophy and theology, there is little systematic study of these phenomena by sociologists. One exception is Barrington Moore (1970) who argues in *Reflections on Human Misery and Upon Certain Proposals to Eliminate Them* that "suffering is not a value in its own right. In this sense any form of suffering becomes a cost, and unnecessary suffering an odious cost. Similarly, general opposition to human suffering constitutes a standpoint that both transcends and unites different cultures and historical epochs" (p. 11). A critic might object that suffering is too variable in its cultural manifestations and too indefinite in its meanings and local significance to provide such a common standpoint. What actually constitutes human suffering might well turn out to be culturally specific. Those who take note of the cultural variability of suffering have made similar arguments against a common standard of disability. Although one could well accept this anthropological argument on the grounds that suffering involves essentially the devaluation of a person as a consequence of accident, affliction, or torture, pain is less variable. Whereas bankruptcy or divorce, for example, could involve some degree of variable psychological suffering, a toothache is a toothache. If we claim that disability is a social condition (the loss of social rights) and thus is relative, we might argue that impairment is the underlying condition about which there is less political dispute. In short, some conditions or states of affairs are less socially constructed than others are. Pain is less variable than suffering, if we regard the latter as an indignity.

The vulnerability thesis can be further criticized because it is very relevant to some human rights but not to others. The view of rights put forward by H. G. Wells and his colleagues in a series of newspaper articles against rearmament and war in the 1930s is specifically pertinent to my position (see Keller n.d.). Human beings are entitled, Wells argued, without any distinction of race or ethnicity to nourishment, housing, and medical care to realize their full potentialities in physical and mental development. In short, human beings have rights that are designed to protect them from their vulnerability—from the afflictions and perturbations to which we are subject as embodied creatures. It could be objected that this claim about vulnerability is relevant to the International Covenant on Economic, Social, and Cultural Rights, but it is not a convincing argument about the civil and political liberties in the Covenant on Civil and Political Rights. It may well be the case that the vulnerability argument will not form the basis of a claim about all rights, specifically rights relating to individual freedoms of expression, privacy, and conscience.

There is, however, a clear relationship between poor socioeconomic conditions and health outcomes. The evidence from public health and epidemiological research demonstrates that human health is significantly influenced by income inequality and democratic participation in society. In particular, social capital (the investments that people make in society in terms of their membership in social clubs, groups, and associations) is a significant causal factor in the determination of morbidity and life expectancy (Turner 2004). It would not be difficult to show that human beings cannot successfully enjoy social rights to health care in societies where civil and political liberties are severely curtailed. For example, the spread of infectious disease with globalization is influenced by the democratic openness of different societies. The reluctance of China's political elite to respond transparently and quickly to the SARS outbreak or the reluctance of some religiously conservative societies to recognize openly the impact of HIV/AIDS infection shows that there are important connections between democracy, inequality, and health. Indeed, nongovernmental organizations in China that have been assisting HIV/AIDS victims continue to be harassed by the authorities. Human Rights Watch reported in 2010 that websites providing information on the disease to homosexual men face closure under regulations prohibiting online pornography. These examples suggest that rights to health and well-being cannot be meaningfully separated from rights to democratic participation, and therefore one can forge a link between social conditions, health, and liberal political rights. While the argument about vulnerability might apply in the first instance to social rights, we can detect important connections between the enjoyment of social rights and access to individual rights or civil liberties.

This claim can be reinforced by an appeal to the work of Amartya Sen and Martha Nussbaum. In reflecting upon the history of postimperial India, Sen (1982) in *Poverty and Famines* came to what looks like a counterintuitive conclusion that democracies were immune to famines. Democratic societies tend not to experience famines because their governments are subject to popular scrutiny and therefore make efforts to ensure that food and other supplies are distributed to poor areas where famines might otherwise occur. Their openness to ideas and criticism tends to promote a timely response. In a similar fashion, the capabilities approach of Martha Nussbaum (2000) in her *Women and Human Development* argues that the most promising development strategy is to improve the education of women. The result is to produce a better management of the domestic sphere with better care for children and improvements in the health of family members, thereby reducing the total fertility rate and slowing women's entrance into the formal labor market. Female literacy is an excellent buffer against poverty. The two approaches—democratic rights and capabilities—were combined in *The Quality of Life* (Nussbaum and Sen 1992). The capabilities approach suggests that the individual rights of liberal democracy and the rights to health care and welfare in social citizenship are not mutually exclusive but in fact are complementary.

This criticism of the vulnerability thesis might, therefore, be summarized by claiming that it is limited by its inability to explain the individual rights of liberalism. Another criticism goes in almost the opposite direction by asking whether there is any difference between human and animal rights. If my argument depends on the fact that human beings as mammalian creatures are vulnerable, then a critic might complain reasonably that one cannot distinguish between animal rights and human rights. Intelligent creatures that are not human are also vulnerable. Do dogs and dolphins have rights? Animal rights activists would probably want to claim that higher-order animals are sentient, rational creatures but not humans. Therefore, some animals enjoy the same right to rights that humans claim. We certainly ascribe animal rights to certain sentient creatures, especially if they are closely associated with human societies, such as working dogs and horses. Some animals that appear to have an elementary communication system (effectively a language), such as dolphins, are thought to be eligible for protection. However, unlike humans, animals cannot exercise these rights directly without our intervention. Animals cannot represent themselves. We might decide to protect animals as an aspect of a set of ecological rights that we have devised to protect our natural environment. Animal rights may thus be an aspect of green or environmental politics, in which protecting animals is seen to be important for protecting human beings. Finally, cruelty to animals is often seen to be a test of the civilizing process.

However, the principal criticism of my argument comes from what I want to regard as the medical technology paradox. The more medical science improves our health condition, the less vulnerable we are. Therefore, technological progress could make this vulnerability thesis historically specific. In principle if we live longer, because we have become less vulnerable with technological advances, then the relevance of human rights to the aging process might be less significant or pressing. This paradox helps me to sharpen my argument, which is that we are human, because we are vulnerable. We could only finally escape our vulnerability by ultimately escaping from our own humanity—by becoming posthuman (Fukuyama 2002). Technological progress promises to create a posthuman world in which, with medical progress, we could in principle live forever. This criticism is a very interesting argument, but there are two potentially important counter-arguments. The first is that, if we could increase our life expectancy, then we would live longer but with potentially higher rates of morbidity and disability. The quantity of life might increase in years, but there would be a corresponding decline in its quality. A posthuman world is a medical utopia that has all the negative features of a "Brave New World." Second, medical improvements in the advanced societies are likely to increase the inequality between societies, creating a more unequal and insecure international order. In such a risk society, where human precariousness increases and human vulnerability decreases, the need for human rights protection would continue. The prospect of living forever might require us to inhabit, in Max Weber's pessimistic metaphor, a biological "iron cage" in which our existence would be by courtesy of life-support machines.

Social Justice and Human Rights

Egalitarian concepts of social justice and human rights have been used in diverse ways in the life-extension debate. Researchers who are sympathetic to the project have both drawn upon and rejected the egalitarian approach in their argumentation. Generally speaking, arguments supporting the quest for radical longevity projects highlight the untenable position of delaying scientific progress that can improve human life in the future while governments and international agencies attempt to resolve existing problems of global social inequality (Post 2004). Arguments against medical progress are easily characterized as absurd; criticizing medical science is equivalent to rejecting apple pie. Hence, these scientific benefits are perceived to outweigh the various social challenges that are brought about by rejuvenation research (Stock and Callahan 2004). In contrast, by supporting the rejuvenation sciences, posthumanist thinking has drawn on egalitarianism to protect the social rights of older adults through interventions in the aging process. The main thrust of this perspective is to reduce the negative consequences of aging, providing equal opportunities for older adults to achieve optimal longevity (by delaying or preventing death). The following quotation clearly illustrates a radical form of antiageism:

> The popular view that saving lives of children in Africa [for example] is more important than curing aging constitutes discrimination in favor of those whose remaining lives will be very short unless we help them but fairly short even if we do, and against those who will probably live a few decades anyway but could live many centuries if we act now. . . . Thus, to prioritize expenditure on

treating diseases of old age . . . and to deprioritize expenditure on curing aging constitutes discrimination against those just young enough to benefit from a cure for aging if we threw more resources now at developing it. (de Grey 2004:166)

These ideas about scientific progress and the right of the elderly to sufficient biomedical expenditure in rejuvenation sciences require a serious response. There may be a right to adequate health care for the elderly, but it is clearly too simplistic to accept the professional autonomy of biogerontologists who want to increase longevity without considering its negative consequences (Hayflick 2000). Indeed, rejuvenation research will affect politics through the prolongation of life, and a series of demographic and social changes will eventually occur as a consequence. These consequences will include the uneven and unequal global distribution of economic and social resources.

In traditional societies, the relationship between resources, especially the food supply and life expectancy, was, more or less, regulated by a Malthusian logic. Although demographic history has not supported this Malthusian pessimism, it is self-evident that powerful groups would benefit more than others from the life-extension technology. If we assume that, while medical sciences could reduce mortality, they would, at least in the short term, increase morbidity as chronic illness and geriatric diseases increased. Life extension would mean, in practice, living longer in discomfort—that is, in a morbid condition. There would therefore have to be increasing investment in resources to solve physiological (chronic illnesses) and psychological problems (depression, ennui, and despair). De Grey's (2004) argument is that rejuvenation can solve these problems by both increasing life expectancy and managing morbidity more effectively. At present we live longer but with more morbidity. The promise of rejuvenative medicine is that we can stay young *and* stay healthy.

The Universal Declaration of Human Rights has much to say, as one might imagine, about life. For example, Article 3 proclaims that "everyone has the right to life, liberty and security of person," and other articles refer to the right to freedom from torture. Article 16 includes "the right to marry and to found a family," and Article 25 talks about "the right to a standard of living adequate for health and well-being" (United Nations 1948). There are many conceptual problems with this list of rights in the declaration (Turner 2008). In the literature, there is much confusion about the rights of humans as humans and the rights of citizens as members of a polity; sometimes this distinction is conceptualized as the difference between the individual rights of people as human beings and the social rights of members of a collectivity. Whereas we might say that all human beings have a right to life regardless of their social memberships, Article 22 refers more specifically to the entitlements of citizens when it proclaims that "everyone, as a member of society, has the right to social security."

Obviously given the period in which it was written, the declaration does not explicitly say that we have a right to live forever or merely for as long as possible. But in declaring that we have rights to "health and well-being" it implies at least that the aspiration to live long, healthy, and satisfactory lives is consistent with our human rights as sentient and reflexive beings. In any case, the declaration was written in the aftermath of the Second World War when its primary concern was to counteract the consequences of the devastation that had been wrought on civilian populations. Since the victims of modern warfare were civilians and not combatants, human rights established new principles to cope with the victims of technological warfare. Neither the possibility nor the desirability that medical science could significantly prolong life was on the minds of politicians and lawmakers in the late 1940s. However, coming toward the end of a long consumer boom in the late twentieth and early twenty-first centuries, the issue of whether there is a right to prolong life indefinitely is now on the horizon and needs attention philosophically, legally, and sociologically. Whether life can be significantly prolonged is still contentious, but the aging of the world's population does as a matter of fact raise critical issues about the equal distribution of natural resources, and this demographic transition brings into focus the particular issue of the rights of children that are part of intergenerational justice.

Before we can tackle these issues directly, we need to clarify some conceptual issues. If we make a distinction between what we might call "mere existence" and "life," then it makes little sense to ask whether we have a right to existence (either prolonged or otherwise). As a member of the human species, it makes little sense for me to ask if I have a right to exist. My existence, like the existence of other creatures, is simply an empirical fact. I simply am. If existence is the mere fact of being alive, then life can be described as the full panoply of my culture, language, social relations, consciousness, and human dignity. It does make sense therefore to ask whether I have a right to life as opposed to mere existence and, second, whether I have a right to extend it without limit. I shall argue further that this right to life only becomes intelligible if one can outline what the duties relating to pro-longevity might be. Legal scholars often argue that there has to be "correlativity" between rights and duties. If I have a right to free speech, it implies duties to protect your right to a voice, to defend the integrity of such institutions as national newspapers and independent journalism, and to defend a democratic civil sphere in which there is a free flow of communication. The relationship between rights and duties is never exact, but we might argue that a strong notion of right carries with it a definite conception of duty. What are or could be the duties of longevity?

A further problem is the discourse of rights and duties itself. We need to clarify whether a right to life can be housed within a human rights discourse or whether it pertains more significantly to the social rights of citizens living within a political community or state. The problem of individual rights, or *my* right to life extension, is related to individualism, namely, whether the rational desire to extend my life is compatible with the needs of the community—that is, with collective rights. If one takes the assumption of classical political economy that human beings cannot escape scarcity, then any (indefinite) extension of life will have serious consequences for collective resources and especially for how those resources are distributed over time. These medical advances raise an inescapable question about justice.

Modern citizenship has been constructed historically around a set of contributory rights and duties that are related to work, public service (e.g., military or jury service), and parenthood or family formation. It defines membership of a society through the entitlements that are associated with service, and is perhaps most clearly evident in a national system of taxation or in conscription into the army. This model of citizenship as contributory social rights has been closely associated with the legacy of the English sociologist Thomas H. Marshall (1950). Marshallian citizenship has been subject to considerable criticism over the last two decades, and the social model of citizenship has been expanded and deepened by approaches that emphasize the flexibility of social membership, by the limitations of citizenship merely as contributory rights, and by perspectives that emphasize identity and difference. This early model of citizenship has been considerably extended, for example, to include, among other things, the idea of sexual citizenship.

Can the long-lasting or everlasting citizen become a reality with some massive increase in economic resources and efficiency? In the Marshallian model, there was an implicit understanding of the normal life cycle in which work, marriage, reproduction, and retirement followed each other in a fairly stable and regular pattern. The deeply aged and the centenarian did not figure into Marshall's scheme of the welfare state and the rights of the "working man," since it was assumed that through savings from employment and with a modest pension, a couple might see out their (relatively short) lives without falling into poverty. All of these assumptions have been rendered obsolete by changes in the nature of work, the decline of adequate work-related pensions, the changing structure of the modern family, high divorce rates, flexible retirement, and longevity.

If citizenship rights are the rights of membership in a discrete political community, human rights are those rights that are held by virtue of being human. These are typically inert and passive rights without matching duties. Human rights are often invoked by reference to victims, especially in relation to genocide. It can be said that citizenship and human rights are fundamentally different kinds of rights that should be analytically and politically kept distinct. Yet, the experience of the last 50 years evolved exactly in the opposite direction. The concern to defend human rights has often outmatched the defense of citizenship as entitlement, status, and social membership. In addition there is increasing confusion about the differences between human and social rights of citizens. For example, in much radical literature in the United States, when sociologists argue that Americans are denied their human rights, they often talk about the inadequacies of health care, education, and housing, but in other political cultures such inadequacies would be described as a failure of citizenship and not a failure of human rights. The American tradition of human rights has been more closely related to social movements against slavery and racial discrimination, on one hand, and the notion of citizenship has, on the other hand, been associated with the autonomy that comes with employment and earnings (Shklar 1991, 1998). As a result the language of human rights has in America been far more prevalent than the language of social rights.

Citizenship is essential for cultivating civic virtues and democratic values. The notion of duty cannot be separated too sharply from rights, and this balance between right and duty, however imperfect, is the essence of social citizenship. Citizenship is vital partly because, when people put investments into their states, they can assume that they have a legitimate claim on that state when they fall ill, or become unemployed, or become too old to support themselves. The past contributions to the community become the basis of legitimate claims on the "commonwealth," and hence an efficient and just system of taxation is necessary to support any collectivized system of welfare and to protect the rights of the elderly (Steinmo 1993). The enthusiasm of populist movements such as the Tea Party for lower personal taxes is a recipe for increasing social inequality, leaving the elderly exposed to the vagaries of financial markets on their savings and pensions. In this respect, there is a clear connection among effort, reward, and virtue. What is the virtue associated with speculation in currency markets as a basis for personal wealth?

Citizenship in this way involves, often covertly, an education in civic culture, and because citizens are patriotically proud of the society to which they belong, they are therefore committed to defending its democratic institutions. In terms of Aristotle's *Nicomachean Ethics,* citizenship creates civic virtues that can only be produced by an education in a particular political and social habitus. It is not clear what virtues flow from human rights, which, following John Rawls (1999), exist to address urgent and immediate crises such as famines resulting from failed states. By contrast, citizenship virtues emerge from the humdrum politics of everyday life in democratic societies. This is where the significance of cities for both cultivating democratic virtues in everyday politics and linking these virtues to cosmopolitan virtues becomes apparent. It is in cities as democratic spaces that "acts of citizenship" unfold and constitute links that bind various sites of becoming citizens (Isin and Nielsen 2008).

I have explored some of the problems that might surround the claim to prolongevity on the part of citizens as a social right. These claims would have an initial plausibility, since a citizen might claim that a government has a duty to provide for the health and security of the members of society. On that basis, one might say that a government has a duty to sustain the lives of its citizens into deep old age and to allow them to live lives that are dignified and meaningful. The problem that I have described is that such a right, without a significant increase in resources and improvements in technology, would have negative Malthusian consequences. I am critical therefore of those theorists of citizenship who assume that there is no resource problem associated with enhanced social benefits (Somers 2008). Various changes might be attempted to cope with this problem of aging and employment. The first would be to expect the elderly to work longer into old age on the basis of flexible retirement. The second would be to force workers to make enhanced savings into state or private retirement funds. The third would be to expect children to make greater contributions to their parents' retirement needs. These assumptions might be feasible if, for example, we were expecting life expectancy to increase on average around two years every decade, but they are not feasible in the scenario described in the immortalist project of gerontologists like Aubrey de Grey in which large numbers of people would be surviving well beyond 120 years. With significant increases in longevity, the social rights framework of Marshallian citizenship will break down, because there will no longer be a balance between rights and duties. More important, the prospects of intergenerational justice would be bleak. No welfare state, as we know it, would cope with the rising health and welfare demands of the deeply aged unless improvements in health could accompany increases in life expectancy. It is claimed, for example, that given the increase in Alzheimer's sufferers in the United States the care costs will destroy the American health care system by 2030. De Grey (2008) has to make the unlikely assumption that not only can we live very long lives, but these extended lives can be free of impairment and disability. We can anticipate therefore that as the framework of citizenship for the elderly fails, people will turn increasingly to some notion that they possess a human right to live forever. What might we say therefore about a *human* right (as opposed to a social right) to living forever? In my view, the real intellectual problem would be to describe a meaningful duty in order to make such a right plausible. This intellectual exercise might not solve the problem of resources, but it would at least provide some *justification* for claims to prolongevity.

How could one reasonably assume that one's use of resources would not reduce the chances of subsequent generations to live satisfactory lives? Given global warming, it seems likely that all future generations will experience serious natural depletion and hence will live lives that are less than optimal. Writing this essay in 2008, it is already clear that the world is facing serious shortages of water, rice, and soybeans. It is very doubtful that an elderly population could be supported without some rapid changes in food production without confronting a Malthusian crisis. The balance between rights and duties is becoming increasingly unbalanced. As sensible and rational beings, we could lead lives that are overwhelmed by guilt and pessimism, but it is difficult to convert this Malthusian pessimism into something resembling a code of conduct. I propose therefore that we cannot easily solve the resource problem without fundamental changes in world governance, over-dependence on oil, the management of water supplies, and collective efforts to address seriously an overwhelming environmental crisis. We can, however, start thinking seriously about developing what we might call an "ethic of longevity"—namely, a set of assumptions or values that might in principle offer some ethical justification not for existence but for life.

Individualism, Suffering, and Virtue

In this discussion of the problems of enhanced longevity, I have sought to distinguish between several types of question: (1) Can we survive forever, (2) can we live forever, and finally (3) ought we to live forever? The answer to the first appears to be negative, but it is the case that with modern medical science we could radically extend life. However, most scientists believe that de Grey's (2004, 2008) exaggerated claims about rejuvenation have little support from modern science and that their application is impractical. In any case, survival or mere existence as such has no significant moral justification. It comes with no moral baggage. We might say, following Descartes, "I eat, therefore I am," but this is not an ethical claim about life and its justification. Mere survival is not in itself virtuous, but rather is a matter of luck in terms of what genetic legacy one has inherited. The struggle for longevity may be merely a product of a competitive consumer society characterized by excessive greed and individualism. By contrast, living may be defined as a creative process of growth and improvement following Simone de Beauvoir's (1972) witty claim that old age is the absence of projects. This suggests the notion that to live forever means to live in such a way that life remains a journey in which there is more or less continuous self-development.

We can expand this idea by borrowing from Nietzsche who argued that the only ultimate purpose to life (as opposed to bare existence or bare life) is to "become who we are"—that is, to develop ourselves into a work of art. To live creatively in the world presupposes a heroic ethic. To live successfully in these terms is to avoid resentment as the basic form of nihilism (Schutte 1984). Such an ethic might be a valuable counterforce to Malthus whose political economy has what Nietzsche would regard as life-denying properties. The justification for life is simply to live life creatively and productively in order to contribute to a shared human existence. To live life to the full in cultural terms is to leave a significant deposit that might add to human culture, making it richer and more diverse. Without such an ethic, it is difficult to see how life could be morally justified. It provides one possible criterion for departing this world not when we are corporeally rigid but when we are culturally and spiritually so. In this ethic, one's life as a work of art needs to be constantly refashioned if it is to be constantly creative.

Malthus was very much caught up in the debate with Condorcet, Mary Wollstonecraft, and William Godwin about whether society could be improved alongside the organic improvement of human beings, and he recognized, however implicitly, that any prolongation of life would require either an increase in available land or an improvement in the productivity of labor through technological advances. He was a pessimist in the sense that he believed that neither land nor technology could ultimately improve the situation of the urban working class—he held somewhat different views of the rural peasantry whose lives, he assumed, were happier and healthier than those of industrial urban workers. By contrast, on the surface of it, Nietzsche does not look like a *social* philosopher. When Nietzsche did overtly address social and political questions, his attitude toward the masses looks as unpromising as Malthus's attitude toward the Poor Laws and the working class. Neither could be accused of harboring democratic values. Nietzsche's ethic is overtly aristocratic, and he condemned modern society as a place where the herd might triumph over the individual, and he therefore bemoaned the loss of a world in which genuinely heroic acts and values could survive.

While we can take from Nietzsche the notion that the justification for extended living might be based on a metaphor of life as a journey or a project, Nietzsche provides no answers—nor should we expect any answers from him—to our current dilemmas that cannot be resolved by exclusively individualistic notions of a satisfying life or, for that matter, by individualistic notions of rights. Rights and duties are social phenomena, and their defense and enjoyment will require collective social solutions. Any worthwhile theory of human rights will have to be cast in a distinctively social framework, and it is for this reason (and others) that we need a sociology of human rights.

Discussion Questions

1. Compare the Convention on the Rights of Persons With Disabilities (see Table 10.1 below) to the Americans With Disabilities Act of 1990.

2. Aristotle's *Nicomachean Ethics* has been translated quite a few times. One that is widely read was translated by W. D. Ross and published by Clarendon Press in 1908. It is available online (http://nicomacheanethics.net/). Close to the beginning is this remarkable statement: "For even if the end is the same for a single man and for a state, that of the state seems at all events something greater and more complete whether to attain or to preserve; though it is worth while to attain the end merely for one man, it is finer and more godlike to attain it for a nation or for city-states." What does this imply about the relationship between citizenship and virtue? What does it imply about democracy?

3. Eighteenth-century debates continue to enliven debates in the twenty-first century. Explore sites on the web to find the many ways that Condorcet, Godwin, and Wollstonecraft stood in opposition to Malthus. In what ways were they drawing from different realms of knowledge and quite different assumptions?

4. There is discussion among United Nations parties to craft a convention on the rights of the elderly. What should be included? Do you want to try your hand in drafting it?

Table 10.1   Excerpts From the Convention on the Rights of Persons with Disabilities

New York, December 13, 2006
Entry into force: May 3, 2008, in accordance with Article 45(1)
Status: Signatories: 147. Parties: 94

(Continued)

(Continued)

Article 1. Purpose

The purpose of the present Convention is to promote, protect and ensure the full and equal enjoyment of all human rights and fundamental freedoms by all persons with disabilities, and to promote respect for their inherent dignity.

Persons with disabilities include those who have long-term physical, mental, intellectual or sensory impairments which in interaction with various barriers may hinder their full and effective participation in society on an equal basis with others.

Article 3. General principles

The principles of the present Convention shall be:

(a) Respect for inherent dignity, individual autonomy including the freedom to make one's own choices, and independence of persons;

(b) Non-discrimination;

(c) Full and effective participation and inclusion in society;

(d) Respect for difference and acceptance of persons with disabilities as part of human diversity and humanity;

(e) Equality of opportunity;

(f) Accessibility;

(g) Equality between men and women;

(h) Respect for the evolving capacities of children with disabilities and respect for the right of children with disabilities to preserve their identities.

Article 5. Equality and non-discrimination

1. States Parties recognize that all persons are equal before and under the law and are entitled without any discrimination to the equal protection and equal benefit of the law.

2. States Parties shall prohibit all discrimination on the basis of disability and guarantee to persons with disabilities equal and effective legal protection against discrimination on all grounds.

3. In order to promote equality and eliminate discrimination, States Parties shall take all appropriate steps to ensure that reasonable accommodation is provided.

4. Specific measures which are necessary to accelerate or achieve de facto equality of persons with disabilities shall not be considered discrimination under the terms of the present Convention.

Article 6. Women with disabilities

1. States Parties recognize that women and girls with disabilities are subject to multiple discrimination, and in this regard shall take measures to ensure the full and equal enjoyment by them of all human rights and fundamental freedoms.

2. States Parties shall take all appropriate measures to ensure the full development, advancement and empowerment of women, for the purpose of guaranteeing them the exercise and enjoyment of the human rights and fundamental freedoms set out in the present Convention.

Article 7. Children with disabilities

1. States Parties shall take all necessary measures to ensure the full enjoyment by children with disabilities of all human rights and fundamental freedoms on an equal basis with other children.

2. In all actions concerning children with disabilities, the best interests of the child shall be a primary consideration.

3. States Parties shall ensure that children with disabilities have the right to express their views freely on all matters affecting them, their views being given due weight in accordance with their age and maturity, on an equal basis with other children, and to be provided with disability and age-appropriate assistance to realize that right.

Source: http://www2.ohchr.org/english/law/disabilities-convention.htm

References

Bourdieu, Pierre. 2000. *Pascalian Meditations*. Cambridge, UK: Cambridge University Press.

Callahan, Daniel. 2009. "Life Extension: Rolling the Technological Dice." *Society* 46(3):214–20.

Centers for Disease Control and Prevention. 2010. "Life Expectancy at Birth, by Race and Sex—United States." September 17. Retrieved January 16, 2011 (http://www.cdc.gov/mmwr/preview/mmwrhtml/mm5936a9.htm?s_cid=mm5936a9_w).

de Beauvoir, Simone. 1972. *Old Age*. London: Deutsch and Weidenfeld and Nicolson.

de Grey, Aubrey. 2004. "Three Self-Evident Life-Extension Truths." *Rejuvenation Research* 7(3):165–67.

de Grey, Aubrey (with Michael Rae). 2008. *Ending Aging: The Rejuvenation Breakthroughs That Could Reverse Human Aging in Our Lifetime.* London: St Martin's Press.

Dubos, Rene. 1959. *Mirage of Health: Utopias, Progress and Biological Change.* London: George Allen & Unwin.

Fukuyama, Francis. 2002. *Our Posthuman Future: Consequences of the Biotechnology Revolution.* New York: Farrar, Straus and Giroux.

Gehlen, Arnold. 1988. *Man: His Nature and Place in the World.* New York: Columbia University Press.

Georgescu-Roegen, N. 1971. *The Entropy Law and the Economic Process.* Cambridge, UK: Cambridge University Press.

Hayflick, L. 2000. "The Future of Aging." *Nature* 408(9):267–69.

Heidegger, Martin. 1962. *Being and Time.* Oxford: Blackwell.

Human Rights Watch. 2010. "The Truth of China's Response to HIV/AIDS." July 1. Retrieved January 16, 2011 (http://www.hrw.org/en/news/2010/07/11/truth-chinas-response-hivaids).

Isin, Engin F. and Greg M. Nielsen, eds. 2008. *Acts of Citizenship.* London: Zed Books.

Keller, Charles. N.d. "H. G. Wells Sees It Through, Posted on the H. G. Wells Society (The Americas) Web Site." Retrieved January 16, 2011 (http://www.hgwellsusa.50megs.com/introduction.html).

Lotka, Alfred J. 1998. *Analytical Theories of Biological Populations.* New York: Plenum Press.

Marshall, Thomas H. 1950. *Citizenship and Social Class, and Other Essays.* Cambridge, UK: Cambridge University Press.

Moore, Barrington. 1970. *Reflections on Human Misery and Upon Certain Proposals to Eliminate Them.* London: Allen Lane.

Nussbaum, Martha C. 2000. *Women and Human Development: The Capabilities Approach.* Cambridge, UK: Cambridge University Press.

Nussbaum, Martha C. and Amartya Sen. 1992. *The Quality of Life.* Oxford, UK: Clarendon Press.

Post, S. G. 2004. "Establishing an Appropriate Ethical Framework: The Moral Conversation Around the Goal of Prolongevity." *Journal of Gerontology: Biological Sciences* 59A(6):534–39.

Rawls, John. 1999. *The Laws of Peoples.* Harvard, MA: Harvard University Press.

Schopenhauer, Arthur. [1850] 2004. *On the Suffering of the World.* London: Penguin.

Schutte, Ofelia. 1984. *Beyond Nihilism: Nietzsche Without Masks.* Chicago: University of Chicago Press.

Sen, Amartya. 1982. *Poverty and Famines.* Oxford, UK: Clarendon Press.

Shklar, Judith N. 1991. *American Citizenship: The Quest for Inclusion.* Cambridge, MA: Harvard University Press.

Shklar, Judith N. 1998. *Political Thought and Political Thinkers.* Chicago: University of Chicago Press.

Somers, Margaret R. 2008. *Genealogies of Citizenship: Markets, Statelessness and the Right to Have Rights.* Cambridge, UK: Cambridge University Press.

Steinmo, Sven. 1993. Taxation and Democracy: Swedish, British and American Approaches to Financing the Modern State. New Haven, CT: Yale University Press.

Stock, G. and D. Callahan. 2004. "Point-Counterpoint: Would Doubling the Human Life Span Be a Net Positive or Negative for Us Either as Individuals or as a Society?" *Journal of Gerontology: Biological Sciences* 59A(6):554–59.

Turner, Bryan S. 2004. *The New Medical Sociology.* New York: Norton.

Turner, Bryan S. 2006. *Vulnerability and Human Rights.* University Park: Penn State University Press.

Turner, Bryan S. 2008. Rights and Virtues: Political Essays on Citizenship and Social Justice. Oxford, UK: Bardwell Press.

Turner, Bryan S. and Chris Rojek. 2001. *Society and Culture: Principles of Scarcity and Solidarity.* London: Sage.

United Nations. 1948. "The Universal Declaration of Human Rights." December 10. Retrieved January 16, 2011 (http://www.un.org/en/documents/udhr/index .shtml).

11

Children's Rights

Brian Gran and Rachel Bryant

It is futile to separate children and their rights from society.

—Martin Guggenheim (2005),
What's Wrong with Children's Rights

What Are Children's Rights?

What are children's rights? Are they a kind of human rights? In this chapter we deliberate on definitions and conceptualizations of children's rights and legal treaties articulating children's rights. We examine types of rights, rights on paper, and rights in practice, and then examine what strengthens or hinders children's rights around the world. Finally, we explore the status of children's rights in the United States.

A variety of definitions shape debates over children's rights. Michael Freeman (2007), a leading expert on children's rights, emphasizes entitlements: that a child's right is an entitlement. Yet what those entitlements are is complicated. Martha Minow (1995) notes that it is possible to argue that children should have the same entitlements as adults, yet others can argue that children are entitled to "special legal protections" adults do not need. Martin Guggenheim (2005) cautions, however, that the complexity observed by Minow is compounded by failures to acknowledge individualization of children's rights. As others (e.g., Williams 1987) have argued, rights do not exist in a social vacuum; rights are only relevant in the context of social interactions. This concern especially applies to children, a social group whose members often rely on others, especially adults.

The United Nations takes seriously this notion of social interaction in its definition of children's rights. For the United Nations, a child is both a human being and a member of society and family. According to the United Nations, children's rights are established so that a young person can reach his or her "full potential, free from hunger and want, neglect and abuse." UNICEF's conceptualization includes that children's rights are age appropriate. UNICEF goes on to split rights into actions a young person may take, and protections from harm. The Council of Europe takes a similar approach, designating *entitlements to* and *freedoms from*. The African Charter on the Rights and Welfare of the Child (African Committee of Experts on the Rights and Welfare of the Child n.d.) makes clear that children hold a unique place in African societies, confirming Minow's (1995) idea that children are different.

Important similarities and differences are found among these definitions. While some conceptualizations are of children as passive recipients of rights, other conceptualizations treat young people as active possessors who can act to enforce their rights. Guggenheim's (2005) reminder that children's rights are based in social interaction highlights a weakness of rights. Rights have limited utility without social interaction. This problem, further discussed below, especially is relevant to young people's rights.

Where Do We Find Children's Rights?

What are sources of ideas of young people's rights? Aristotle, whose concepts form the basis of western government, also contributes to contemporary ideas about family law. In his *Politics* (1885), Aristotle presents a conceptualization of the state and its organization. One component of Aristotle's conception is the family. In Aristotle's family, the father should govern his children as a king should rule his subjects. In turn, his children should expect to be treated as royal subjects. Only if the father does not govern his children as royal subjects can the state, consisting of male citizens, intervene into the father-children relationship. In many ways, Aristotle's conception is similar to family arrangements found in some contemporary societies, including that government will only intervene in the family when a child is improperly governed by parents.

More recent notions of children's rights are found in the work of Save the Children, currently known as the Save the Children International. With roots back to the First World War, the organization first focused on economic injustices and harms children experienced during war. Established in 1920, the International Save the Children Union initially concentrated on children's rights, with one of its founders drafting the first Declaration of the Rights of the Child, also known as the Declaration of Geneva. The League of Nations adopted this declaration in 1924. While the declaration does not use the term *rights*, except in its title, it declares that "mankind" owes duties to young people. The 1924 Geneva Declaration primarily focused on a child's development, relief from distress, protection from exploitation, and the opportunity to learn to serve other people.

The 1959 Declaration of the Rights of the Child clearly built upon the 1924 declaration. Adopted by the UN General Assembly, it notes that children need special care, including legal protections. It declares 10 principles, which move beyond the 1924 declaration. These principles delineate various rights, such as the right to education and social security, and the right to nationality.

The next major international treaty on children's rights is the UN Convention on the Rights of the Child (UNCRC). While declarations are not binding, ratification of a convention indicates a government's commitment to implementing rights detailed in the treaty. The UNCRC is the most ratified of all human rights treaties. Only the national governments of Somalia and the United States have yet to ratify the convention. Adopted in 1989, with over 50 articles, the convention not only articulates children's rights but also identifies others who are responsible for implementation of children's rights, such as parents, governments, and the United Nations. The UNCRC permits a government to file a reservation to the convention, which indicates a government's unwillingness or inability to implement a specific article.

Since UNCRC adoption, regional authorities have introduced treaties on children's rights. A paramount example is the African Charter on the Rights and Welfare of the Child (African Committee of Experts on the Rights and Welfare of the Child n.d.). Adopted in 1990, the African charter has a parallel format and identifies similar rights to the UNCRC, such as the best interests of the child. Nevertheless, it has important differences, among which are that this charter pertains to African children, it identifies a child's welfare as predominant, and the monitoring committee of the African charter can receive communications from groups and individuals, including children. The UNCRC does not permit such communications.

Are Children's Rights Needed?

The UNCRC (1989) declares, "Childhood is entitled to special care and assistance." Proponents of children's rights include the United Nations,

Amnesty International, and nonprofit groups such as Child Watch and the Child Rights Information Network. Groups such as Child Watch focus on issues specifically affecting children, such as education and violence against children.

Some experts such as Paulo Sérgio Pinheiro, as well as Peter Newell (2008), contend children are a vulnerable population in need of special protection around the world, with specific regard to violence against children. Children's rights are needed because as a vulnerable population, children are not able to advocate for their own needs and rights. For example, children across the world are recruited into armed forces. Often they are abducted or choose to enlist because they see few alternatives. Girls are at high risk of rape and sexual abuse (Amnesty International 2010).

Another concern for those who advocate for children's rights is empowerment of children. To some degree, children do not possess autonomy to make decisions for themselves. Instead, they rely on adults such as parents, guardians, teachers, or school administrators to make decisions on their behalf. Some advocates call for inclusion of children in decision making, political and otherwise, on issues affecting children.

Some groups, specifically parental rights groups in the United States, contend children's rights are unnecessary. Opponents of children's rights argue that childhood is a time of innocence and children should be protected from the adult world (Parental Rights 2011). They seek to preserve and protect a child-parent relationship in which the "parent knows best" and government should remain outside of the family home. In the United States, opponents of children's rights are concerned about specific articles of the UNCRC, such as Article 14, which articulates the rights to freedom of thought, conscience, and religion. Opposition has been voiced against Article 19 and General Comment 8, which require protection from all forms of violence, including corporal punishment. This is not an uncommon reservation to have about the UNCRC; in fact, only around 30 states have outlawed corporal punishment in the home, in schools, and in prisons (Global Initiative to End All Corporal Punishment of Children n.d.).

The concept of the "best interests of the child"—which has been part of U.S. law for 100 years—is also challenged (Gran 2008). Parents who oppose children's rights fear that it challenges their parental authority and that it could allow courts to override their parental decisions. The UNCRC does not give states or the United Nations the authority to police parenting.

Parental rights groups are also concerned that ratification of the treaty would challenge U.S. sovereignty and would overrule federal and state laws.

This opposition has proposed a bill, SR 519, to block ratification of the UNCRC in the Senate. These groups are also petitioning for a parental rights amendment. Interestingly, the UNCRC is not a self-executing treaty; specific legislation would need to be enacted to execute the principles in the UNCRC.

Types of Children's Rights

In his seminal work *Class, Citizenship, and Social Development* T. H. Marshall (1964) defined citizenship as a status indicating an individual is a full member of society. For Marshall, citizenship consisted of three types of rights: civil, political, and social. Civil rights are based in the legal system and enable an individual to speak and think freely, to obtain due process when another person tries to restrict civil rights, and to defend one's civil rights.

Political rights are rights to participate fully in a political system (Marshall 1964). Key political rights are the right to vote, the right to assemble, and the right to run for political office. Social rights enable individuals to enjoy a level of socioeconomic well-being. Social rights include the right to an education and the right to social security. According to Marshall, social rights are key to citizenship as a status. Without an education, for instance, individuals will struggle to implement their right to vote.

Marshall's definition of political rights has been extended to include the ability to shape governing institutions through participation in other institutions, such as schools (Gran 2010). In many countries such as the United States, minors are excluded from voting in elections. However, young people have representation in schools through student councils. In the United Kingdom, young people are represented through the United Kingdom Youth Parliament (UKYP). The UKYP is composed of 600 members ages 11 to 18 who are elected in annual youth elections throughout the United Kingdom. Any young person aged 11 to 18 can run for election or vote (UKYP 2011).

Economic rights have been added to Marshall's (1964) conception of citizenship. Economic rights include freedoms from encroachments on individuals' lives and harms to their welfare (Gran 2010; Turner 1993). Key examples of economic rights are freedoms from economic exploitation and hazardous work. Participation rights have been incorporated into discussions of citizenship. Participation rights are rights to participate in decision-making processes and vary depending on the extent to which children share decision-making power with adults (Smith 2007; Thomas 2007).

Rights on Paper Versus Rights in Practice

Children's rights are set out in a variety of treaties, constitutions, and laws. Sometimes rights are articulated as specifically belonging to children. Other times they are available to everyone, and children are not precluded from employing them.

In Norway, Article 2 of the Child Welfare Act stipulates that the Norwegian government will implement the UNCRC (Norwegian Forum on the Rights of the Child n.d.). On the other hand, despite the U.S. government not yet ratifying the UNCRC, some federal laws coincide with the UNCRC. For instance, imprisonment of children with adults is prohibited in Article 37(c) of the UNCRC, which states,

> Every child deprived of liberty shall be treated with humanity and respect for the inherent dignity of the human person, and in a manner which takes into account the needs of persons of his or her age. In particular, every child deprived of liberty shall be separated from adults unless it is considered in the child's best interest not to do so and shall have the right to maintain contact with his or her family through correspondence and visits, save in exceptional circumstances.

The 1974 Juvenile Justice and Delinquency Prevention Act (JJDPA), a federal law, requires separation in prisons of juveniles from adults by sight and sound. This separation does not apply to juveniles to be tried as adults, an important distinction from the UNCRC.

Rights on paper do not necessarily mean rights work in practice. An important example again is imprisonment of children. A U.S. Department of Justice Bureau of Justice Assessment (2000) report finds that many U.S. states do not comply with the JJDPA law. Some states permit imprisonment of children with adults for up to six hours, as well as provide exceptions for cleaning of cells and transport of prisoners. While this Department of Justice report is 12 years old, our research indicates that many states continue practices that conflict with the federal law (also see Act 4 n.d.).

Since children's rights in practice are difficult to measure, some scholars use proxies of rights, or indicators. These indicators may focus on structure, process, or outcome.

Structural indicators include the ratification and adoption of legal instruments as well as the existence of basic institutional mechanisms that facilitate human rights. Structural indicators capture commitments or the intent of states in undertaking measures for the implementation of human rights. This is particularly important since while providing an indication on the commitment of the state, structural indicators may also provide relevant benchmarks for holding the state accountable for its acts of commission or omission regarding human rights.

Process indicators include state policy instruments with milestones that cumulate into outcome indicators. Process indicators are more sensitive to changes than outcome indicators and hence are better at capturing progress toward implementation of human rights. Outcome indicators capture attainments, individual or collective, that reflect the status of the realization of a human right. It is a more direct measure of the realization of a human right that is actually experienced by individuals (United Nations International Human Rights Instruments 2008).

For example, when examining safe working conditions, some structural indicators would be the number of international human rights treaties relevant to the right to work ratified by the state, the maximum number of working hours per week allowed by law, and the minimum age for employment by occupation type. A process indicator would be the proportion of employed persons whose salary level is covered under legislation (e.g., minimum wage) and wage setting procedures involving social partners such as unions. Outcome indicators would be the incidence of accidents at work, the incidence of occupational diseases, and the ratio of women's to men's wages, by sector and by other target groups (United Nations International Human Rights Instruments 2008).

Scholars have introduced innovative measures of children's rights. A new academic society, the International Society for Child Indicators, publishes a journal, *Child Indicators Research*, and holds an international conference. Individual scholars have introduced measures of children's rights. Elizabeth Heger Boyle (University of Minnesota 2010) and her team are constructing "Child Rights National Law Indexes," a systematic approach to defining and measuring national law that promotes children's rights. Brian Gran and his team (Case Western Reserve University 2004a) have developed the Children's Rights Index (CRI). The CRI is an international measure of children's formal rights for over 190 countries. Gran and Rachel Bryant (Case Western Reserve University 2004b) are developing a parallel measure for U.S. states and territories. Despite these contributions, great needs exist in systematically assessing children's rights. Both Boyle's and Gran's projects focus on rights on paper; research on rights in practice at the international level requires attention.

What Strengthens and What Hinders Children's Rights?

Evidence of what factors promote and hinder children's rights is limited. At the international level, the UN Committee on the Rights of the Child has examined implementation of the UNCRC according to national laws. Once a state party ratifies the UNCRC, it is obligated to file an initial report within 2 years, and then every 5 subsequent years. The Committee on the Rights of the Child reviews the reports and issues concluding observations. It is not uncommon for states parties to be tardy in filing these reports, especially initial reports, which may not be filed until 5 or 10 years after ratification. For example, Albania's initial report was filed in 2005, 13 years after its national government ratified the UNCRC.

In its general comments, which the committee publishes to guide states parties in their implementation of the UNCRC, the committee has focused on the rights to education, to adolescent health, and to be heard, as well as issues facing unaccompanied children and children who have disabilities. General Comment 5, "General measures of implementation of the Convention on the Rights of the Child," identifies steps the committee considers essential to implementation. Systematic evidence on whether these steps have been fulfilled is lacking. The committee calls for different efforts at implementation. The committee wants to see states parties make the UNCRC part of national legislation. The committee wants states parties to establish governmental and independent bodies that will coordinate and monitor children's rights. The committee wants to see states parties undertake data collection, "awareness-raising and training," and establishment of policies, services, and programs that will implement the UNCRC. The authors of this chapter are not aware of systematic research on all components, but are aware of studies, described above, on different aspects of this call from the committee.

Other research indicates the importance of some factors to children's rights advancement. One is economic resources. General Comment 5 does acknowledge challenges states parties face in UNCRC implementation. The committee calls for progressive realization of the UNCRC; that is, states parties should demonstrate that they have implemented the UNCRC "to the maximum extent of their available resources" (para. 7). Another is independent children's rights institutions. Through its General Comment 2, the UN committee calls on states parties to establish independent children's rights institutions—for instance, children's ombudspersons and children's commissioners. The UN committee asserts that these institutions are essential to implementing and advancing children's rights in each country. Ongoing research conducted by Gran and Alberti (2003), Thomas et al. (2010), and UNICEF Innocenti Research Centre (2011) examines the impacts these independent children's rights institutions have for children's rights.

In addition to the work of the UN committee, research on factors critical to implementation of children's rights has tended to focus on specific types of rights, such as freedom from violence. These studies have tackled questions about why young people's right to bodily control depends on where they live. In her book, *Female Genital Cutting*, Elizabeth Heger Boyle (2002) studies why, despite international treaties, national policies vary on the right a young woman possesses to control her body.

Children's Rights in the United States: An Ideal Type?

An important variable to discussions of children's rights in the United States is the U.S. federal system of government. State-level differences in children's rights are significant in the United States. While some federal laws govern children's rights across states, state laws may strengthen, weaken, or even preclude implementation of a children's right. The right may not be addressed in the state law at all, or the state law may implement a weaker right than federal law. As noted above, the Juvenile Justice and Delinquency Prevention Act is a federal law that prevents incarcerating juveniles with adults. Some state laws allow prison administrators to hold juveniles with adults for up to six hours in some situations or in the same facility as long as they are separated by sight and sound.

Ratification of the UNCRC by the United States does not look especially favorable in the immediate future. The Campaign for U.S. Ratification of the Convention of the Rights of the Child is a national coalition led by the leadership of the Child Welfare League of America and composed of supporters from over 200 organizations and academic institutions. The campaign has led lobbying and advocacy efforts to ratify the UNCRC since 2003 and has been hopeful that ratification would be on the table during the Obama administration.

The campaign's efforts have sparked opposition from small groups that oppose ratification of the UNCRC because that ratification would endanger national and state sovereignty, undermine parental authority by allowing the UN to dictate how parents raise and teach their children, and enable children the right to do as they please (Gran 2010). While these are misconceptions about the UNCRC, the opposition has nevertheless proposed SR 519, the bill to block ratification of the UNCRC, and a parental rights amendment, which would guarantee parents' supreme authority over their children. These bills in conjunction with the declining approval rating of the Obama administration make ratification unlikely in the immediate future especially since proposing ratification may be a risky political move. If the UNCRC is not ratified during the Obama administration, it is not likely to be ratified in the near future especially if the next administration is conservative.

An Overview

Two views of children's rights seem to predominate. One view sees children as a vulnerable population in need of special protection who deserve a set of specifically articulated human rights to protect them. Advocates of this view point toward children in difficult circumstances such as children in armed conflict, children denied education, street children, and orphans and unaccompanied children.

Another view of children's rights understands children as active, potentially empowered users of rights. This view sees children as members of a social group who can advocate for their own needs and goals. Supporters of this view argue for lowering the voting age, establishing youth parliaments, and giving young people a stronger voice in their educations.

International treaties on children's rights do not choose one view over another. Instead, these treaties, as well as other texts, including general comments published by the UN Committee on the Rights of the Child, seem to accept both views.

As these views are debated all over the world, the importance of social interaction to children's rights becomes clear. No matter the child, rights do not operate in a social vacuum. Rights frequently are important to people in precarious situations. Indeed, rights can be used to change social structures that produce inequality and other harms. Implementing rights not only requires social interaction; rights only matter if people are doing things together.

As a social group, young people living in contemporary societies must often rely on adults to articulate, advance, and implement their rights. How these societies respond to children's rights may indicate their willingness to change social structures that foster growth, or limit the potential, of their young people.

Useful Resources and Websites

Amnesty International: http://www.amnesty.org/en/children

Campaign for U.S. Ratification of the Convention on the Rights of the Child: http://childrightscampaign.org/

Child Watch: http://www.hrw.org/en/category/topic/children's-rights

Children's Rights Index: http://www.case.edu/artsci/soci/Gran/childrights.html

Child Rights Information Network: http://www.crin.org/

Global Initiative to End All Corporal Punishment of Children: http://www.end corporalpunishment.org

International Society for Child Indicators: http://www.childindicators.org/

Parental Rights: http://www.parentalrights.org

Save the Children: http://www.savethechildren.net/alliance/index.html

UNICEF: http://www.unicefusa.org

UNICEF Innocenti Research Centre: http://www.unicef-irc.org

United Kingdom Youth Parliament: http://www.ukyouthparliament.org.uk/4655/index.html

United Nations Documents: http://www.un-documents.net

University of Minnesota Human Rights Library, Rights of the Child: http://www1.umn.edu/humanrts/instree/auok.htm

Discussion Questions

1. Since 1924, when the Geneva Declaration of the Rights of the Child was adopted, the conception of the child has changed, and it even has changed since 1989 when the Convention on the Rights of the Child was approved by the General Assembly. Part of this relates to changes in families. For example, there are fewer stay-at-home moms these days, and LGBTQ couples can legally adopt children in many states. There is also evidence that children are more autonomous and independent now compared with, say, 1924. How would you "tweak" the following documents to take these changes into account?

2. Globalization has been accompanied by a dramatic rise in child trafficking and reliance on child soldiers. The following declarations and treaty might not fully reflect contemporary levels of such horrific child abuse. Again, are there any ways you would strengthen the language in any of these documents?

3. Do the language and perspective of these documents reflect the biases of one part of the world over others? For example, are they Western?

4. How do these documents balance protection of children and opportunities for children?

GENEVA DECLARATION OF
THE RIGHTS OF THE CHILD

Adopted 26 September, 1924, League of Nations

By the present Declaration of the Rights of the Child, commonly known as "Declaration of Geneva," men and women of all nations, recognizing that mankind owes to the Child the best that it has to give, declare and accept it as their duty that, beyond and above all considerations of race, nationality or creed:

1. The child must be given the means requisite for its normal development, both materially and spiritually;

2. The child that is hungry must be fed; the child that is sick must be nursed; the child that is backward must be helped; the delinquent child must be reclaimed; and the orphan and the waif must be sheltered and succored;

3. The child must be the first to receive relief in times of distress;

4. The child must be put in a position to earn a livelihood, and must be protected against every form of exploitation;

5. The child must be brought up in the consciousness that its talents must be devoted to the service of fellow men.

Source: www.un-documents.net/gdrc1924.htm.

DECLARATION OF THE RIGHTS OF THE CHILD

Whereas the peoples of the United Nations have, in the Charter, reaffirmed their faith in fundamental human rights and in the dignity and worth of the human person, and have determined to promote social progress and better standards of life in larger freedom,

Whereas the United Nations has, in the Universal Declaration of Human Rights, proclaimed that everyone is entitled to all the rights and freedoms set forth therein, without distinction of any kind, such as race, colour, sex, language, religion, political or other opinion, national or social origin, property, birth or other status,

Whereas the child, by reason of his physical and mental immaturity, needs special safeguards and care, including appropriate legal protection, before as well as after birth,

Whereas the need for such special safeguards has been stated in the Geneva Declaration of the Rights of the Child of 1924, and recognized in the Universal Declaration of Human Rights and in the statutes of specialized agencies and international organizations concerned with the welfare of children,

Whereas mankind owes to the child the best it has to give,

Now therefore,

The General Assembly

Proclaims this Declaration of the Rights of the Child to the end that he may have a happy childhood and enjoy for his own good and for the good of society the rights and freedoms herein set forth, and calls upon parents, upon men and women as individuals, and upon voluntary organizations, local authorities and national Governments to recognize these rights and strive for their observance by legislative and other measures progressively taken in accordance with the following principles.

Source: www.un-documents.net/a14r1386.htm.

CONVENTION ON THE RIGHTS OF THE CHILD

General Assembly Resolution 44/25 of 20 November 1989
http://www2.ohchr.org/english/law/crc.htm
Preamble

The States Parties to the present Convention,

Considering that, in accordance with the principles proclaimed in the Charter of the United Nations, recognition of the inherent dignity and of the equal and inalienable rights of all members of the human family is the foundation of freedom, justice and peace in the world,

Bearing in mind that the peoples of the United Nations have, in the Charter, reaffirmed their faith in fundamental human rights and in the dignity and worth of the human person, and have determined to promote social progress and better standards of life in larger freedom,

(Continued)

(Continued)

Recalling that, in the Universal Declaration of Human Rights, the United Nations has proclaimed that childhood is entitled to special care and assistance,

Convinced that the family, as the fundamental group of society and the natural environment for the growth and well-being of all its members and particularly children, should be afforded the necessary protection and assistance so that it can fully assume its responsibilities within the community,

Recognizing that the child, for the full and harmonious development of his or her personality, should grow up in a family environment, in an atmosphere of happiness, love and understanding,

Considering that the child should be fully prepared to live an individual life in society, and brought up in the spirit of the ideals proclaimed in the Charter of the United Nations, and in particular in the spirit of peace, dignity, tolerance, freedom, equality and solidarity,

Bearing in mind that the need to extend particular care to the child has been stated in the Geneva Declaration of the Rights of the Child of 1924 and in the Declaration of the Rights of the Child adopted by the General Assembly on 20 November 1959 and recognized in the Universal Declaration of Human Rights, in the International Covenant on Civil and Political Rights (in particular in articles 23 and 24), in the International Covenant on Economic, Social and Cultural Rights (in particular in article 10) and in the statutes and relevant instruments of specialized agencies and international organizations concerned with the welfare of children,

Bearing in mind that, as indicated in the Declaration of the Rights of the Child, "the child, by reason of his physical and mental immaturity, needs special safeguards and care, including appropriate legal protection, before as well as after birth,"

Taking due account of the importance of the traditions and cultural values of each people for the protection and harmonious development of the child,

Recognizing the importance of international co-operation for improving the living conditions of children in every country, in particular in the developing countries,

Have agreed as follows:

PART I

Article I

For the purposes of the present Convention, a child means every human being below the age of eighteen years unless under the law applicable to the child, majority is attained earlier.

Article 3

In all actions concerning children, whether undertaken by public or private social welfare institutions, courts of law, administrative authorities or legislative bodies, the best interests of the child shall be a primary consideration.

Article 5

States Parties shall respect the responsibilities, rights and duties of parents or, where applicable, the members of the extended family or community as provided for by local custom, legal guardians or other persons legally responsible for the child, to provide, in a manner consistent with the evolving capacities of the child, appropriate direction and guidance in the exercise by the child of the rights recognized in the present Convention.

Article 9

States Parties shall ensure that a child shall not be separated from his or her parents against their will, except when competent authorities subject to judicial review determine, in accordance with applicable law and procedures, that such separation is necessary for the best interests of the child. Such determination may be necessary in a particular case such as one involving abuse or neglect of the child by the parents, or one where the parents are living separately and a decision must be made as to the child's place of residence.

Article 12

States Parties shall assure to the child who is capable of forming his or her own views the right to express those views freely in all matters affecting the child, the views of the child being given due weight in accordance with the age and maturity of the child.

(Continued)

(Continued)

Article 13

1. The child shall have the right to freedom of expression; this right shall include freedom to seek, receive and impart information and ideas of all kinds, regardless of frontiers, either orally, in writing or in print, in the form of art, or through any other media of the child's choice.

2. The exercise of this right may be subject to certain restrictions, but these shall only be such as are provided by law and are necessary:

   (a) For respect of the rights or reputations of others; or

   (b) For the protection of national security or of public order (ordre public), or of public health or morals.

Article 14

1. States Parties shall respect the right of the child to freedom of thought, conscience and religion.

2. States Parties shall respect the rights and duties of the parents and, when applicable, legal guardians, to provide direction to the child in the exercise of his or her right in a manner consistent with the evolving capacities of the child.

3. Freedom to manifest one's religion or beliefs may be subject only to such limitations as are prescribed by law and are necessary to protect public safety, order, health or morals, or the fundamental rights and freedoms of others.

Article 15

States Parties recognize the rights of the child to freedom of association and to freedom of peaceful assembly.

Article 16

1. No child shall be subjected to arbitrary or unlawful interference with his or her privacy, family, or correspondence, nor to unlawful attacks on his or her honor and reputation.

2. The child has the right to the protection of the law against such interference or attacks.

Article 18

States Parties shall use their best efforts to ensure recognition of the principle that both parents have common responsibilities for the upbringing and development of the child. Parents or, as the case may be, legal guardians, have the primary responsibility for the upbringing and development of the child. The best interests of the child will be their basic concern.

Article 19

States Parties shall take all appropriate legislative, administrative, social and educational measures to protect the child from all forms of physical or mental violence, injury or abuse, neglect or negligent treatment, maltreatment or exploitation, including sexual abuse, while in the care of parent(s), legal guardian(s) or any other person who has the care of the child.

Article 21

States Parties that recognize and/or permit the system of adoption shall ensure that the best interests of the child shall be the paramount consideration and they shall:

(a) Ensure that the adoption of a child is authorized only by competent authorities who determine, in accordance with applicable law and procedures and on the basis of all pertinent and reliable information, that the adoption is permissible in view of the child's status concerning parents, relatives and legal guardians and that, if required, the persons concerned have given their informed consent to the adoption on the basis of such counselling as may be necessary;

(b) Recognize that inter-country adoption may be considered as an alternative means of child's care, if the child cannot be placed in a foster or an adoptive family or cannot in any suitable manner be cared for in the child's country of origin.

Article 24

States Parties recognize the right of the child to the enjoyment of the highest attainable standard of health and to facilities for the treatment of illness and rehabilitation of health. States Parties shall strive to ensure that no child is deprived of his or her right of access to such health care services.

Article 26

1. States Parties shall recognize for every child the right to benefit from social security, including social insurance, and shall take the necessary measures to achieve the full realization of this right in accordance with their national law.

(Continued)

(Continued)

2. The benefits should, where appropriate, be granted, taking into account the resources and the circumstances of the child and persons having responsibility for the maintenance of the child, as well as any other consideration relevant to an application for benefits made by or on behalf of the child.

Article 27

States Parties recognize the right of every child to a standard of living adequate for the child's physical, mental, spiritual, moral and social development.

Article 28

1. States Parties recognize the right of the child to education, and with a view to achieving this right progressively and on the basis of equal opportunity, they shall, in particular:

   (a) Make primary education compulsory and available free to all.

1. States Parties agree that the education of the child shall be directed to:

   (a) The development of the child's personality, talents and mental and physical abilities to their fullest potential.

Article 32

States Parties recognize the right of the child to be protected from economic exploitation and from performing any work that is likely to be hazardous or to interfere with the child's education, or to be harmful to the child's health or physical, mental, spiritual, moral or social development.

Article 35

States Parties shall take all appropriate national, bilateral and multilateral measures to prevent the abduction of, the sale of or traffic in children for any purpose or in any form.

[Part II lays out a system for state party compliance and monitoring of adherence to the treaty.]

References

Act 4. N.d. "Fact Sheet: Jail Removal and Sight and Sound Core Protections." Retrieved September 30, 2010 (http://www.act4jj.org/media/factsheets/fact-sheet_60.pdf).

African Committee of Experts on the Rights and Welfare of the Child. N.d. "About the African Charter on the Rights and Welfare of the Child." Retrieved January 20, 2011 (http://www.africa-union.org/child/home.htm).

Amnesty International. 2010. "Children and Human Rights." Retrieved September 30, 2011 (http://www.amnesty.org/en/children).

Aristotle. 1885. *Politics*. Forgotten Books.

Boyle, Elizabeth Heger. 2002. *Female Genital Cutting*. Baltimore: Johns Hopkins University Press.

Case Western Reserve University. 2004a. "Department of Sociology: Dr. Brian Gran: The Children's Rights Index." Retrieved January 20, 2011 (http://www.case.edu/artsci/soci/Gran/childrights.html).

Case Western Reserve University. 2004b. "Department of Sociology: Dr. Brian Gran: U.S. Children's Rights." Retrieved January 20, 2011 (http://www.case.edu/artsci/soci/Gran/uschildrensrights.html).

Freeman, Michael. 2007. "Why It Remains Important to Take Children's Rights Seriously." *International Journal of Children's Rights* 15:5–23.

Global Initiative to End All Corporal Punishment of Children. N.d. Accessed September 29, 2010 (www.endcorporalpunishment.org).

Gran, Brian. 2008. "The Rights of the Child." Pp. 47–59 in *The Leading Rogue State: The US and Human Rights*, edited by Judith Blau, Alberto Moncada, Cathy Zimmer, and David Brunsma. Boulder, CO: Paradigm.

Gran, Brian K. 2010. "Comparing Children's Rights: Introducing the Children's Rights Index." *International Journal of Children's Rights* 18:1–17.

Gran, Brian, and Dawn Aliberti. 2003. "The Office of the Children's Ombudsperson: Children's Rights and Social-Policy Innovation." *International Journal of the Sociology of Law* 31(2):89–106.

Guggenheim, Martin. 2005. *What's Wrong with Children's Rights*. Cambridge, MA: Harvard University Press.

Juvenile Justice and Delinquency Prevention Act. 1974. 42 U.S.C. 5601.

Marshall, T. H. 1964. *Class, Citizenship, and Social Development*. Garden City, NY: Doubleday.

Minow, Martha. 1995. "Whatever Happened to Children's Rights?" *Minnesota Law Review* 80:267.

Newell, Peter. 2008. *Challenging Violence against Children*. London, England: Save the Children.

Norwegian Forum on the Rights of the Child. N.d. "Submission by the Norwegian Forum on the Rights of the Child Related to Norway for Universal Periodic

Review 6th Session. Children's Rights in Norway: Key Issues of Concern." Retrieved September 30, 2010 (http://lib.ohchr.org/HRBodies/UPR/Documents/Session6/NO/FFB_NOR_UPR_S06_2009_NorwegianForumOnTheRightsOf TheChild.pdf).

Parental Rights. 2011. "Protecting Children by Empowering Parents." Retrieved September 29, 2010 (http://www.parentalrights.org).

Smith, Anne B. 2007. "Children and Young People's Participation Rights in Education." *International Journal of Children's Rights* 15:147–64.

Thomas, Nigel. 2007. "Towards a Theory of Children's Participation." *International Journal of Children's Rights* 15:199–218.

Thomas, Nigel, Mandy Cook, Josey Cook, Hannah France, Joanne Hillman, Cerys Jenkins, Toby Pearson, Rhodri Pugh-Dungey, Ben Sawyers, Matthew Taylor, and Anne Crowley. 2010. "Evaluating the Children's Commissioner for Wales: Report of a Participatory Research Study." *International Journal of Children's Rights* 18(1):19–52.

Turner, Bryan S. 1993. "Contemporary Problems in the Theory of Citizenship." Pp. 1–18 in *Citizenship and Social Theory*, edited by B. S. Turner. London: Sage.

UNICEF Innocenti Research Centre. 2011. *Global Study on Independent Human Rights Institutions for Children*. Florence, Italy: Author.

United Kingdom Youth Parliament. 2011. "Welcome." Retrieved September 29, 2010 (http://www.ukyouthparliament.org.uk).

United Nations International Human Rights Instruments. 2008. "Report on Indicators for Promoting and Monitoring the Implementation of Human Rights." HRI/MC/2008/3* Retrieved January 21, 2011 (http://www2.ohchr.org/english/bodies/icm-mc/docs/HRI.MC.2008.3EN.pdf).

University of Minnesota. 2010. "Department of Sociology: Elizabeth Heger Boyle." Retrieved January 20, 2011 (http://www.soc.umn.edu/people/boyle_e.html).

U.S. Department of Justice Bureau of Justice Assessment. 2000. "Juveniles in Adult Prisons and Jails: A National Assessment." Washington, DC: U.S. Department of Justice.

Williams, Patricia. 1987. "Alchemical Notes: Reconstructing Ideals from Deconstructed Rights." *Harvard Civil Rights-Civil Liberties Law Review* 22:401–33.

PART IV

The Global and the Local

12

Growing and Learning Human Rights

Judith Blau

A mazingly, after Eleanor Roosevelt helped to craft what became the 1948 Universal Declaration of Human Rights—for *all* the world's peoples—she gave a speech a decade later, in 1958, at the United Nations in which she stated,

> Where, after all, do universal human rights begin? In small places, close to home—so close and so small that they cannot be seen on any maps of the world. Yet they are the world of the individual person; the neighborhood he lives in; the school or college he attends; the factory, farm, or office where he works. Such are the places where every man, woman, and child seeks equal justice, equal opportunity, equal dignity without discrimination.

In this chapter I describe how I along with many others have started to discover and nurture human rights in one small place. By "many others" I refer to my students, student groups with which we partner, community nonprofits, and, most of all, the residents of the Abbey Court apartment complex where the Human Rights Center (HRC) is located.[1] Our Hispanic neighbors teach all of us at the HRC what human rights entail because *derechos humanos* run deep in Latino culture. Our Burmese neighbors teach all of us at the HRC that tenacity and emotional strength are required to

245

overtake the experiences of dislocation and resettlement. They are refugees. Our African American neighbors teach us how Americans experience discrimination and marginalization. Our neighbors do not lecture or educate us in any formal sense. They teach by example, in the gracious ways they treat one another and treat us.

Another inspiration for founding the HRC came from the People's Movement for Human Rights Learning.[2] As the founder, Shulamith Koenig, insists, human rights are not charity; they are achieved through people's equal and informed participation in the decisions that affect their lives. This nonprofit organization was pivotal at the United Nations in founding a Decade for Human Rights Education and in helping to draft resolutions for the World Conference on Human Rights, and it played an active role at the Fourth World Conference on Women. Shula Koenig was awarded the UN Prize in the Field of Human Rights in 2003, an award of distinction that is given only occasionally. She, like Eleanor Roosevelt before her, applauds progress in human rights laws, but the seedbeds for transformative change are in those small places "where every man, woman, and child seeks equal justice, equal opportunity, [and] equal dignity without discrimination." In Shula Koenig's words, "Day after day human rights are given new life by the experiences and efforts of communities to recognize and claim their right to live in dignity and security."[3] Before founding the HRC I invited Koenig to come to Chapel Hill, North Carolina, to meet with students and the mayors of Chapel Hill and Carrboro. Her charisma is amazing.

I had three objectives in mind when I founded the HRC: first, for all of us to learn together how we could deepen our understanding of human rights through social interaction across cultural and class lines; second, to help defend the most vulnerable people, especially in their dealings with disreputable employers and overzealous police; and, third, to provide my undergraduates with authentic experiences as to how the most marginalized could realize their fundamental human rights.

In class we discuss the conceptual and philosophical depth of human rights. That is, we refer to rights that are indivisible, interdependent, and inherent in persons. They include, but are not limited to, civil and political rights, nondiscrimination, the rights of vulnerable people, cultural rights, migrants' rights, and environmental rights. We discuss how white, rich Americans take these for granted, but migrants, refugees, and persons of color do not (Blau and Moncada 2009). We also discuss *collective goods* and ask what goods are not collective. My answer is that even sex is a limited, dyadic collective good and that psychological well-being and personal health depend on the overall supply of collective goods in the community and society. In caring communities and societies, people are happier and healthier.[4] There has been a sea change on my campus and, I suspect, on the campuses of other U.S. universities and colleges. The contemporary "we-we" generation has displaced the "me-me" generation of the 1980s and 1990s. National survey polls support my conjecture. They indicate, for example, that young Americans are repudiating racism and embracing a vision of a multiracial and multiethnic society (Taylor 2008).

In large part the transformation was due to the forces that accompanied globalism, such as multiculturalism, and a new cosmopolitanism that accompanied international travel and studies. In class we also consider that the United States does not ratify human rights treaties, most environmental and climate treaties, and the Rome Statute that implements the International Criminal Court.[5] In these respects, the United States is on a par with Somalia, which does not have a government. We also consider that the United States has excessively high poverty rates compared with most other industrialized countries,[6] and greater disparities in wealth and income (Reich 2010). Yet the implications of such facts and statistics are hard for anyone to process in the absence of grounded experiences. My university, along with many others, developed service learning in the 1990s and, later, experiential learning, which is learning from direct experience. In practical terms I prefer the term *experiential learning* since it does not have the connotation of charity but rather can imply democratic experiential learning where, in our case, both students and community residents learn from one another.

I should also note that there are transformations in American society that affect students' learning in and out of the classroom and deepen their understanding of what participatory community activism entails. These include a variety of social movements that are both national and local: fair trade, local food, slow food, green economies, local economies, and sustainability. These all draw from residents' awareness of collective welfare and what they can accomplish through participatory democracy. From our perspective, an awareness of human rights clarifies why these movements are important and why deeper forms of democracy depend on such efforts and relations. In other words, such community practices are grounded in human rights, and they also strengthen community bonds, interpersonal obligations, and local democracy, all of which are necessary for the advance of human rights. I am convinced that how we practice human rights at the local level will help shape a national human rights culture.

In this chapter I describe how one community-based organization, the HRC, along with University of North Carolina college students and community residents, attempts to sow the seeds of human rights in one American community—in "one small place," as Eleanor Roosevelt described it. We must insist with her and the other committee members who drafted the Universal Declaration of Human Rights that human rights are indivisible and inalienable. For this reason the HRC takes on many challenges that come our way.

Migrants in the United States and Elsewhere Do Not Have Human Rights

Migrants have historically been welcomed in the United States for their labor and to do work that Americans will not do—in construction, agriculture, housekeeping, and landscaping. Yet migrants to the United States are not protected by the Constitution and do not benefit from federal, state, and most local programs, although most immigrants, both documented and undocumented, pay taxes (Urban Institute 2005). In other parts of the world governments have pushed for freer migration policies, according migrants many of the rights that citizens have. The European Union, for example, has made it possible for citizens of member countries to move without restriction from one member state to another. In 1994 EU countries went further than this, reconfirming their commitment to protect migrant workers from discrimination (Organization for Security and Co-operation in Europe 2008).[7] EU citizens, therefore, no matter where they live in the European Union, are entitled to social welfare. Nevertheless, EU countries are struggling to accommodate non-EU citizens just as the United States is doing with non-U.S. citizens. The tragic irony everywhere is that trade, finance, and multinationals know no borders and roam freely around the globe whereas few people have this right. In some states in the United States, notably Arizona, migrants are treated like criminals, as clarified in the chapter by Rogelio Sáenz, Cecilia Menjívar, and San Juanita Edilia Garcia (Chapter 8). Migration is one of the defining global issues of the early twenty-first century since more people are on the move today than at any other time in human history. According to the International Organization of Migration, there are now about 192 million people living outside their place of birth, which is about 3 percent of the world's population.[8]

Few constitutions spell out migrants' rights, although they are sometimes explicit that everyone who resides in their country, including migrants, has freedom of movement. The constitution of the Virgin Islands is such an example. Beyond this, there are now regional efforts being made to protect migrants, the most comprehensive of which is the Colombo Process, an agreement signed by 11 Asian countries.[9] The Colombo Process is a regional consultative process on the management of overseas employment and contractual labor for workers from Asian countries. One of its concerns is the working conditions of Asian workers in the context of globalization driven by the Global North, and these countries invite to their meetings representatives of the International Labour Organization, UNIFEM (the United Nations Development Fund for Women), and the Human Rights Council. The reason I attach particular importance to the Colombo Process is that regional bodies to ensure migrants' rights are needed throughout the world, and since the flow of migrants is often regional in nature, countries need to cooperate.

It is also the case that other regional bodies attempt to promote and protect the rights of migrants. The Organization of American States (OAS) has a Special Rapporteur on Migrant Workers and Their Families, and engages country representatives and groups in developing programs that will better protect migrants.[10] Yet the overarching global normative standard is the International Convention on the Protection of the Rights of All Migrant Workers and Members of Their Families (United Nations 1990).

Day Laborers

Special attention will be paid to day laborers and their families because many, if not most, of the men who live in Abbey Court work as day laborers, and wait for employers to pick them up right outside the apartment complex, at "the corner." In fact, it is the side of the highway, but *the corner* is their somewhat affectionate term for the place where they gather, talk with one another, and wait (and wait, and wait, and wait) for a contractor, restaurant owner, or landscaper to pick them up.

It is important to clarify why Mexicans come to the United States. First, Mexicans were here first, before Americans, at least in much of what is now U.S. territory. That is, Mexico owned the present-day states of California, Nevada, and Utah, as well as portions of Arizona, Colorado, New Mexico, and Wyoming. As a result families put down roots, and this sense of belonging has continued. Second, Mexicans have historically been welcome to work in the United States, and with the wage differential persisting between the two countries, Mexicans migrated to the United States, at first without border controls, and then later taking advantage of the *Bracero* Program (1942–1964). After the end of the *Bracero* Program, U.S. recruiters continued to go to Mexico to enlist low-wage workers. The North American Free Trade Agreement (NAFTA) accelerated migration because it further opened up interstate markets. Yet NAFTA failed to include labor protections and allowed American firms to invest in Mexican industries and agricultural land. As these companies streamlined production, they threw millions out of work. Adding insult to injury the traditional *ejidos* laws that protected collective farming were repealed, and to take advantage of cheaper labor in Asian and African countries, many factories next to the border—*maquiladoras*—closed, laying off millions of workers. The result, inevitably, was a spike in migration to the United States (Passel and Suro 2005).[11]

INGOs, NGOs, and CBOs

The HRC is a nonprofit (by American tax law), which in the rest of the world is called a nongovernmental organization (NGO), but it is also a community-based organization (CBO)—namely, an NGO that is based in one community.[12] The HRC[13] was recognized by the U.S. Internal Revenue Service as a 501(c)(3) nonprofit on February 2, 2009, and in March we moved into our current location, in Abbey Court in Carrboro, North Carolina. Our world is very small indeed. Most of our activities focus on that community of about 800 people, although we occasionally make forays into the larger community, as I will describe. I need to distinguish the HRC from university-based human rights centers, such as those at Columbia University, Duke University, and the University of Minnesota. University-based human rights centers typically focus on human rights abuses in countries other than the United States, and their objective is research. In contrast, although the HRC selectively supports university graduate students working on research projects, the HRC is an advocacy organization that also tries to empower residents. Like other nonprofits, we provide services, but we call this solidarity, not services.

Human Rights Center of
Chapel Hill and Carrboro: Its Origins

The founding of the Human Rights Center of Chapel Hill and Carrboro was motivated by three major considerations. First, teaching a course on human rights, I wanted to provide my students with an opportunity to engage human rights directly instead of abstractly. Second, I felt it was possible to create an organization that would engage the breadth of human rights issues in the community, from education to wages. Third, it was evident that migrants in the community enjoyed few rights and experienced discrimination, which worsened with the economic recession. I wanted my students to better understand why people from Mexico and Central America migrated to the

United States and the ordeals they faced once they were here. There inevitably grows a sense of comradeship between my students—working with migrants in computer classes, tutoring the children of migrants, and occasionally working on a car engine with migrants—and the residents of Abbey Court. In the language of human rights, my students discover what equality is and its significance.

What formally justifies the founding of such a center? In a sense the entire international human rights framework justifies what we do, but this framework does not clarify the practical implementation of human rights. However, one UN human rights declaration deals specifically with the responsibilities of individuals and CBOs in promoting human rights. It is the Declaration on the Right and Responsibility of Individuals, Groups and Organs of Society to Promote and Protect Universally Recognized Human Rights and Fundamental Freedoms. It was not long until this declaration became commonly known as the Declaration on Human Rights Defenders.[14] Portions of it are replicated in Figure 12.1.

This declaration is especially noteworthy for its insistence that local organizations and people themselves defend, advocate, and advance human rights against governments and powerful economic actors. The declaration defends the rights—indeed, the obligations—of people to protest human rights violations and to advance human rights in their communities. This declaration provides the rationale and justification of the HRC. As noted above, it quickly acquired the title—a nickname, really—of the Declaration on Human Rights Defenders. It is fully a focus of the UN Human Rights Council with its own Special Rapporteur and a complaints procedure.

The premise of the Declaration on Human Rights Defenders is that people are themselves empowered to act to advance human rights on their own behalf but, more especially, in solidarity with others. Shack/Slum Dwellers International (SDI) uses another term, *incrementalism*. In Figure 12.2 an extract from a published letter written by SDI Secretariat Benjamin Bradlow is reproduced. It is hard to distinguish what Americans call "grassroots movement" (or "empowerment," or "participatory democracy") from incrementalism since Bradlow contrasts incrementalism with top-down approaches and state intervention. And it is also important to remember that the rich believe the poor create the conditions of their poverty. To paraphrase activist Sheela Patel who organized SPARC—the Society for the Promotion of Area Resource Centres[15]—one of the persistent myths is that the poor are not improving their lot because they lack the skills to do so and that if they were trained they would stop suffering and start prospering.

Figure 12.1 Declaration on the Right and Responsibility of Individuals, Groups and Organs of Society to Promote and Protect Universally Recognized Human Rights and Fundamental Freedoms (Extracts)

Adopted by General Assembly resolution 53/144 of 9 December 1998

The General Assembly,

Reaffirming also the importance of the Universal Declaration of Human Rights and the International Covenants on Human Rights as basic elements of international efforts to promote universal respect for and observance of human rights and fundamental freedoms and the importance of other human rights instruments adopted within the United Nations system, as well as those at the regional level,

Stressing that all members of the international community shall fulfill, jointly and separately, their solemn obligation to promote and encourage respect for human rights and fundamental freedoms for all without distinction of any kind, including distinctions based on race, color, sex, language, religion, political or other opinion, national or social origin, property, birth or other status,

Reiterating that all human rights and fundamental freedoms are universal, indivisible, interdependent and interrelated and should be promoted and implemented in a fair and equitable manner, without prejudice to the implementation of each of those rights and freedoms,

Declares:

Article 6

Everyone has the right, individually and in association with others:

(a) To know, seek, obtain, receive and hold information about all human rights and fundamental freedoms, including having access to information as to how those rights and freedoms are given effect in domestic legislative, judicial or administrative systems;

(b) As provided for in human rights and other applicable international instruments, freely to publish, impart or disseminate to others views, information and knowledge on all human rights and fundamental freedoms;

(c) To study, discuss, form and hold opinions on the observance, both in law and in practice, of all human rights and fundamental freedoms and, through these and other appropriate means, to draw public attention to those matters.

Article 7

Everyone has the right, individually and in association with others, to develop and discuss new human rights ideas and principles and to advocate their acceptance.

3. To the same end, everyone has the right, individually and in association with others:

   (a) To complain about the policies and actions of individual officials and governmental bodies with regard to violations of human rights and fundamental freedoms, by petition or other appropriate means, to competent domestic judicial, administrative or legislative authorities or any other competent authority provided for by the legal system of the State, which should render their decision on the complaint without undue delay.

Article 12

Everyone has the right, individually and in association with others, to participate in peaceful activities against violations of human rights and fundamental freedoms.

Article 13

Everyone has the right, individually and in association with others, to solicit, receive and utilize resources for the express purpose of promoting and protecting human rights and fundamental freedoms through peaceful means.

Article 16

Individuals, non-governmental organizations and relevant institutions have an important role to play in contributing to making the public more aware of questions relating to all human rights and fundamental freedoms through activities such as education, training and research in these areas to strengthen further, inter alia, understanding, tolerance, peace and friendly relations among nations and among all racial and religious groups, bearing in mind the various backgrounds of the societies and communities in which they carry out their activities.

Article 18

1. Everyone has duties towards and within the community, in which alone the free and full development of his or her personality is possible.

2. Individuals, groups, institutions and non-governmental organizations have an important role to play and a responsibility in safeguarding democracy, promoting human rights and fundamental freedoms and contributing to the promotion and advancement of democratic societies, institutions and processes.

Source: Office of the High Commissioner for Human Rights: http://www2.ohchr.org/english/law/freedom.htm.

Figure 12.2   What Is Incrementalism? (Extracts)

By Benjamin Bradlow, SDI Secretariat

Top-down strategies for "eradicating slums" are seemingly always in vogue. Planners, government officials, commentators, and most non-governmental civil society actors, all aim for State-conceived, State-driven solutions to the "problems" of slums. Occasionally, we might hear about the potential of the social energy and even the density of informal settlements. But the solutions, we hear, must always come from the State.

But we can consider for a moment where these "formal" actors are headed, and from where they get their ideas. It is not the State. Governments of the Global South are quite evidently incapable of conceiving and implementing solutions without the people such policies are intended to address. The slums of the South are growing. And in the absence of effective State interventions, the poor—the world of the "informal"—are providing the vast majority of shelter solutions.

So "formal" actors—the State, planners, etc.—are getting their ideas from those who populate the world of the "informal"—the urban poor themselves. Instead of centrally-planned, green-fields housing developments, governments from South Africa to Kenya are talking about "slum upgrading" or "informal settlement upgrading." In India, the term that most closely mirrors this is "redevelopment." To varying degrees, policies that deploy these terms in each country are rooted in "informal" practice. Improvements in the living spaces where people already live.

The poor know this, and address it on a daily basis in the only way they can: incrementalism. To build incrementally is to live within one's means, adding on and improving one's dwelling and environment bit-by-bit. There are obstacles to this approach, namely lack of security of tenure. How can a person save to upgrade when he or she faces the constant threat of being evicted? But even without total security of tenure (i.e. full title), the poor are willing to build incrementally.

Source: Courtesy of Benjamin Bradlow, Shack/Slum Dwellers International (SDI). http://www .sdinet.org/.

The Evolution of the HRC

December 10, 2008, was the 60th anniversary of the Universal Declaration of Human Rights (UDHR), and since we were in motion to found the HRC, my students and I decided to have community meetings devoted to human rights in both Chapel Hill and Carrboro. We covered the waterfront of topics that dealt with human rights, including labor rights, women's rights, racial justice, health care, diversity, sustainability, local food, and fair trade.

We managed to cram into the week musical performances and theater. I like to think that we conveyed to the residents of Chapel Hill and Carrboro the idea that human rights are indivisible and that ultimate responsibility for ensuring them rests with people themselves, not governments. Right after acquiring our 501(c)(3) status, we filed a petition with Chapel Hill and Carrboro to adopt the Universal Declaration of Human Rights. The Carrboro town manager asked me to make revisions in the UDHR, "to bring it up to date." I couldn't do it. For me the UDHR is like the Declaration of Independence or the Communist Manifesto, which is to say that its language may be in some sense antiquated but in no way detracts from its contemporary and enduring significance. But to give the town manager credit, updating the UDHR would make it more relevant to today's realities. Changes that Carrboro officials made include the following:

a. Make reference in the Preamble to "humankind" rather than "mankind"

b. Include in Article 2 the statuses of ethnicity, sexual orientation, and gender expression

c. Acknowledge in Article 10 the rights of all persons to enter into civil marriage

d. Make reference to "people" rather than "men and women" in Article 16(1)

e. Acknowledge in Article 18(3) the great variation in social units that today serve family functions

f. Revise Article 25(2) to include "fatherhood"

g. State, throughout the document, any reference to "his" or "himself" as "them" or "themselves"

Carrboro adopted the Universal Declaration of Human Rights, as revised, on April 21, 2009, making it the second city in the country to have done so, and Chapel Hill followed suit and adopted it on November 23, 2009, also with the same revisions enacted by Carrboro, making it the fifth city in the country to have adopted the UDHR.

What, really, is the worth of such exercises? What gets accomplished? There are now four other Human Rights Cities in the United States that have adopted the UDHR—namely, Washington, DC; Eugene, Oregon; Richmond, California; and South Bend, Indiana. It is also useful to mention that worldwide there are about 26 Human Rights Cities, thanks to the energy and commitment of Shulamith Koenig, director of People's Decade of Human Rights Education (PDHRE), which now goes by the name of People's Movement for Human Rights Learning.[16] The human rights cities movement empowers people in communities to challenge elite structures, patriarchy, and unfair and discriminatory laws. It also seeks to affirm the culture and language of all groups while celebrating the equality of all human beings. The Human Rights Center strives to advance these two goals, and we do so through our partnerships, including with the American Civil Liberties Union (ACLU), schools, urban farming groups, organizations devoted to food security, computer groups, and arts organizations.

Moving Into Abbey Court

When we moved into Abbey Court in February 2009, loitering or simply standing around was *forbidden*. As we discovered, Tar Heel Realty, which owns the property, stipulated that people could only walk between their cars (or the bus stop) and their apartments and could not linger or socialize. We appealed to the town of Carrboro, and although the answer was that Abbey Court was a privately owned property and the town could do little, things did change and did so suddenly. The antiloitering rules were relaxed, and to test this new regime, we started playing soccer on the weekends with the kids.

Maybe this is the context to explain why I decided the center should be located in Abbey Court. In January 2009, I along with Rafael Gallegos, teaching assistant and now associate director of the HRC, and a couple of my students went to Abbey Court to hand out brochures for El Centro, a Latino advocacy organization. As we made our way from building to building, a security guard followed us yelling to get off of private property. Eventually he called the police and sheriff. I motioned the students to stand back and introduced myself as "Professor Blau" to the law enforcement officers. They said they would arrest me if I did not leave the property. Had I not had students with me, I may not have left, but instead I told them we would have to leave. I sent an e-mail to the mayor who replied I would have to contact the chief of police. When I met with her she said, "You were lucky we did not trespass you." We still have disagreements with the police, but to her credit, Carolyn Hutchison, the chief of police, has always met with us when we have asked. Right about that time I met Hugo Olaiz, an Argentinean, who lives in Abbey Court. He had long been protesting the unreasonable towing of cars, the failure of the owner to maintain the property, and the town's failure to protect the residents. I later asked him to serve on the executive committee of the HRC.

Right after acquiring our 501(c)(3) status, we moved into an apartment in Abbey Court in Carrboro in March 2009. Home to day laborers, Burmese refugees, and a few African and African American families, Abbey Court is an impoverished community. Residents contend with economic hardships and discrimination that native-born Americans cannot possibly imagine. But in a sense, the lives of the day laborers and Burmese are totally different from one another. The day laborers are undocumented, and even in the best of times they are poorly paid, are often cheated of their wages ("wage theft"), and receive no benefits whatsoever. At the corner, there is no shelter and no restrooms. There is no protection from the sweltering sun in the summer months, and no protection from the sleet storms, freezing rain, and cold during the winter months. We have petitioned the town for a workers' center and portable toilets, but to no avail, perhaps because of tight budgets during the economic recession.

On the other hand, the refugees struggle to adapt to their new country, often working two minimum-wage jobs. I think they are at least more hopeful about their futures than the migrants are. What the Latinos, the Burmese, and the small number of African and African American families have in common is they adore their children and want the best for them. As I will describe, there is nothing like the after-school program to win friends and for them to make friends with one another.

The first semester of 2009 we were trying to find our legs. Hugely helpful were Alfonso Hernandez, assistant director of the HRC and the assistant teacher, who lives at the HRC, and Rafael Gallegos. My goal that semester was to find ways of bridging my classes with Abbey Court and the HRC. As hard as I tried, that first semester was rocky. One day one of the University of North Carolina (UNC) students, a tall male, arrived at the HRC, visibly shaken, saying he was scared of the men at the corner. However, one should never underestimate student culture. Word got around, apparently, since my courses are now extremely popular and students are now casual about coming to the HRC. Some work with Rafael and me on projects that hopefully will improve the lives of the day laborers. For example, one group of students is working on a microfinancing project for the day laborers. Such projects as these are underscored by compassion and empathy for the workers.

Additionally, Rafael, Alfonso, and I do several things to bridge the divide between our students and Abbey Court residents. Each semester, for example, Rafael, Alfonso, and I take turns distributing flyers in Abbey Court that describe our programs, and we always take at least one student. Personal contacts, however fleeting, are helpful. Also, Rafael invites several of the day laborers to our class. Students are moved by their accounts of the ordeals they encounter as migrants and as workers.

Undocumented residents are highly vulnerable. The men routinely experience "wage theft"; that is, contractors, restaurant owners, and landscapers often cheat them out of their wages. Rafael often represents them in court or intervenes with the North Carolina Department of Labor. (We have been unsuccessful in our attempts to get the town to adopt an ordinance against wage theft.) If day laborers face constant uncertainty and anxiety about where and when their next job is, the Burmese also experience marginalization. Typically, at least in Abbey Court, parents in both Latino and Burmese households work as much as they can, giving them little time for schooling and classes in English as a second language (ESL). Language barriers are, of course, a great challenge. Were we pleased when a Burmese father, Mr. Kyaw Maung,[17] came to the center, with his son and daughter, to join us for an ice cream party. He beamed from ear to ear, and we beamed from ear to ear, as we all grasped hands. One by one, we gain the trust of our neighbors.

One day I walked into the center, and Rafael was there working on his computer. With him, working at separate computers, were two day laborers. One was on Skype, with a camera and microphone, talking with a relative in Guatemala. The other, Socrates,[18] was typing on his blog—entering text from sheaves of paper. The poem, which Alfonso later translated, is deeply passionate, filled with love and yearning. One of his poems is reproduced in Figure 12.3, along with a translation into English.

Figure 12.3   A Poem by Socrates Morales Mendoza

Orgullosa

eres altiva y orgullosa te crees mariposa

el epidermis de tus alas son tan suaves

como la espuma y los petalos de una rosa

y la trasparencia de tu ser y alma,

hacen perder mis sentidos ya perdidos

y a mi corazon la razon y la calma

eres orgullo de un capullo mi linda diosa

te miras planeando tus alas elegante y bella

cuando yo te veo, veo en el cielo

luces de colores y bellas estrellas

tu eres mi ilusion, mi fe y mi anhelo

tu haces que mi corazon, tenga algo de consuelo

tu haces que mi corazon no sea de roca ni de hielo

tu haces que mi corazon sienta amor

Proud

haughty and proud you believe you are a butterfly

the epidermis of your wings are so soft

like the foam and the petals of a rose

and the transparency of your being and soul,

making me lose my senses already lost

and my heart my reason and my calmness

you are the pride from a cocoon beautiful goddess

you look planning your wings elegant and beautiful

when I see you I see the sky

you light up with colors and beautiful stars

you are my illusion, my faith and my longing

you make my heart , have some comfort

you make my heart not be rock or ice

you make my heart feel love

Translated by Alfonso Hernandez

Source: Courtesy of socrates morales mendoza; http://socratesmorales.blogspot.com/.

The center has four rooms (excluding Alfonso's), plus a kitchen. The rooms are decorated with learning posters for the children, wall hangings from Brazil and Korea, photographs from one of our festivals, and, as I will describe, gold stars on the ceiling. Outside the center are usually exuberant chalk drawings that cover the walls, the walkways, and the sidewalks. It rains, and by the next day there is an even more exuberant display. This is a collective effort. For me it is a leading indicator that we are on the right track.

Programs

Here I describe the programs we have launched, the festivals we have sponsored, and some of our partnerships. As far as I am aware, we are the first CBO devoted to human rights in the country, and for that reason we do a lot of improvising, as we attempt to clarify human rights principles to suit the needs of Abbey Court residents, and provide learning experiences for my students. There have been challenges we could not meet, along with some successes, sometimes when we didn't expect them (such as when our neighbors organized a monthly cleanup campaign; self-determination is terribly important). For the most part, volunteers come from the courses I teach in which I include an experiential-learning component. Teaching human rights without hands-on experience is somewhat like teaching astrophysics without giving students the opportunity to look through telescopes at the sky.

Most of our enduring partnerships are with groups (committees) from UNC's Campus Y, a 150-year-old student-run organization that is committed to the pursuit of social justice.[19] Campus Y houses many student groups, some of which provide programs specifically designed for the HRC, and some of which are in the process of developing partnerships with us. These include the following: Linking Immigrants to New Communities (LINC, which provides ESL classes at the center); Homeless Outreach Poverty Eradication (HOPE, which empowers the poor, including the homeless, to write stories that are annually published in a large booklet); a know-your-rights committee; the Community Empowerment Fund (CEF), which will give residents in Abbey Court access to microloans; and Techs without Borders (TWOB).

To clarify our partnership with TWOB, I need to say a bit more. The two cochairs approached us to ask if we would be their partner in making Abbey Court Wi-Fi compatible. "Of course!" I said. They applied for a grant, and received it, at which point we contacted Renny Johnson of Chapel Hill-Carrboro City Schools, and he, in turn, obtained nearly 50 computers from a local nonprofit to give to families in Abbey Court. TWOB continues to troubleshoot computer problems and give computer classes.

Finally, there is another campus group, WhyEquals, spearheaded by David Iberkleid, a graduate student in information sciences. David brings his Bolivian background with him when he acknowledges Latino culture in his technical collaborations with our neighbors. Recognizing that our neighbors are very talented mechanics, he is collaborating with them to make a video of their repairing a car.

We don't partner exclusively with student groups. We also work with local NGOs, including a variety of partners in a food distribution program that secures fresh fruit and vegetables every Saturday from the farmers' market. In addition, we collaborate with TABLE, which gives workshops about nutrition and provides food for children, and with the Orange County Partnership for Young Children's Healthy Kids Campaign, which provides small plots of land to families for growing vegetables. We have been fortunate in having an attorney from the ACLU and a migrant advocate give know-your-rights workshops.

After-School and Summer School Programs

Nothing has been as successful as our collaboration with Scroggs Elementary School. The Scroggs teacher who runs the after-school program, Nancy Hilburn, and her assistant, Alfonso, have made an immense difference, not only at the HRC, but in the entire community. Besides, the after-school program is the main bridge between my classes and the HRC. I have learned never to underestimate student culture. For example, usually one of my African students volunteers to be the head math tutor. Why? This started with Daniel Tesfu, an Ethiopian student, who first volunteered to be the math tutor, and then at the end of the semester, he passed the torch to another African student, who at the beginning of the summer session passed it to another. More typically, student tutors switch around from math to reading.

We have all grown to love Zaw Zeya (not his real name). Zaw Zeya is a Burmese refugee youngster who has been in the United States for about two years. He has many family responsibilities, with two younger siblings and parents who speak and read very little English. He is an exceptionally good math student. Nancy and Alfonso put a gold paper star on the ceiling whenever a child scores 100 on a test at school, and Zaw Zeya has several gold stars. He is very, very proud. He is also an amazing soccer player, often running circles around my students, playing barefoot. Nine times out of ten when I have stopped by the HRC when it is closed, Zaw Zeya is there patiently waiting for Alfonso to open the door to use the computers (since our computers are faster than the one he has at home).

Another elementary school student is Array (not his real name), an African American who is exceedingly good at computer chess, and the story at the center is that he taught himself. Array flips the board with each move, and what I find astonishing is that he captures the same number of black and white pieces over the course of two moves. "Fair chess" is what we might call it. He is always eager to teach my students to play computer chess.

All the children are unique and special, whether as precocious readers, talented artists, or little computer geeks. They adore my college students, and my college students not only adore them but are also ambitious toward their success in school. And Nancy and Alfonso have amazing pedagogical talent skills. They are warm and nurturing, and provide each child with challenges.

The HRC's partnership with Scroggs is a complete success. It is also a great success with my students. Their presentations in class offer abundant proof of that. Most important, we see spectacular academic gains, as well as their bonding across race and ethnic lines. And, it is a great success not only in fostering cooperative learning but in fostering cooperative play. One indicator is the exuberance of the children. Figure 12.4 is a photograph of one of the children, Gabriela (not her real name), virtually swimming in the chalk art that she and the other girls worked on one day. Although I schedule a weekly visit to the HRC sometime during the after-school program, I often go at other times just for a pickup. What my students and I find especially amazing is how cooperative the children are and how they develop such inclusive relations among themselves.

Nancy and I had dinner together one evening in the late spring of 2010. I asked her to describe the after-school program, and she replied, "It's magic. How would you describe it?" she asked. I replied, "It's magic." It dawned on us that we were actually developing a new model—an after-school, neighborhood program. Three things happened that semester that helped to confirm that speculation. First, Frank Porter Graham Elementary School's principal asked us if we would like to collaborate on an after-school program in Carolina Apartments, a housing complex near Abbey Court.

Figure 12.4   Gabriela

She said she would like it to be tailored after our program. We agreed, and this became another after-school program and an experiential-learning opportunity for my UNC students. Second, we were asked to give a presentation at a school board task force meeting, where Nancy and I both described the HRC's after-school program, and acknowledged the help that Renny Johnson had provided in securing computers for our neighbors and also for the HRC. And, third, word got around the school district that our neighborhood after-school program was somewhat unique. For about two weeks we had a steady stream of visitors: teachers and principals. Figure 12.5 is a photograph of our teacher, Nancy Hilburn, and our assistant teacher, Alfonso Hernandez.

My own (social science) explanation as to why the after-school program is such a success is that poor children feel more secure when they are close to their parents and families. Latino and Burmese families are very close-knit. In contrast, public schools can feel impersonal, and in the case of our children they are districted in a faraway school that is in an extremely affluent neighborhood.

Nancy recommended that the after-school program continue through the summer. I agreed and signed up to teach in both summer sessions at UNC.

Figure 12.5   Nancy Hilburn and Alfonso Hernandez

The compelling reason for offering summer school is that poor children fall behind in the summer while their affluent counterparts are engaged in enriching programs (Alexander, Entwisle, and Olson 2007).

She designed the summer school programs to provide a balance of opportunities that were fun and educational. Included in these programs were trips to the Carrboro Branch Library where children read books and checked some out. The children also participated in a tennis program sponsored by the town of Carrboro's Department of Parks and Recreation, and they went to the UNC campus where they visited a dorm room. The biggest treat of all was the trip to the zoo. Over 110 people, including the children, many parents, and some of my students, piled into two charter buses to journey across the state to enjoy sharing watching the lions, elephants, giraffes, tigers, monkeys, camels, and gorillas.

Festivals

One of our goals is to give residents a chance to come together to celebrate and socialize. The housing complex is austere, and sociability is difficult in Abbey Court. There are no benches in Abbey Court, and no playgrounds for young children. Our neighbors, I thought, needed opportunities to celebrate.

The first festival we had at Abbey Court in 2009 was Las Posadas. It was a huge success. Primarily a Mexican festival, it lasts for nine days, beginning December 16 and ending December 24,[20] although we only celebrated one evening. It is a saga of Mary and Joseph's quest for an inn where Mary can deliver her baby. For this occasion, the center hired mariachi bands and a horse, and an Abbey Court resident made tamales that were out of this world. All of the children had an opportunity to ride the horse, and then "Mary" got on it, with "Joseph" at her side, to go from one apartment to another in search of an inn. Part of the magic, of course, was that University of North Carolina (UNC) students and Abbey Court residents intermingled, and children from the after-school program introduced the students to their families.

Because Burmese refugees make up a sizeable minority of Abbey Court residents, we decided to celebrate Thingyan. This is the background:

> When the Sun enters the constellation Aswini in sign Aries, the *Thingyan* period begins, and continues for three days. The popular belief, however, is that during the *Thingyan* period *Thagyamin* (who is the same as the Vedic deity Indra) descends to make his annual visit to the realms of the earth. He

begins with him a golden book wherein he inscribes the names of those who [did] good deeds and he has with him another book made of dog's skin wherein he puts down the names of those who did wicked deeds.[21]

That is the theological background, but the festival itself is an orgy of water—water throwing, water games, water balloons, water pistols, water sprinklers, and, of course, dunking. In Burma even huge water hoses pulled by trucks are deployed (but we skipped this particular part of Thingyan). We had the same mixture of attendees as we had for Las Posadas: Latino, Burmese, and African American residents; teachers from Scroggs Elementary School; and UNC students. The little kids were gleeful as they drenched their tutors. My students had just as much fun, but by the end of the afternoon there was no question that the little kids had the upper hand. Then they all went to the top of a little knoll to fly kites together. At about this time one of our Mexican neighbors joined the mariachi band, took out a mic, and burst into song. He sang the most beautiful and sorrowful songs. Alfonso and I looked at each other in disbelief. We have some very talented neighbors, and are making very dear friends.

Relations With the Towns

Besides being successful in getting the two towns to adopt the Universal Declaration of Human Rights, we also launched a fair trade campaign in Chapel Hill and Carrboro, with retailers, consumers, and large institutions, such as the university. We successfully got a resolution passed in Chapel Hill.[22] We have ongoing relations with the town departments. I call the police—dial 911 to complain—when I see that their presence in Abbey Court is threatening, or when they are needed, but then I also call the chief of police to ask her if the Abbey Court kids can visit the police station. My students have gone to various town meetings to understand the relations between developers and the towns, and have occasionally spoken out in opposition to a proposed project that harms minority communities. I cannot say that our relations with Carrboro police are completely smooth. None on the police force speaks Spanish, Burmese, or Karen. I have complained to the chief of police when I see police cars "herding" the day laborers, and I think it is confusing that the security guards, who are off-duty police, are indistinguishable from on-duty police. They wear the same uniforms, have the same badges, and carry the same guns. Still, the chief of police has told us she wants to start community policing in Abbey Court. This would be good, Rafael and I told her, especially if she hired someone to speak Spanish, which the majority of residents speak.

Conclusion

Several very large cities, including Washington, D.C., have embarked on human rights programs usually launched by a coalition of organizations.[23] Besides, academic associations are adopting human rights statements,[24] and there are national human rights organizations, including Human Rights First and the US Human Rights Network. Another is the Human Rights Campaign, which is dedicated to the equal rights of lesbians, gays, bisexuals, and transgendered individuals. These efforts will make a difference, introducing Americans to human rights and to the fundamental idea that all people are equal, entitled to their dignity and freedoms.

After teaching a college class on human rights for about five years, it became clear to me that for students to experience human rights firsthand, they need to see human rights violations close up—that is, to understand how people are deprived of their human rights in an impoverished community and where people struggle daily with food insecurity, lack of health care, joblessness, and discrimination. In Abbey Court, my students learn the value of human rights. The pathway to this realization is partly my students' interaction with the children whom many tutor. But it's much more than tutoring: My students play chess with the children, play soccer with them, turn the ropes for Double Dutch, set up logo games, and tell stories, as well as work on improving reading and math.

Why do these practices fall into the category of human rights? Occasionally one of my students gives a presentation to the children on the Convention on the Rights of the Child and reminds them they have the full array of rights that are spelled out in that international treaty. And, in a profound sense, the after-school program, like the HRC itself, embraces the principles of human rights and applies them on a day-to-day basis. Everyone is treated as an equal and with dignity.

Why is this sociology? I believe that sociology is the pursuit of understanding what a decent society is. We attempt to make a decent community in Abbey Court, in collaboration with our neighbors. For reasons having to do with poverty and discrimination, it is a struggle. We learn together. But one thing I am certain of is that what we bring back to the university classroom greatly enhances students' understanding of human rights in a sociological context.

What are the challenges ahead? Both towns adopted the Universal Declaration of Human Rights, yet both towns, like every town in America, subordinate people's rights to property; in many respects the university is not helpful; and nonprofits, although geared to advancing particular human rights, do not frame their missions in those terms. The people of Chapel Hill and Carrboro have many challenges ahead, as do Americans everywhere. I think the Human Rights Center will be helpful in our very smallest of places.

Discussion Questions

1. In America we tend to believe that the only grassroots movements that exist are political in character. In contrast, the Human Rights Center is sociological in that it focuses more on individual well-being and community. Do you know of communities similar to Abbey Court? What is happening in these communities?

2. What is the appropriate role of human rights defenders?

3. How can we bridge poor and nonpoor communities in the United States?

Notes

1. http://humanrightscities.org/about_us.html

2. http://www.pdhre.org/index.html

3. http://www.pdhre.org/about.html

4. There have been many studies of what constitutes a "happy society"; for a summary see http://en.wikipedia.org/wiki/Gross_national_happiness

5. The United States is not a party to the International Criminal Court: http://www.icc-cpi.int/Menus/ICC/About+the+Court/

6. Organization for Economic Co-operation and Development: http://www.oecd.org/home/0,3305,en_2649_201185_1_1_1_1_1,00.html

7. http://www.osce.org/odihr/49752

8. http://www.iom.int/jahia/Jahia/about-migration/lang/en

9. http://www.colomboprocess.org/

10. OAS actions to protect migrants: http://www.summit-americas.org/sisca/mig.html

11. However, with the severe economic recession in the United States, migration has dramatically declined.

12. NGOs and INGOs (international nongovernmental organizations) play a critical role in the United Nations, and comprise what is termed the global civil society. There are over 3,000 NGOs and INGOs that have consultative status with

the UN Economic and Social Council. They include ones with which Americans are familiar, such as Amnesty International, Human Rights Watch, and Habitat for Humanity, and also ones that evolved in the context of the Global South, such as Choike (a hub for Latin American NGOs), Via Campesina (an international advocacy organization for peasants), and Shack/Slum Dwellers International. What differentiates the HRC from other nonprofits in the United States is a commitment to advancing all human rights, at least in the community in which we are located.

13. Human Rights Center of Chapel Hill and Carrboro: http://www.human rightscities.org/

14. http://www2.ohchr.org/english/issues/defenders/declaration.htm

15. SPARC: http://www.sparcindia.org/about.html#SPARC

16. People's Movement for Human Rights Learning: http://www.pdhre.org/

17. Residents of Abbey Court are given fictitious names in this chapter.

18. This is his nom de plume.

19. Campus Y of UNC Chapel Hill: http://campus-y.unc.edu/

20. Mexconnect: http://www.mexconnect.com/articles/2816-las-posadas

21. http://www.seasite.niu.edu/burmese/Culture/thingyan.htm

22. http://chapelhillpublic.novusagenda.com/Bluesheet.aspx?itemid=838& meetingid=80

23. These include Carrboro, North Carolina; Chapel Hill, North Carolina; Eugene, Oregon, Richmond, California; and South Bend, Indiana.

24. See, for example, the American Sociological Association Statement Affirming and Expanding the Commitment of the American Sociological Association to Human Rights: http://www.asanet.org/about/Council_Statements/Council%20State ment%20on%20Human%20Rights%20%28August%202009%29.pdf.

References

Alexander, K. L., D. R. Entwisle, and L. S. Olson. 2007. "Lasting Consequences of the Summer Learning Gap." *American Sociological Review* 72:167–80.

Blau, Judith, and Alberto Moncada. 2009. *Human Rights: A Primer*. Boulder, CO: Paradigm.

Organization for Security and Co-operation in Europe. 2008. "OSCE Meeting Starts with Call for Stronger Institutions to Tackle Discrimination." May 29. Retrieved January 19, 2011 (http://www.osce.org/odihr/49752).

Passel, Jeffrey S., and Roberto Suro. 2005. "Rise, Peak and Decline: Trends in U.S. Immigration 1992–2004." Pew Hispanic Center. Retrieved January 12, 2011 (http://pewhispanic.org/reports/report.php?ReportID=53).

Reich, Robert B. 2010. *Aftershock: The Next Economy and America's Future*. New York: Alfred A. Knopf.

Roosevelt, Eleanor. 1958. "The Great Question." Remarks delivered at the United Nations in New York on March 27. Retrieved January 12, 2011 (http://www .udhr.org/history/Biographies/bioer.htm).

Taylor, Paul. 2008. "Race, Ethnicity and Campaign '08." Pew Research Center, January 17. Retrieved January 12, 2011 (http://pewresearch.org/pubs/694/race-ethnicity-and-campaign-08).

United Nations. 1990. "International Convention on the Protection of the Rights of All Migrant Workers and Members of Their Families." Retrieved January 12, 2011 (http://www2.ohchr.org/english/law/cmw.htm).

Urban Institute. 2005. "Undocumented Immigrants: Myths and Realities." Retrieved January 12, 2011 (http://www.urban.org/url.cfm?ID=900898).

13

Going Forward

Judith Blau

The objective in this final chapter is to argue that a human rights revolution is afoot in America and elsewhere that is *epistemological* as well as social, and therefore profoundly practical in its implications. It has been launched "on the ground," at the grassroots level, at the level of the state, by global civil society actors, and internationally, in the United Nations and in interstate relations. This revolution is not political in the sense of pitting left against right, but it is political in the sense that it advances every human being's self-determination and exerts demands on nation-states to protect and respect everyone's human rights. Perhaps we can be most certain that this revolution has validity because it is taken up by scientists in (as I will explain) a revolution of their own making. What is most uncertain is whether or not economic practices and institutions allow for progressive change.

Human Rights: Local, Global, and International

With increasing global interdependencies, the benchmarks for meeting human rights standards have become increasingly rigorous in various respects. First, these benchmarks are thoroughly international—through the United Nations and its various agencies—and thoroughly global—through the coordination of local nongovernmental organizations (NGOs), international nongovernmental organizations (INGOs), and global networks and media. Second, these benchmarks refer not only to constitutions but also to international human rights doctrine and laws. It is important to recognize that because of new complex interdependencies—that is, new with globalism—action at any given level ricochets throughout other levels. I draw on two instances to illustrate how this happens.

During the week of July 26, 2010, many global networks were broadly broadcasting two seemingly unrelated events.[1] First, the General Assembly adopted a resolution on July 28 declaring that access to clean water and sanitation is a human right (United Nations Department of Public Information 2010). Second, it was announced—also on global networks—that Laotian and Northern Thai villagers living on the Mekong River banks were mobilizing, along with civil society groups, to oppose the planned cascade of 11 dams to be built on the mainstream of Southeast Asia's largest body of water (see Macan-Markar 2010). These two events are independent of one another, and it is only coincidently that they both deal with water. However, these two events do shed light on how international human rights efforts and local-global human rights campaigns reinforce one another.

The General Assembly's resolution that access to clean water and sanitation is a human right also was broadly broadcast around the world within moments of its approval. Included in these global e-mails was the text of the resolution, which was accompanied by a statement expressing the concern that some 884 million people were without access to safe drinking water and more than 2.6 billion lacked access to basic sanitation. The statement also expressed alarm that 1.5 million children under five years old died each year as a result of water- and sanitation-related diseases, acknowledging that safe, clean drinking water and sanitation are integral to the realization of all human rights. Lack of access to water killed more children annually than AIDS, malaria, and measles combined.

This resolution did not come out of the blue. NGOs, such as the Centre on Housing Rights and Evictions (COHRE), had earlier launched an international campaign focused on water and sanitation as a human right, and the World Health Organization (a UN body) concluded quite a while ago that water, like food and access to vaccines and health care, is essential for human health and survival.[2] In spite of all of the scientific evidence that clean water and sanitation are indispensable for human health and for local and national development, the United States abstained in the vote taken in the General Assembly.

This process that led to the General Assembly resolution was carried on at multiple levels, and included NGOs, INGOs, states, research institutes, and UN agencies. In contrast, initial protests against dam construction on the Mekong River were led by local groups, and the protest spread to students and university scientists, who in turn attracted the attention of NGOs and INGOs. There is currently a standoff between the government and protestors, but if the government and private corporations are successful, residents of 40 villages will have to be relocated, and there will be a great loss of fish on which the villagers depend. If the dam project goes through, electricity will be sold to a Thai electric company. The villagers contend their fundamental human rights will be violated if this project is undertaken and completed.

These two instances—one involving the UN General Assembly (and a great variety of organizations, agencies, and countries) and the other a grassroots movement spearheaded by Thai and Laotian villagers—together help to illustrate the growing power of the global human rights movement. It is important to point out that people who live in the most remote villages and hamlets of the world have an especially profound understanding of human rights. In that respect they help Westerners understand the deeper significance of human rights.

Human Rights and Social Processes

Scholars have described how international transformative social and economic processes have spurred the global human rights movements and intensified people's demands for the realization of their rights (Cardenas 2009; Dunoff and Trachtman 2009; Falk 2009). What lies behind these processes was, to oversimplify a bit, the development of the Internet. On the one hand, the Internet was used by multinationals and financial institutions to enhance and concentrate wealth and power, at the expense of people everywhere. On the other hand, the Internet provides a remarkable tool for activists, grassroots movements, and human rights advocates. No doubt, the World Social Forum best exemplifies how a people's movement reaches around the globe, gathering up the energies of people everywhere.[3] Yet, there are other visionary social movements. These include international alliances that connect grassroots groups, such as Via Campesina, the international peasants' movement;[4] Shack/Slum Dwellers International;[5] and Grassroots International.[6] These social movements complement the ongoing efforts of international advocacy groups, such as the Center for Economic and Social Rights.[7] It is hard to estimate the total number of NGOs and INGOs in the world today.[8] There are at least a million.

A general principle here is that social processes that are inherent in networks often have multiplier effects. That is, if, say, a local network is successful, it expands and grows, sometimes activating other local networks and sometimes expanding to become a regional or global network.[9] This is not always the case, of course, but the key point to make is that networks have multiplier effects unlike top-down and centralized networks. For that reason they are the potential vehicles for social movements.

It is perhaps not surprising to learn that civil society actors (NGOs, INGOs, CBOs, and faith-based groups) protest when multinationals and businesses violate people's fundamental human rights. Nor is it surprising that these civil society actors protest governments when these governments fail to protect their fundamental human rights. But what can these civil society actors expect from the academy and research institutes, and, more specifically, from the scientists who carry out their work in academic and research settings? On the face of it, we might assume they can expect very little. Scientists, after all, put their values aside as they pursue objective knowledge. This is changing.

Science and Scientific Revolutions

Thomas Kuhn published a book in 1962 titled *The Structure of Scientific Revolutions* that rocked the scientific establishment. In this book he argued that science undergoes periodic *paradigm shifts* instead of progressing in a linear fashion and that these paradigm shifts open up new possibilities in science that scientists never could have previously recognized. For this reason scientists are never fully objective and bring a subjective perspective to their work. One of Kuhn's main examples was the slow but dramatic turn in science when Galileo Galilei, Johannes Kepler, and Isaac Newton over the course of a century overturned the Ptolemaic model that posited that the earth was the stationary center of the universe. In more recent times, we might say that the double-helix model of DNA published by James D. Watson and Francis Crick in 1953 led to a paradigm shift in molecular biology and biotechnology.

There is a new scientific revolution afoot, or at least some believe that to be the case. Let's assume for the moment that young people are attracted to science in order to pursue "truth and beauty" and, more specifically, to take on the mathematical and modeling challenges as well as to enjoy the aesthetics of a carefully designed study or experiment. Science is rigorous, but there is also a sense of deep satisfaction in the process of scientific discovery. But let us be frank. As young scientists mature, they find themselves caught up in scientific careers that are driven by the relentless competition for grants and promotions and that depend on corporate funding that is part and parcel of universities' promotion ladders. Too often the quest for "truth and beauty" is undermined by the systems in which scientists find themselves. Worse, science itself can diminish in social value as it becomes an end in and of itself or a means to further profits. This trend has been aggravated by the growing dependence of corporate-funded science on intellectual property rights, which are essentially forms of monopoly over a new product, such as a written work, or over nature, such as medicinal plants and animals. Claiming intellectual property rights over nature is often referred to as biopiracy.[10]

The revolution that is afoot is to harness science to the end of promoting human rights and a healthy environment, and to reduce science's prominent role in corporate wealth creation. We are already beginning to see that. Oceanography is in part dedicated to protecting the world's oceans and the species that inhabit them; climatology, to understanding how to slow global climate change; ecology, to protecting biodiversity; and glaciology, increasingly, to understanding how the melting of glaciers affects humans and their habitats.

More specifically, there are now champions of human rights within the scientific community. Hugh G. Gauch (2003), a crop and soil scientist, argues for a "humanities-rich-science," and Richard Pierre Claude (2002), a political scientist and statistician, argues not only that science and human rights are interdependent, but that science also is central to the welfare of all humankind. This is not a new idea, of course, since there has always been a debate within scientific circles as to whether the purpose of science is to seek better understanding (for the sake of understanding) or to improve people's lives and welfare. What is new—with revolutionary implications—is the specificity of the argument regarding science and human rights. Interestingly and importantly, scientists have "discovered" what has been there all the time—or at least since December 16, 1966: Article 15 of the International Covenant on Economic, Social, and Cultural Rights.[11] Article 15 joins culture and science because science always has a cultural context, and the flourishing of each culture and science depend on an open society with free and open exchange. Article 15 does not privilege any scientific tradition over others and by implication does not privilege knowledge obtained through the methods of Western science over indigenous knowledge:

Article 15

1. The States Parties to the present Covenant recognize the right of everyone:
   (a) To take part in cultural life;
   (b) To enjoy the benefits of scientific progress and its applications;
   (c) To benefit from the protection of the moral and material interests resulting from any scientific, literary or artistic production of which he is the author.

2. The steps to be taken by the States Parties to the present Covenant to achieve the full realization of this right shall include those necessary for the conservation, the development and the diffusion of science and culture.

3. The States Parties to the present Covenant undertake to respect the freedom indispensable for scientific research and creative activity.

4. The States Parties to the present Covenant recognize the benefits to be derived from the encouragement and development of international contacts and co-operation in the scientific and cultural fields.[12]

In 2009, the United Nations Educational, Scientific, and Cultural Organization hosted a conference on Article 15 in Venice, Italy, and what emerged from that conference was an important document—*Venice Statement on the Right to Enjoy the Benefits of Scientific Progress and Its Applications.* In the same year, the American Association for the Advancement of Science (AAAS) launched its Science and Human Rights Coalition. Its mission, in part, is as follows:

> The protection and advancement of human rights require the active engagement of scientists—their knowledge, tools, and voices. While some scientific associations and scientists have made vital contributions to human rights, as a group they have lacked a forum in which to learn from colleagues with experience in human rights, explore new areas of human rights work, and develop together new contributions to human rights efforts. The AAAS Science and Human Rights Coalition was formed to fill this gap. It will also finally make it possible to advance the right to *"the benefits of scientific progress and its applications"* by combining the efforts of scientific associations across disciplines to tackle this long-neglected human right [italics added].[13]

In other words, central to the mission of the AAAS Science and Human Rights Coalition is Article 15. Scientists who participate in the coalition's activities represent many specialties and are open to dialogue with human rights activists.

If we accept the idea that the objective of science is to benefit everyone and promote human welfare, as spelled out in Article 15.1(b), we need to question many scientific practices, including the use of science to pursue profits, and, perhaps more controversially, to question the use of intellectual property rights to limit access to a scientific idea or product, in the pursuit of profits. Scientists also get caught up in esoteric projects that have harmful aspects, such as biowarfare, genetic engineering, biopiracy, and nanotechnology. Saving polar bears from extinction may not be as "sexy" as devoting one's career to mammalian cloning. Yet Western science has evolved in a way that privileges the pursuit of problems that are esoteric and profitable rather than being publically accessible and that promote human welfare. There are many indications that a scientific revolution is afoot that involves scientists' questioning the pursuit of esoteric research and research that is devoted to corporate profits (and high salaries for scientists). The planet is facing critical challenges from global climate change, a dramatic reduction in biodiversity, ocean warming and sea level rising, food and water scarcity, desertification, and an increase in weather turbulence.

Conclusion

Human rights, as laid out in treaties—such as the Convention on the Rights of the Child, the Convention on the Elimination of All Forms of Discrimination Against Women, and the Convention on the Rights of Persons With Disabilities—are most often interpreted, at least in the United States, in terms of individual rights. But even a glance at the text of any human rights treaty shows that they are also framed as collective rights. Let's take as an example the treaty that draws most from the Western tradition of liberal, individual rights, namely the International Covenant on Civil and Political Rights. Included in the short preamble is this statement:

> In accordance with the Universal Declaration of Human Rights, the ideal of free human beings enjoying civil and political freedom and freedom from fear and want can only be achieved *if conditions are created whereby everyone may enjoy his civil and political rights.*

There is a mirror statement in the preamble of the International Covenant on Economic, Social, and Cultural Rights. A premise, in fact, of all human rights treaties and declarations is that rights are embedded in collectivities, namely communities and societies, and the members of all communities and societies have the responsibility to create the conditions whereby fundamental human rights are protected. Governments are the allies of people in this ambitious project, but the action is on the ground. Ordinary citizens do the heavy lifting, holding enterprises and governments responsible. Importantly, citizens create spaces in their communities to protect the most vulnerable—minorities, migrants and refugees, children, the handicapped, and the aged. Increasingly important in this age of globalism, transnationalism, migration, and multicultural diversities is the human capacity for empathy across lines of difference, and the recognition of human equality.

Without question the advance of human rights depends on a deep understanding of what a *decent society* is and how that understanding can be widely shared.[14] The knowledge bases and methodologies of the social sciences as well as many other fields, including those that are interdisciplinary, will be extremely useful to people, enterprises, organizations, and governments in their pursuit of a decent society. It can be stressed here that a scientific revolution is now under way that posits that the realization of human rights is the objective (*telos*) of any scientific endeavor. Although academic institutions have not retooled in all respects to accommodate this revolution-in-the-making, it is very likely that the great divide between science and the humanities can be bridged. None can predict now how in any detail the intellectual, practical, and institutional dimensions of this revolution-in-the-making will unfold, but there is little question that they will. The human costs of economic inequality, the degradation of the earth's ecosystem, and the destruction of cultures and languages are now too great for scientists to continue to pursue knowledge-for-the-sake-of-knowledge. Yet, there is no question that challenging times are ahead for all of the sciences, and as the pace of globalism continues, interdependencies will increase. It is already evident that countries are rapidly adopting human rights provisions into their constitutions, and these inevitably trickle down to local governments, while at the same time, local grassroots activists and movements push upward, demanding that governments responsibly put humans first. What remains unclear is how communities, societies, nation-states, and the global community will advance economic practices that prioritize human welfare. In the eighteenth century, Adam Smith struggled to understand this; in the nineteenth century, Karl Marx did; and in the twentieth century, John Maynard Keynes did. An immense challenge for the world's peoples in the twenty-first century is to create frameworks for *decent economies*. Such frameworks are part and parcel of decent societies. Recognizing all the environmental and climatological changes—even crises—that will confront us in the remaining decades of the twenty-first century, human rights must play the central role in promoting justice not only in courts but also practically in promoting decent economies and decent societies. To repeat, by *decent*

I refer to societies and economies in which there is mutual recognition of human equality and mutual respect across lines of difference.

Discussion Questions

1. How would you contrast epistemology with scientific practice? How are these interdependent and interrelated?

2. What is the controversy over intellectual property rights?

3. There is debate within the scientific community as to whether science should have a *telos* or, better put, be teleological or not. This is somewhat separate from the widely held view that scientists should be ethical. Find some examples of ethical and unethical science, and explore the question about *telos*, or the ultimate end(s) of science. Discuss why the latter is controversial but may have some usefulness in human rights discourse.

4. How would you go about reconciling science with the humanities? Is this a doable project?

Notes

1. Illustrations of these global networks include ESCR-Net (http://www.escr-net .org/subscription) and H-Net (H-HUMAN-RIGHTS@H-NET.MSU.EDU).

2. World Health Organization Guidelines for Drinking-Water Quality: http:// www.who.int/water_sanitation_health/dwq/guidelines/en/index.html

3. World Social Forum: http://www.forumsocialmundial.org.br/index.php?cd_ language=2&id_menu=

4. Via Campesina: http://viacampesina.org/en/

5. Shack/Slum Dwellers International: http://www.sdinet.org/

6. Grassroots International: http://www.grassrootsonline.org/

7. Center for Economic and Social Rights: http://www.cesr.org/

8. The number of INGOs and NGOs that have both staying power and an international dimension is best reflected in the number affiliated with the Economic and Social Council of the United Nations. On August 1, 2010, there were 3,051: That is the tip of the iceberg. In Kenya alone there were approximately 1,200 that were registered with the NGO board (http://www.un.org/esa/coordination/ngo/faq .htm).

9. We have been caught up in these processes with Sociologists without Borders (http://www.sociologistswithoutborders.org/; http://www.ssfthinktank .org/).

10. Global Issues: http://www.globalissues.org/issue

11. http://www2.ohchr.org/english/law/cescr.htm

12. Several countries, including South Africa and Spain, have adopted Article 15 in their constitutions.

13. In part this is notable because AAAS is the largest scientific society in the world, and its activities and policy statements are widely disseminated. The webpage of the coalition is http://shr.aaas.org/coalition/index.shtml.

14. I use the commonsense understanding of a *decent society*—namely, a society (community) where people treat all others as equals while recognizing their individuality

References

Cardenas, Sonia. 2009. *Human Rights in Latin America: A Politics of Terror and Hope.* Pennsylvania Studies in Human Rights Series. Philadelphia: University of Pennsylvania Press.

Claude, Richard Pierre. 2002. *Science in the Service of Human Rights.* Philadelphia: University of Pennsylvania Press.

Dunoff, Jeffrey L. and Joel P. Trachtman, eds. 2009. *Ruling the World? Constitutionalism, International Law, and Global Governance.* Cambridge, UK: Cambridge University Press.

Falk, Richard. 2009. *Achieving Human Rights.* New York: Routledge.

Gauch, Hugh G., Jr. 2003. *Scientific Method in Practice.* Cambridge, UK: Cambridge University Press.

Kuhn, Thomas. S. 1962. *The Structure of Scientific Revolutions.* Chicago: University of Chicago Press.

Macan-Markar, Marwaan. 2010. "Thailand Faces Flak for Backing Mekong Dams." *Interpress Service*, July 29. Retrieved January 12, 2011 (http://ipsnews .net/news.asp?idnews=52314).

United Nations Department of Public Information. 2010. "General Assembly Adopts Resolution Declaring Access to Clean Water, Sanitation a Human Right." July 28. Retrieved January 12, 2011 (http://www.un.org/apps/news/story.asp?NewsID =35456&Cr=SANITATION&Cr1=).

United Nations Educational, Scientific, and Cultural Organization. 2009. *Venice Statement on the Right to Enjoy the Benefits of Scientific Progress and Its Applications.* Paris: Author.

Watson, James D. and Francis Crick. 1953. "A Structure for Deoxyribose Nucleic Acid." *Nature* 171:737–38.

Index

About the Editors

Judith Blau is a professor at the University of North Carolina, and from 2000 to 2010 she served as the director of the Social and Economic Justice program, which includes over 60 courses. She is president of Sociologists without Borders and founding editor of its journal, *Societies without Borders*. She has published 18 books, including four with Alberto Moncada, *Human Rights: Beyond the Liberal Vision* (2005), *Justice in the United States* (2006), *Freedoms and Solidarities* (2007), and *Human Rights* (2009). She has served as president of the Southern Sociological Society and now serves on the executive committee of the Science and Human Rights Coalition of the American Association for the Advancement of Science. She is the director of the Human Rights Center of Chapel Hill and Carrboro (North Carolina).

Mark Frezzo is an assistant professor of sociology at the University of Mississippi. He has published book chapters in *Overcoming the "Two Cultures": Science versus the Humanities in the Modern World-System* (2004), *The World and US Social Forums: A Better World Is Possible and Necessary* (2008), and *The Leading Rogue State: The U.S. and Human Rights* (2008), articles in *Perspectives on Global Development and Technology* and *Societies without Borders*, and a book, *Deflecting the Crisis: Keynesianism, Social Movements, and US Hegemony* (2009). He serves as secretary/treasurer of the Section on Human Rights of the American Sociological Association, coeditor of the journal *Societies without Borders*, and vice president of public relations for Sociologists without Borders.

About the Contributors

Rachel Bryant is a doctoral student in the Department of Sociology at Case Western Reserve University. She is currently the project director of the U.S. Children's Rights Index. Her dissertation focuses on children's participation in medical decision making.

Rebecca Clausen is a professor of sociology at Fort Lewis College in Durango, Colorado. Her interest in environmental sociology and political economy has informed her research on the social structural drivers of environmental change. Themes of human rights and environmental rights weave throughout her work as a teacher and an activist.

Louis Edgar Esparza is a lecturer in human rights at the Josef Korbel School of International Studies at the University of Denver. His dissertation, *Grassroots Human Rights Activism in Contemporary Colombia*, is the winner of the 2010 Latin American Studies Association/Oxfam America Martin Diskin Dissertation Award. His work has attracted grants from the Andrew W. Mellon Foundation and the National Science Foundation. He publishes in the areas of contentious politics, human rights, and development.

Bruce K. Friesen is an associate professor of sociology at the University of Tampa in Florida. He received his PhD in sociology from the University of Calgary (Canada) in 1993, and is author of *Designing and Conducting Your First Interview Project* (Jossey-Bass, 2010). He teaches courses in global sociology and has led study-abroad courses in Geneva, Switzerland, and Florence, Italy. Dr. Friesen continues to agitate for respect for human rights. He is the recipient of several teaching excellence awards.

San Juanita Edilia García is a doctoral student in the Department of Sociology at Texas A&M University and an American Sociological Association Minority Fellowship Program Fellow. Her areas of specialization include Latino sociology, immigration, race and ethnic relations, sociology of mental health, and social psychology. She received a bachelor of arts degree, double-majoring in criminal justice and Spanish with a minor in sociology. She received her master's degree from Texas A&M University, where her thesis examined the relationship between nativism and depression among undocumented Mexican immigrant women.

Brian Gran is on the faculty of the Department of Sociology and School of Law at Case Western Reserve University. His research focuses on how law is used to designate public-private boundaries in social life. Gran currently directs the Children's Rights Index project. He is completing a book on independent children's rights institutions.

Tugrul Keskin is an assistant professor of international and Middle Eastern studies and Turkish studies at Portland State University. Previously, Dr. Keskin served as instructor of sociology and Africana studies at Virginia Tech University and as visiting assistant professor of sociology at James Madison and Radford universities. He received his PhD from Virginia Tech in sociology, with certificates in Africana studies, social and political thought, and international research and development. He is the editor of *The Sociology of Islam: Secularism, Economy and Politics* (Garnet/Ithaca Press, 2011). He also is a board member of Sociologists without Borders and a book review editor of *Societies without Borders*

Shulamith Koenig is the recipient of the 2003 United Nations Prize in the Field of Human Rights. For the last 20 years she has developed public policy on learning about human rights as a way of life across communities, reaching out to 100 communities and dialoguing with grassroots organizations in more than 50 nations. She is the founding president of PDHRE, the People's Movement for Human Rights Learning, and deputy of the International NGO Committee on Human Rights in Trade and Investment. To develop viable models and an ongoing process of learning and acting, she is facilitating the development of an international institute for learning human rights as a way of life, and a national corps to pursue such learning throughout members' countries and in their communities.

Cecilia Menjívar is the Cowden Distinguished Professor of Sociology in the School of Social and Family Dynamics at Arizona State University. In recent years she has examined the effects of immigration laws on different aspects of immigrants' lives, including family dynamics, educational aspirations, religious activities, and artistic expressions. Her publications include the books *Fragmented Ties: Salvadoran Immigrant Networks in America* (University of California Press, 2000); *Through the Eyes of Women: Gender, Social Networks, Family and Structural Change in Latin America and the*

Caribbean (edited; De Sitter, 2003); *When States Kill: Latin America, the U.S. and Technologies of Terror* (coedited with Nestor Rodriguez; University of Texas Press, 2005); and *Enduring Violence: Ladina Women's Lives in Guatemala* (University of California Press, 2011) and numerous articles in academic journals.

Rogelio Sáenz is a professor in the Department of Sociology at Texas A&M University. He is also a Fellow of the Carsey Institute at the University of New Hampshire and writes occasionally on demographic trends for the Population Reference Bureau. His research focuses on the areas of demography, immigration, sociology of Latinos, and inequality. Sáenz is a coeditor of *Latinas/os in the United States: Changing the Face of América.* His articles have also appeared in a variety of journals including *Demography, Du Bois Review, International Migration Review, Journal of Marriage and Family, Race & Society, Social Science Quarterly,* and *Social Science Research.*

Laura Toussaint is a member of the academic core faculty at Lake Washington Technical College and a research affiliate for the "Globalization, Gender, and Development" project in the Department of Sociology at American University. She is the outreach coordinator for the global and transnational section-in-formation of the American Sociological Association and a member of the editorial collective of *Societies without Borders.* She has published articles for *Sociologists for Women in Society* and *Bharatiya Samajik Chintan,* the academic journal of the Indian Academy of Social Sciences. Her book, *The Contemporary U.S. Peace Movement,* was published by Routledge in 2009.

Bryan S. Turner is the Presidential Professor of Sociology at the City University of New York Graduate Center and the director of the Committee on Religion. He was previously the Alona Evans Distinguished Visiting Professor at Wellesley College (2009–2010). He published *Vulnerability and Human Rights* (Penn State University Press, 2006) and *Rights and Virtues* (Bardwell Press, 2008). He is the founding editor of the journal *Citizenship Studies.* He edited the *Routledge International Handbook of Globalization Studies* (2009) and the *New Blackwell Companion to the Sociology of Religion* (2010). Professor Turner was awarded a Doctor of Letters by Cambridge University in 2009.